A guide to the

Ordnance Survey

one-inch Third Edition maps, in colour

Dedicated to the memory of

Kenneth Guy Messenger

born 27 February 1920, died 25 November 1993

botanist and cartobibliographer

A guide to the

Ordnance Survey

one-inch Third Edition maps,

in colour

England and Wales, Scotland, Ireland

Roger Hellyer

and

Richard Oliver

London
The Charles Close Society
2004

First published in 2004 by The Charles Close Society for the Study of Ordnance Survey Maps, c/o The Map Library, British Library, 96 Euston Road, London NW1 2DB

A catalogue record for this book is available from the British Library

ISBN 1-870598-21-0

Typeset by Roger Hellyer

Printed and bound by CPI Bath

Contents

Cartobibliography

Appendices

Illustrations

Acknowledgements and abbreviations

The compilation of a cartobibliography can never be work of a single individual, and I would like to thank friends and colleagues who have assisted in the making of this book in many different ways: David Archer, Mike Ashworth, Christopher Board, Chris Bull, Peter Clark, Graham Cornell, Mike Cottrell, John Cruickshank, Richard Dean, Richard Evans, Peter Gibson, Yolande Hodson, Paul Laming, Maria Mealey, Ian Mumford, Mike Nolan, Ian O'Brien, Bridget Oliver, Barry Phillips, Tim Sanderson, Peter Stubbs, John Taylor, Andrew Teed.

I would also like to thank the staff in the map rooms of the British Library, Royal Geographical Society (with the Institute of British Geographers) (Francis Herbert), Royal Scottish Geographical Society (Kerr Jamieson), Ordnance Survey's Historical Mapping Archive (Pete Clark), National Library of Scotland (Peter Milne and Chris Fleet), National Library of Wales (Huw Thomas), Birmingham Central Library (Richard Abbott), The National Archives (Public Record Office), Library of Congress; also map librarians in universities and university geography departments in Aberdeen (Jackie Brown), Birmingham (James Peart), Bristol, Cambridge (Anne Taylor and Philip Stickler), Dublin (Paul Ferguson and Richard Haworth), Edinburgh (Kerry Watt), Exeter (Terry Bacon), Glasgow (John Moore and Mike Shand), Leeds, Liverpool (Antonio da Cruz), London (Moira Courtman), Manchester (Chris Perkins), Newcastle upon Tyne (Ann Rooke), Oxford (Nick Millea and Linda Atkinson), Reading (Robert Parry) and Sheffield (Val Clinging), all of whom extended me every courtesy on my visits to inspect the map collections in their charge. I would especially like to thank Anne Taylor and her staff in the University Library at Cambridge, who made the lengthy business of inspecting Guy Messenger's enormous private collection as straightforward as possible for me.

Finally, Richard and I would like particularly to thank Professor Roger Kain for making the photographic facilities in the School of Geography, Archaeology and Earth Resources at the University of Exeter available to us, to Brian Adams for overseeing the mathematical content of this book, and especially for contributing appendix 7, to David Archer, who took great care in proof reading the text, footnotes, and lists, and weeded out many errors and inconsistencies. Any that remain are the fault of the authors. And lastly we would like to thank Chris Higley, who designed with such clarity the index diagrams and undertook the layout and compilation of the illustration pages, and who prepared the digital camera ready copy.

List of abbreviations

Cpt: the copyright collections (British Library, National Library of Scotland, Bodleian Library, Oxford, University Library, Cambridge, Trinity College, Dublin).

Additional copies held by these libraries are denoted by the following abbreviations:

BL-c: additional England and Wales LSS copies in the British Library copyright set, at Maps 1175(130); **BL-d**: the Military Survey (now Defence Geographic Centre, DGIA) collection transferred in 2001 from Tolworth to the British Library; **BL-r**: the British Library record copy set of England and Wales LSS sheets – coloured sheets at Maps 1175(255), Black Outline edition at Maps 1175(256), district maps at Maps 1175(303). **Cu**: England and Wales LSS maps donated to the University Library, Cambridge, at Maps c.G.038. The library also houses Guy Messenger's collection, listed as **Cu-m**. Printings in copyright collections also in the Messenger collection are denoted **Cpt-m**. **NLS**: National Library of Scotland, **Ob**: Bodleian Library, Oxford – additional copies with their copyright sets.

Other collections: **Bc**: Birmingham Central Library; **Dm**: Military Archives, Cathal Brugha Barracks, Dublin; **Dtc**: Map Library, Trinity College, Dublin; **Dtf**: Freeman Library, Trinity College, Dublin; **NLW**: National Library of Wales, Aberystwyth; **NYp**: New York Public Library; **OSNI**: Ordnance Survey of Northern Ireland, Belfast; **PRO**: The National Archives (Public Record Office); **RGS**: Royal Geographical Society; **RSGS**: Royal Scottish Geographical Society, Glasgow; **Wc**: Library of Congress, Washington D.C.. University libraries: **Gu**: Glasgow; **Lu**: London. University geography department libraries: **Ag**: Aberdeen; **Bg**: Birmingham: **BSg**: Bristol; **Cg**: Cambridge; **Eg**: Edinburgh; **EXg**: Exeter; **Gg**: Glasgow; **LDg**: Leeds; **LVg**: Liverpool; **Mg**: Manchester; **NTg**: Newcastle upon Tyne; **Og**: Oxford; **Rg**: Reading; **Sg**: Sheffield. **PC**: private collection.

The history of the one-inch Third Edition coloured map

Part I – The development of the mapping

The most significant event in the development of the Ordnance Survey one-inch (1:63,360) and 1:50,000 map families was the adoption of colour printing by lithography, in place of monochrome printing from engraved copper plates. The first and third generations of OS one-inch coloured maps of England and Wales have recently been studied by Tim Nicholson, and Yolande Hodson.[1] As these together provide detailed studies of the development of the one-inch map, it is only necessary here to describe briefly its development prior to the genesis of the second generation, the 'Third Edition', which is the subject of the present publication.

The development of the one-inch mapping of Great Britain to 1900[2]
The Ordnance Survey came into being in the late eighteenth century with the twofold objectives of providing a national geodetic framework and making a national military topographic survey. In the 1780s and 1790s several areas of military importance were surveyed by the Board of Ordnance at scales of between two inches and six inches to one mile (1:31,680 and 1:10,560), and in 1795, following the outbreak of war with France two years earlier, the decision was taken to extend these nationally. By the end of the French wars in 1815 the Ordnance's surveyors had made manuscript maps of roughly the southern half of England and Wales, mostly at 1:31,680. After some mapping of Sussex and Kent had been issued by private publishers, using Ordnance materials, the Ordnance decided to engrave and publish its own maps, and the first of these appeared in 1805. Although military in origin, the main justification for continuing survey and publication after 1815 was civil. The published maps were engraved on copper and showed relief by hachures. Up to the 1830s they were published in 'full sheets', varying in size inside the neat line from about 29 to 35.5 inches (about 73.5-90.0cm) west-east, but all about 23.5 inches (about 60.0 cm) south-north; thereafter they were usually published as 'quarter sheets'. By 1840 the survey had reached the southern parts of Lancashire and Yorkshire, and publication of the mapping, known later as the Old Series, was completed up to a line from Preston to Hull in 1844 (Hi.2.1).[3]

Between 1825 and 1842 the Ordnance surveyed Ireland at the six-inch scale for fiscal purposes, and in 1840, following requests from geological and other interests in Scotland and northern England, the scale of survey in Britain was changed to the six-inch. From 1853 surveying was mostly at 1:2500, with publication also at six-inch and one-inch. From 1856 the one-inch of northern England, and the whole of Scotland, was published in two forms: as before, with hachures (Hi.2.1, Hi.13.2 respectively), and in an alternative form without hachures but with contours,

[1] Tim Nicholson, *The birth of the modern Ordnance Survey small-scale map.* London: Charles Close Society, 2002; Yolande Hodson, *Popular maps.* London: Charles Close Society, 1999.
[2] Strangely enough, there is still no satisfactory summary history of the OS one-inch map. The most accessible modern summary for England and Wales to 1919 is that in Yolande Hodson, *Popular maps.* London: Charles Close Society, 1999, chapter 1, with other earlier accounts cited in footnote 33. The earlier period is covered in detail in the introductory essays by J.B. Harley and others in *The Old Series Ordnance Survey.* Lympne Castle: Harry Margary, 8 vols, 1975-92, and for Ireland in J.H. Andrews, *History in the Ordnance map.* Dublin: Ordnance Survey, 1974 (reissued Kerry: David Archer, 1993) and J.H. Andrews, *A paper landscape: the Ordnance Survey in nineteenth-century Ireland.* Oxford University Press, 1975 (reissued Dublin: Four Courts Press, 2002); see also Roger Hellyer, *Ordnance Survey small-scale maps indexes: 1801-1998.* Kerry: David Archer, 1999, and Richard Oliver, 'What's what with the New Series', *Sheetlines* 5 (1982), 3-8. But there is no comprehensive monograph.
[3] The 'Hi' numbers refer to the serial numbers in Roger Hellyer, *Ordnance Survey small-scale maps indexes: 1801-1998.* Kerry: David Archer, 1999.

usually at 100 feet intervals between 100 and 1000 feet and at 250 ft intervals thereafter (Hi.2.2, Hi.13.1). Engraving effort was minimised by using electrotyping to produce duplicate plates, so that only the contours and hachures had to be engraved separately. Publication of England was completed in 1869 and of Scotland with contours in 1887 and 'with hills' in 1895. The remaining English sheets were published as 'quarter sheets', 18 inches (45.7 cm) west-east by 12 inches (30.4 cm) south-north within the neat lines, and the Scottish one-inch, laid out and numbered as a completely separate series, was published in what were sometimes referred to as 'half-sheets', 24 inches west-east by 18 inches south-north. (The Isle of Man was published in 1873 in outline but without contours, and 'with hills' in 1874, as a 'full' sheet, 24 inches west-east by 36 inches south-north.) Ireland was published in 18 by 12 inch sheets in outline, mostly without contours, between 1855 and 1862 (Hi.22.1) and 'with hills' between 1856 and 1895 (Hi.22.2). The six-inch was engraved in full sheets, 36 by 24 inches, until the early 1880s; thereafter it was usually published in photozincographed quarter-sheets. The various sheet sizes have a bearing on the development of the Third Edition.

The mapping of England, Wales, Scotland and Ireland was generally similar in approach, but whereas for the two former the Cassini projection was used, for Scotland and Ireland the Bonne projection was employed instead.[4] Thus as separate meridians and sheet line systems were used for Scotland and Ireland, it was possible to treat them differently in details of design. Enduring features of both were a much narrower and simpler margin than was used on the maps of England, railway names in italic sans-serif capitals, and names of hills in lower-case Egyptian. A few sheets in both Scotland and Ireland used reverse-italic for water names.

In 1870 Captain Charles Wilson, a Royal Engineer officer who had previously served on the Ordnance Survey, was sent by the War Office to report on aspects of the Franco-Prussian War. He noted that whilst the French had good maps of the areas beyond their frontiers, their own 1:80,000 was seriously out of date. The following year the War Office drew attention to the similar out-datedness of the Old Series, and Colonel Sir Henry James, the Director General of the Ordnance Survey (DGOS), presented a scheme for complete replacement of the pre-1844 mapping, to be published in both outline and hachured forms. As he had ready a complete specimen sheet at very short notice, it is apparent that he was only awaiting his chance. The Treasury duly authorised the new map in July 1872.[5] The first outline sheet of the 'New Series' was published early in 1874 (Hi.3.2), and the first 'with hills' (Hi.3.4, Hi.3.5) in 1878; the outline version was completed in 1896 and the hills version in 1902-3, but neither was in the form envisaged in 1871-2.

Between 1861 and 1868 the OS had produced for the War Office a series of six-inch maps of hilly ground to the south and west of London, in which the outline was printed in black and the hachures in brown, using zincography: other colour was added by hand, as for the 1:2500.[6] In the later 1870s a few one-inch manoeuvre maps, based on New Series material, were published using zincography, with black outline and brown hills, and in 1887 two one-inch sheets were issued with coloured water and contours (Hi.3.7). In 1889 work began on preparing completely separate hachure plates for the New Series, and from 1893 all newly published one-inch hill maps were available with the hachures in either black or brown. As a stopgap, between 1892 and 1897 about a third of England and Wales was published with the engraved outline, printed from zinc, combined

[4] Brian Adams, 'The projection of the original one-inch map of Ireland (and of Scotland)', *Sheetlines* 30 (1991), 12-15.

[5] For the report, see National Archives, Public Record Office (PRO) WO 33/22; for Treasury papers and map specimens, see papers in file 11660 in PRO T1/7200B.

[6] There is such a set in the British Library: Maps 144.e.12. The OS's limited use of colour-printing in the later nineteenth century is explored in Ian Mumford, 'Monochrome to polychrome at the Ordnance Survey in the 19th century', *Ordnance Survey past, present and future*. Chichester: Survey and Mapping Alliance, [1991] [unpaginated]. (Proceedings of the symposium held to celebrate the Ordnance Survey bicentenary, held at the Royal Geographical Society, London, 23 May 1991).

with photozincographed hachures, obtained by pen-drawing (Hi.3.3): the results were of variable quality and did not find wide favour.[7]

Thus by 1892 printing two-colour hill-maps by zincography was a well-established technique at the OS. In the spring of that year two committees were appointed: one by the War Office, to consider military mapping of the United Kingdom, and the other, by the Board of Agriculture (which had had ministerial responsibility for the OS since 1889) to inquire into the state of the OS generally. The War Office Committee, under Sir T.D. Baker and including Charles Wilson, now knighted, a colonel, and DGOS, was appointed after the Dorington Committee, but got its report in first. For present purposes, its important recommendations were that the one-inch should be the principal military map, that it should be improved for military purposes by including new data on roads, railways, church steeples, post and telegraph facilities, smithies and some other details, and that there should be some additional contouring.[8] The other Committee, under Sir John Dorington, M.P., recommended that the one-inch map should be revised every fifteen years, independently of the larger scales, which would be revised every twenty years, and that the one-inch should be published in a multi-colour version.[9]

There was no difficulty in getting the Treasury to authorise one-inch revision, and a special OS section of 80 Royal Engineers was formed for this purpose early in 1893.[10] Their work included both general updating and adding the additional information requested by the Baker Committee. Nor was there any difficulty in persuading the Treasury to authorise large-scale revision. The one-inch revision of Britain was carried out between 1893 and 1898 and published in outline between 1895 and 1899 (England & Wales Hi.4.1, Scotland Hi.14.1). (Large-scale revision had begun in a modest way in 1891, and got into its stride by 1895: the first cycle was completed in 1914, although most of the work had been completed by 1906.) For most of southern Lancashire and southern Yorkshire the 'revised' New Series was also its first publication.[11] The first priority appears to have been southern England, much of which was at least 15 and sometimes 25 or 30 years out of date; then Scotland, which was equally or more out of date, particularly in the south; then northern England, and finally those parts of England which had been surveyed at 1:2500 from about 1880 onwards. Although this made sense in terms of military needs and age of existing mapping, it was not a straightforward unidirectional geographical progress, and reflected to an extent the priority given in the 1:2500 survey to south-east England, Cheshire, and the Welsh coalfields. Once Britain was completed Ireland was taken up, with revision in 1898-1901 and publication in 1899-1902 (Hi.23.1). Both in Britain and Ireland only the outline plates were revised; the engraved hills versions continued on sale, unrevised.

More problematic than revision were the additional contours, which were only realised after 1910, and the coloured version of the one-inch. Experiment with colour was authorised in 1894, after pressure on the Treasury from General Sir Redvers Buller (his reputation as yet untarnished by the Boer War), who wrote that 'The want of such a map is... more than an inconvenience, it is an evil...'.[12] Following some experiments, a manoeuvre map of Aldershot was issued in 1896 and the first series sheets appeared in September 1897 (Hi.5). Outline and names

---

[7] Roger Hellyer, 'One-inch engraved maps with hills: some notes on double-printing', *Sheetlines* 44 (1995), 11-20.

[8] *Report of Committee on a military map of the United Kingdom*. London: War Office, 1892, 8-11 (War Office number A.237). [Chairman Sir T.D. Baker. Copies RGS, Ordnance Survey Library].

[9] *Report of the Departmental Committee appointed by the Board of Agriculture to inquire into the present condition of the Ordnance Survey*. London: HMSO, 1893. British Parliamentary Papers (House of Commons Series) [hereafter BPP (HC)] 1893-94 [C. 6895], LXXII, 305, report, x, xxix-xxx. [Chairman Sir J. E. Dorington].

[10] Copy minute of Board of Agriculture, December 1893 [printed], in PRO OS 1/2/5.

[11] Sheets 74-78, 83, 84 and 87 were not published at all in unrevised form; sheets 79-81, 85, 86, 88 and 96-100 were published in 1886-90 with the Lancashire and Yorkshire portions left blank, as was sheet 101 which was, however, republished in 1895 with the Yorkshire portion added, apparently unrevised. Sheet 357.360, covering the Isles of Scilly, was published initially in a photozincographed version in 1892; its appearance in 'revised' form in 1896 was also its first appearance in engraved form.

[12] Tim Nicholson, *The birth of the modern Ordnance Survey small-scale map*. London: Charles Close Society, 2002, 16, citing file 10077 in PRO T1/8834C.

were in black, contours in red, water in blue, hachures in brown, and roads in burnt sienna. The original intention seems to have been to cover only south-east England, as the most likely seat of operations in the event of a hostile invasion, but by 1899 cover was being extended into the south-west, and true sienna was being substituted for burnt sienna. Given the semi-experimental nature of the map, and the modest sales to the public, this seems to be unlikely to be due to public demand; it seems more likely to be due to military influence, and it may owe something to the interest in printing techniques of Col (later Sir) Duncan A. Johnston, DGOS 1899-1905.[13] It is also possible that it was felt that the experiment had not been allowed enough time to produce results: whilst waiting to see if there really was a demand cover could be extended, and there would come a point when cover was so extensive that it might as well be pushed to completion. Whatever the explanation, the coloured one-inch was pushed forward vigorously, with coverage of the mainland of England and Wales completed in March 1904.

By that time separate hachure plates had been produced for all those sheets in England which had been published originally with the hachures combined with outline, and it is apparent that the publication of coloured one-inch sheets followed very closely on the availability of separate hachure plates. Where the hachures were combined with outline they could be separated by taking a electrotype 'negative', from which the unwanted outline and names were scraped away, and then a positive was taken in which any consequent gaps or damage in the hachuring were made good.[14] In 1900 no such separate hachure plates were available for northern England, Scotland or Ireland. Production of separate hill-plates was completed for England by early 1904, when work started on those of Scotland: those of Ireland only started to appear from about 1909. (Apparently none were prepared for the Isle of Man.)

An alternative to producing hill plates by engraving was to take a print of the combined hachures and unrevised outline in lithographic ink on transfer paper, scrape away the unwanted detail, make good the hachures by drawing, and lay down the amended transfer on stone or zinc, for printing in brown combined with revised outline in black. This technique was used to produce a revised hill-map of Scotland, issued between 1898 and 1903, with most of the sheets dated 1900 (Hi.14.2). This was a variation on a technique used to produce some of the plates for the coloured one-inch of England.[15] Col John Farquharson (DGOS 1894-9) apparently expected that this technique would also be used to produce a revised hill-map of northern England (sheets 1-73), but what actually happened was rather different.[16] In February 1901 there appeared the first coloured one-inch sheets of northern England. They differed from those published hitherto in that a sixth colour was employed: green, for woods. Separate hachure plates were produced as they had been for the revised hill-map of Scotland, by transfer, scraping and making good. This apparent change of plan from providing northern England with an outline-and-hills map, as in Scotland, suggests that by 1900-01 the OS was minded to complete coloured one-inch cover for England and Wales. The need for a hill-map of northern England was made the opportunity for producing a fully-coloured map which happened to include the hills.

However, only a few sheets of northern England had been issued by December 1901, when there seems to have been another change of plan, in favour of not proceeding further with the fully-coloured one-inch doubling as a hill-map, and instead of waiting for separate engraved hill-plates to be prepared. Thus the coloured one-inch of northern England was only completed in 1903-4. These later sheets were assimilated to the earlier ones by having woods in green and tree symbols in brown, though these last appeared in black on some reprints. The brown trees were on the hachure plate, and may have been used so as to avoid the trouble of scraping and making good

---

[13] Brian Adams, 'The projection of the original one-inch map of Ireland (and of Scotland)', *Sheetlines* 30 (1991), 12-15, 12.

[14] H.StJ.L. Winterbotham, *A key to maps*. London & Glasgow: Blackie, 1936, 73.

[15] The methods used for both the coloured map and for the hill-map of Scotland are described in Duncan A. Johnston [ed], *Account of the methods and processes adopted for the production of the maps of the Ordnance Survey of the United Kingdom*, revised edition. London: HMSO, 1902, 185-7.

[16] See Sir John Farquharson, 'Twelve years work of the Ordnance Survey, 1887 to 1899', *Geographical Journal* XV (1900), 565-98, esp. 584.

the hachures in wooded areas on plates which would only be a short-term expedient. The coloured mapping of northern England would appear to have been partly justified by accountancy, being paid for from funds for maintaining the one-inch, which evidently embraced producing separate hill-plates. These plates would have had to be produced anyway, even if there had been no coloured publication.[17]

In 1901 production of a coloured one-inch of Ireland began; it was completed in 1906 (Hi.24).[18] It used the same transfer-scrape-and-make-good method of producing hill plates as had been used in Scotland, and with woods in green with brown tree-symbols, as in northern England. Presumably priority was given to Ireland over Scotland for coloured one-inch cover partly because Scotland already had its interim revised hill-map, and partly because fieldwork for a further revision of the one-inch of Britain was starting, whereas the first revision of Ireland was only just completed. Thus an Irish one-inch coloured map produced in the early 1900s using first-revision materials might be expected to have a much longer 'shelf-life' than one of Scotland produced on the same basis, though it is unlikely that anyone expected the Irish map to last, as it did, well into the third quarter of the twentieth century.

The Third Edition: inception, revision and publication[19]
Completion in Ireland of the first general revision of the one-inch mapping of the United Kingdom in 1901 coincided with the start of a 'second national revision' in both England and Scotland. The results were published from 1903 onwards as the 'Third Edition', and before proceeding further it may be helpful to summarise the main forms which the Third Edition took. (The more experienced may wish to pass over the next paragraph.)

The most comprehensive in cover was the engraved outline form, which was based on the existing copper plates. This covered the whole of England and Wales on 346 plates (Hi.6.1), and Scotland on 131 plates (Hi.15.1), and less than two-thirds of Ireland on 128 plates (Hi.25.1).[20] The engraved plates were also issued overprinted with engraved hachures in black or brown, but publication of this form was discontinued in 1911-12, and so only 325 plates of England and Wales (Hi.6.2), 110 in Scotland (Hi.15.3) and 50 in Ireland (Hi.25.3) were issued in this form. A third form, probably the most important from the point of view of the map-using public by 1914, was the colour-printed style which is the subject of this book. For England and Wales this took two forms: an incomplete series in 96 'small' sheets, with sheet lines based on those of the engraved plates, which is often referred to as the 'small sheet series' (Hi.7.1), and a complete 'Large Sheet Series', with a standard sheet size of 27 by 18 inches, in 152 sheets (Hi.8.1). There was a single series for Scotland, in 98 sheets, based on the sheet lines of the engraved map, but omitting cover of the Outer Hebrides (Hi.16.1). Only fragmentary coloured Third Edition cover was published in Ireland: three sheets based on the engraved sheet lines (Hi.24.A.3), two on 'large' sheet lines (Hi.26.1, Hi.26.3), and two district maps (Hi.26.2, Hi.26.4). A considerable number of district maps for Great Britain were published, in various styles (Hi.6.3, Hi.7.3, Hi.8.8-13, Hi.16.2-5). There was an incomplete lithographed 'Black Outline Edition' of England and Wales, using the Large Sheet Series plates, issued in 1918-19 (Hi.8.2), and a similarly incomplete lithographed Black Outline Edition for Scotland, but based directly on the engraved plates (Hi.15.2).

The progress of this second revision was somewhat different from the first in 1893-8. There were two starting-points, along the border around the Tweed, and around the Hampshire-Surrey border. Progress was more straightforward in Scotland: the revisers worked west and north, so that as a rule the further north the mapping was, the later it was revised and published. Revision of Scotland was completed in 1910 and publication of the 'Third Edition' was in 1903-12.

---

[17] Minute by Duncan A. Johnston, 1901: copy in PRO OS 1/20.
[18] Roger Hellyer, 'A cartobibliography of the one-inch map of Ireland, in colour, 1901-1956', *Sheetlines* 63 (2002), 12-38.
[19] For further discussion of one-inch revision see Yolande Hodson, *Popular maps.* London: Charles Close Society, 1999, 55-64.
[20] 'Plates' has been used here because in each series a few plates bore more than one sheet-number.

What was published between 1903 and 1913 as the Third Edition of England and Wales progressed in a less straightforward way. It was certainly not a case of revision parties setting off from Aldershot and Berwick and meeting somewhere half-way. The flow of revision had reached Furness by 1904 and the Humber by 1905-6, but instead of moving into Lancashire and the West Riding the revisers bypassed these and worked instead in Cheshire, north Wales and the north midlands. Nor was Wales revised systematically: the north and most of the south-east were completed by 1906, leaving the remainder to be completed in 1908-9. Whilst the revision of Cheshire and north-east Wales might be justified as a legacy of the original order of large-scale survey which had fathered the New Series, this does not explain why north-west Wales was revised at the same time. The result of this can be seen by contrasting sheet 118, *Nevin*, with sheet 75, *Preston*: 118 was published in 1895, republished in 1899 and again in the Third Edition in 1905; 75 was published in 1896 as one of the small group where initial and revised publication were effectively fused into one, and only republished in the Third Edition in 1913. Publication in the south-east was somewhat more regular but, even so, there was a break between Surrey and west Sussex (revised 1901-2) and Kent and east Sussex (revised 1903-4).

The decision to defer Lancashire and the West Riding must have been taken by 1904-5. It seems strange in view of the propensity of industrialised areas such as these to more rapid development than in predominantly rural areas, and it undermined the concept of separate one-inch revision so that no one-inch sheet would be more that fifteen years out of date when issued to the public. The actual average interval between the fieldwork for the revised New Series and the publication of the Third Edition was about ten years: in Lancashire it was up to eighteen years.

The problematic relationship of Third Edition revision with *ad hoc* one-inch revision and large-scale revision is further emphasised by its successor generations of the one-inch. In 1909 a Third National Revision began, although its predecessor was still incomplete; it was suspended a couple of years later, but not before seven sheets of east Kent and one of Berwickshire had been published as 'Fourth Edition' (Hi.9, Hi.17 respectively), and more had been revised in the field.[21] All these were in areas which had recently been subject to large-scale revision; as the second revision of the 1:2500 of Kent preceded that of Surrey, so the Fourth Edition cover of that county would have preceded that of Surrey, thus inverting the order of the Third Edition.

The explanation for this appears in an OS internal circular of 8 April 1909, which opens by noting that until 'quite recently' it had been the practice to revise the one-inch on a fifteen-year cycle, but that now 'it has been approved that this fifteen year cycle be extended to twenty years', as for the larger scales. Each one-inch sheet would be taken up for revision immediately revised six-inch cover was available; it was expected that this would 'materially' lighten the work of one-inch field revision, as it would only be necessary to note changes which had taken place since the parent 1:2500 survey.[22] In principle this is what small-scale revisers had been doing since 1893, but in the revision of 1893-8 they had worked on six-inch sheets which were rarely less than ten years and sometimes over forty years out of date. Whilst much of the revision for the Third Edition was made using six-inch sheets which were no more than three to seven years out of date, the pattern of large-scale revision was such that in a few areas the one-inch revisers were working, as in 1893-8, on pre-1888 six-inch mapping. In west Cornwall and north Lincolnshire in 1905 the large-scale and small-scale revisers must have been working practically alongside each other.

The progress of large-scale revision seems to have been determined partly by the pattern of the original 1:2500 survey, which as noted before was not in an orderly geographical progression, and partly by an attempt so to arrange things that such a geographical progression might eventually develop. Thus London, Surrey and Kent were revised in the mid 1890s; by 1902 revision had

---

[21] Sheets published: England 273, 274, 289, 290, 305, 306, 321; Scotland 26. A diagram in *Report of the progress of the Ordnance Survey to the 31st March 1911* (BPP (HC) 1911 [Cd. 5873], XXXVII, 577) indicates that the following were also revised: England 271, 272, 287, 288, 304, 320, 330, 344, 345; Scotland 1-5, 33, 34.

[22] Circular by Col S.C.N. Grant, 8 April 1909, in 'Southampton Circulars', Book 2 (formerly at Ordnance Survey Office, Dublin; now in National Archives of Ireland, Dublin; photocopy in Ordnance Survey library, Southampton).

reached Leicestershire, but had already taken place in Derbyshire and Nottinghamshire, by 1908 it had reached the East Riding of Yorkshire, but had begun in the West Riding in 1901, and by 1911 it had reached the Tees, from which it flowed neatly into the second revision of Durham and Northumberland. The second national revision of the 1:2500 began in Cheshire in 1904, and this county, Kent and Hampshire were revised roughly simultaneously over the next few years.

The policy in force by April 1909 of one-inch revision 'shadowing' that of the larger scales may not have applied in 1904, when presumably the decision was taken to defer Lancashire and the West Riding. However, it does seem to explain why these areas were only revised for the Third Edition in 1910-12. By the time this revision was completed there had been a further change of policy, and whilst this does not directly affect the publication of the maps which are the subject of this book it does have an effect on the chronology of their replacement. There was no explicit reference to the change of small-scale revision policy in the published annual reports, but in the 1908-9, 1909-10 and 1910-11 reports the customary reference hitherto to a fifteen-year cycle is omitted; it is reinstated in that for 1911-12.[23] Although this would appear to be a departure from the policy recommended and adopted in 1892-3, in practice by the later 1900s the intervals between the first and second national revisions of the large scales was less than fifteen years. Those responsible for the change of policy may have reasoned that, with existing resources, and given the comparatively small number of changes on many published Third Edition sheets as compared with their predecessors, there was no practical difficulty in maintaining the one-inch in a satisfactorily up-to-date condition.

A decision in 1908-9 that in future one-inch revision would be carried out on recently-published six-inch sheets might explain the delay in revising Lancashire and the West Riding, if it had been decided in 1904 to wait until 1908-9 before revising these areas, which would have been the limit under the fifteen-year cycle. There then might have been a further delay until 1910-12 whilst waiting for the revised six-inch mapping, consequent upon the 1:2500 revision of these areas in 1904-8, to be published.

The orderly tenor of large-scale revision was broken in 1911-12 as a result of the Finance (1909-10) Act, 1910, which introduced taxation of land values.[24] Consequently, it was necessary to undertake a national land valuation, and to facilitate this ordinary OS large-scale revision was virtually suspended in order to bring the 1:2500 up-to-date in respect of details such as buildings and roads which would have a bearing on the valuers' work. This experience must have raised doubts in some minds as to the advisability of rigid cyclic revision for the large-scales, in favour of one whereby rapidly-changing areas would be revised more frequently than slower-changing ones. At any rate, it can hardly be a coincidence that the revision for the Fourth Edition seems to have been abandoned at the same time as the special revision for land valuation was started: in 1934 H.StJ.L. Winterbotham referred to 'releasing from office duties every available man under the age of 50', which can be taken to suggest that small-scale revisers were redeployed on large-scale work.[25] However, it is also noticeable that the abandoning of the revision for the Fourth Edition seems to coincide with the appointment of Colonel Charles Close as DGOS, and Yolande Hodson has argued that it was due to this, rather than Land Valuation.[26]

So when the Third National Revision of the one-inch resumed in 1912 it was evidently with a view to a smooth geographical progression from south to north, rather than a patchwork determined by the complexities of large-scale and earlier small-scale revision. This can be

[23] Ordnance Survey annual reports: *Report of the progress of the Ordnance Survey to the 31st March 1909.* BPP (HC) 1909 [Cd. 4830], XXXV, 727; *...to the 31st March 1910.* BPP (HC) 1910 [Cd. 5241], XLIV, 445; *...to the 31st March 1911.* BPP (HC) 1911 [Cd. 5873], XXXVII, 577; *...to the 31st March 1912.* BPP (HC) 1912-13 [Cd. 6372], XLII, 641, 4.

[24] Brian Short, *The geography of England and Wales in 1910: an evaluation of Lloyd George's 'Domesday' of landownership,* Historical Geography Research Series, 22, April 1989; Brian Short, *Land and society in Edwardian Britain.* Cambridge University Press, 1997.

[25] H.StJ.L. Winterbotham, *The national plans (the ten-foot, five-foot, twenty-five-inch and six-inch scales).* London: HMSO, 1934, 79. (Ordnance Survey Professional Papers. New Series, No.16).

[26] Yolande Hodson, *Popular maps.* London: Charles Close Society, 1999, 60.

interpreted as a fresh start by Close, who instigated a rationalisation of both large-scale county meridians and small-scale sheet lines; it can also be considered as at least desirable in view of Close's espousal of a new style of one-inch mapping, which would include a quite different road classification from that used on the Third Edition. The revision began around Aldershot and in the south-west; it was disrupted by the outbreak of war in August 1914, but by 1920 it had reached southern Lancashire and Yorkshire, by 1923 it was in southern Scotland, and in 1930 it was completed, in Orkney. The results of the revision of 1912-30 were published between 1919 and 1932 as the 'Popular Edition' (Hi.10.1, Hi.18.1 respectively). Consequently, Third Edition maps, at any rate coloured ones, had a much shorter currency (1910-11 to 1919) in Devon than they did in Northumberland (1907 to 1925-6) or Scotland.

Revision for a Third Edition of the one-inch of Ireland began in 1908 but was abandoned in 1914 and never resumed. 128 sheets were published in outline (Hi.25.1): as will be related later, very few appeared in colour.

The Third Edition in colour
The first Third Edition sheets, in outline, were published in July 1903 in England and a month later in Scotland. The first of England in colour appeared some four months later, but four months before the completion of the initial publication of the revised New Series one-inch of England in Wales in colour, based on the revision of 1893-8.[27] The Third Edition coloured sheets differed in two essential particulars from the original design of 1896-7. They were in six colours, as for the northern English coloured sheets being published at this time, but though woods were in green, tree symbols were in black. Railways were now shown as on the engraved maps, with single lines by 'ladders' and others by 'chequers', whereas the coloured maps derived from the revision of 1893-8 had used chequers and solid lines respectively. Was the earlier redrawn style considered too bold, or was the extra litho-drawing considered not worth the effort? Personal preference of War Office or OS officers may have contributed. In other respects the earlier Third Edition sheets were similar to their predecessors, with yellowy sienna road infill, a comparatively low ratio of mapped area to total printed area, inclusive of marginalia (1:1.48 for a standard sheet), and the latitude and longitude values and dicing in the border replaced by alpha-numeric referencing, though without any squaring on the map face. As with the first coloured one-inch, the nominal total of 360 sheets was reduced by combining some sheets in coastal areas, though the combinations proposed for the Third Edition often differed noticeably from its predecessor, and some of the combinations would have resulted in strangely-shaped sheets: for example, sheet 72.73 would have had a map area of about 29 inches west-east by 12 inches south-north (about 737 by 304 mm).[28] It is possible that the preference for combined sheets of standard height south-north was so that as many as possible would suit the new folding pattern and marginalia adopted in 1904-5, and discussed below.

One fundamental difference, invisible on the maps themselves, was in terms of function. The coloured one-inch which had begun series publication in 1897 had been a creature of the military. The Dorington Committee might recommend a coloured one-inch, but it was General Sir Redvers Buller who had persuaded the Treasury to authorise it. Ideally, in the 1890s the military would have liked a coloured map at a somewhat larger scale, but they were prepared to work with the one-inch, and when in 1900 they decided that they needed comparatively large mobilisation stocks they were prepared to take a three-colour version.[29]

In 1900 Britain was in the midst of the South African war and there was a possibility that 'splendid isolation' might lead to difficulties with some other European power. The mapping used

---

[27] Unless noted otherwise, references to months of publication in this essay are taken from OS publication reports, at the time properly entitled *Supplement to catalogue of* [eg] *England and Wales. Publications issued from* [eg] *1st to 31st May, 1911.*

[28] Indexes to these proposed combinations appear in OS catalogues for 1905 and 1906.

[29] Tim Nicholson, *The birth of the modern Ordnance Survey small-scale map.* London: Charles Close Society, 2002, 34, and papers in group 17794/00 in file 19069 in PRO T1/9744.

in South Africa was very different in quality from that available at home, and the experience seems to have convinced the War Office of the worth of the half-inch (1:126,720) scale:

'…the Boer War had, as everyone knows, a chastening and sharpening effect on the British Army. We learnt to earmark the largest ant heap in sight for our next step forward, to regard every fold in the ground with deep suspicion, and to look on a good map as at once unexpected and heaven sent. In the period which followed that war the officer studied ground and maps as never before nor since. Now Bartholomew had just produced a very excellent ½-inch, based upon the Ordnance 1-inch. It offered an attractive layer system, and a wider opportunity for the strategically minded and brass-hatted, than the 1-inch. He bought, but grumbled, and so it was that the Ordnance Survey was charged with making a national ½-inch.'[30]

Whether military purchasers were quite so reluctant as Winterbotham implies is perhaps open to question, but the OS, the Board of Agriculture, and the Stationery Office (HMSO) certainly 'grumbled'. Their objection was less to the fact that the Bartholomew map, completed for Scotland in 1896 and for England and Wales in 1903, was a straightforward reduction of the OS one-inch, and more to its title 'Reduced Ordnance Map'. The upshot was that in 1902 the OS was authorised to produce its own half-inch map and at the same time Bartholomew adopted the title 'New Reduced Survey'. Pending completion of the OS offering, the War Office purchased Bartholomew's in quantity, much to the distress of HMSO and the Treasury.[31] So did the general public: there is an argument from known print-runs for the standard civil topographical map of Edwardian Britain being, not the OS one-inch, but the Bartholomew half-inch.[32]

The story of the OS half-inch map has yet to be told in the detail which it deserves, but by 1914 it could be described as 'the principal military map of Great Britain', and the War Office seems to have maintained considerable control over its design.[33] This was apparently not the case with the one-inch, although it would be wrong to suppose that the War Office completely lost interest in it: apart from surviving copies bearing the stamps of various military units, it was widely used for such purposes as staff college entrance examinations.[34] In 1909, in a report on mapping for the Australian government, Close noted that 'In the United Kingdom, the scale for general issue is ½ inch to 1 mile… with a very small issue of 1 inch maps…', and that the standard military scales elsewhere were 1:80,000 in France, 1:100,000 in Germany and Italy, 1:125,000 in Orange River Colony, and 1:126,000 in Russia; in Canada no decision had yet been made whether to standardise on one-inch or half-inch.[35] Whereas the half-inch passed through several design phases including, from 1908, publication in two forms, hill-shaded (mainly, it would seem, for the civil market) and layered (evidently more favoured by the military), the design of the one-inch remained fundamentally unchanged until a replacement for the Third Edition came under consideration, in 1911-12. Road infills were affected by a small change effected on all the OS's small-scale colour-

[30] H.StJ.L. Winterbotham, *A key to maps*. London & Glasgow: Blackie, 1936, 82-3.

[31] For a War Office requisition of Bartholomew maps, the dispute with Bartholomew and the authorisation of the OS half-inch map see file 19069/01 in PRO T1/9744, and file 13984/02 in PRO T1/9850B.

[32] See Tim Nicholson, *The birth of the modern Ordnance Survey small-scale map*. London: Charles Close Society, 2002; Eugene Burden, 'Early issues of Bartholomew's Reduced Ordnance Survey of England & Wales Scale 2 Miles to an Inch', *Sheetlines* 56 (1999), 22-26; Tim Nicholson, 'Bartholomew and the half-inch layer coloured map 1883-1903', *Cartographic Journal* 37 (2000), 123-145; and Yolande Hodson, *Popular maps*. London: Charles Close Society, 1999, 214.

[33] Comment by Col C.F. Close in *Report of the Departmental Committee on the sale of small-scale Ordnance Survey maps,* [1914], report, 30. [Chairman Sir S. Olivier. Copy PRO OS 1/6/5].

[34] R.C. Wheeler, 'Military use of UK maps 1900-1913: an examiner's perspective', *Sheetlines* 45 (1996), 32-3.

[35] Report by C.F. Close, 29 March 1909, in Australian Archives, Brighton, Victoria, 133/2 item 143/10/29, quoted in John D. Lines, *Australia on paper: the story of Australian mapping.* Box Hill, Victoria: Fortune publications, 1992, 41-3.

printed mapping from about August 1904 onwards: the yellowy sienna favoured since 1899 was replaced by burnt sienna, as used on the earliest one-inch coloured sheets.

Although there was stability in design inside the neat line, there was a change early in 1905 when the marginalia of the coloured one-inch were redesigned. Hitherto the border had been about 0.575-inch (14.6 mm) wide; now it was reduced to 0.25-inch (6.4 mm). The conventional signs were rearranged, and the publication and other footnotes were simplified and compressed. The compression continued the omission of the words 'track or footpath' from the rights-of-way disclaimer on sheets of England and Wales, which had been used since late in 1902 on the coloured one-inch and which would have made sense on the half-inch, which did not show these, but not on the one-inch, which did. The result was an increase in the ratio of mapped area to total printed area from 1:1.48 to 1:1.19 for a standard inland sheet.[36] The reason for the change would seem to be the adoption of a new 'concertina' style of fold which, for a standard sheet, would enable any part of the map to be inspected without having to open it out fully. It is unclear whether the initiative for this came from the War Office or the Ordnance Survey. What is more certain is that the change in colour of cover, from red to white (officially 'colourless') made probably in March 1906, was the result of pressure from the War Office.[37] Apparently the red was prone to run when wetted, which must have been unsightly when the British army had comparatively recently adopted khaki.[38]

Meanwhile, in March 1905 publication began of a coloured one-inch Third Edition of Scotland. In content it was similar to the Third Edition of England and Wales. Differences in design were partly a legacy of the parent engraved plates: apart from the marginalia, distinctive writing for hill and railway names, and reverse italic for water on a few sheets,[39] parishes were named in shaded capitals and districts were named in open block. A difference peculiar to the coloured version was that water-lining was replaced by a tint, thus necessitating a seventh printing: the coloured maps of England and Wales and Ireland retained water-lining. Water-tint was standard on half-inch and smaller-scale maps of the period, perhaps because it was less troublesome to produce and arguably better-looking. Whilst this may have been a good reason for using the technique on newly-created mapping, such as the half-inch, it does not explain why the OS went to the trouble of scraping out the water-lining and drawing the tint for the one-inch of Scotland. Was it because there was so much more inland water in Scotland that the trouble was felt worth it on aesthetic grounds? In contrast, the marginalia seem to have been the outcome of minimalism; the latitude and longitude values and dicing were replaced by graduations for alpha-numeric referencing, as on the English map, but the border retained its original width, sheet names remained top right, with 'Ordnance Survey of Scotland' top centre (and 'Third Edition', rather apologetically, top left), the rights-of-way disclaimer continued to refer to paths and tracks as well as roads, and the engraved map's publication notes and diagrams showing constituent six-inch sheets were retained. (So was 'Expansion', with arrows, to the left of the legend on some sheets: the meaning of this is baffling.[40]) Given the larger size of the Scottish sheets, and the necessity for a third fold, redrawing all the marginalia to suit the 'compact' style of later English, Welsh and Irish coloured maps was perhaps not felt to be worth the trouble. The Scottish sheets covered twice the area of standard one-inch sheets elsewhere in the United Kingdom, and there were a few combined sheets of coastal areas. Cross-border areas falling in England were left blank, unlike on OS half-inch and quarter-inch coloured mapping.

---

[36] These wide (0.575-inch) and narrow (0.25-inch) borders and associated marginal layout are indicated by 'w' and 'n' in column 9 in the list below.

[37] Copy, War Office to Board of Agriculture, 17 April 1905, papers in group 9263/05 in file 14847 in PRO T1/10667A.

[38] Comment by Col Pitt in W.J. Johnston, 'The new one-inch and quarter-inch maps of the Ordnance Survey', *Geographical Journal* LV (1920), 192-200, 199.

[39] Used in the Wigtown and Kirkcudbrightshire portions of sheets 1-9, and the small portion of Harris on sheet 90. (It was also used on the outer Hebridean sheets, but these were not published in colour.)

[40] Examples will be found on some printings of Scotland 8, 25, 26, 30, 34, 37, 42, 44, 48, 49, 52, 53 and 54.

The Large Sheet Series

It may be no coincidence that the advent of the first Scottish coloured Third Editions was quickly followed by the War Office requesting a larger sheet size, at any rate for the half-inch. That map now covered over half of England and Wales, with a basic sheet size of 18 by 12 inches, formed by grouping four standard New Series engraved sheets, though, as with the coloured one-inch, there were combined sheets in coastal areas, considerably reducing the nominal total of 104 sheets (Hi.35). It is also perhaps no coincidence that, a few weeks after the first Scottish sheets were published, the Topographical Section of the General Staff (TSGS; renamed Geographical Section, General Staff (GSGS) in 1908) got a new head, Major Charles Close, who in December 1904 had delivered a paper to the Royal Geographical Society on 'The ideal topographical map'.[41] Colonel Sir Duncan Johnston, DGOS, who retired at about the same time as Close was appointed to TSGS, was in the audience. Close, who had had OS experience, most recently in 1901-2, did not criticise the Ordnance Survey directly, but here was an original mind at work which wanted to design maps. Although he only became DGOS in August 1911, his influence on OS map design can be traced back to his appointment to TSGS in April 1905.

Almost as soon as Close took up his new post a War Office committee was appointed to consider aspects of mapping policy.[42] Its desire for map covers to be other than red has already been noted, its wish for map indexes on back covers is discussed below, and its need for a layered half-inch, rather than the hill-shaded one which the OS was currently producing, does not belong to the one-inch story. The other main item on its shopping-list was a larger standard sheet size. It suggested perhaps 24 by 16 inches within the neat line. It is unclear how this was arrived at, unless as a consequence of grouping sixteen standard six-inch full sheets of 36 by 24 inches; just such a 24 by 16 inch sheet had been produced in 1901 as an index to a set of sixteen 'War Game' maps of the Thames Valley. After some demur by the Treasury, the half-inch Large Sheet Series was authorised. The War Office's attitude did not please everyone: Sir Thomas Elliott, the permanent secretary of the Board of Agriculture and Fisheries, after discussing mapping matters with Close, remarked 'I thought him quite capable of forming a sound opinion as to what was really required but of course one never knows what the next man may think in a department in which there is so very little continuity of policy.'[43]

An outcome of this was that the one-inch of England and Wales, described by the War Office in February 1906 as 'an excellent military map', though the sheets were 'somewhat small', was also issued in large sheets: the OS annual report for 1906-7 remarked that 'As revision progresses, the coloured map is now being issued in larger sheets to meet the views of the War Office, and it is hoped that there will be a convenience to the general public as well.'[44] The War Office was evidently still more important to the one-inch that were the civilians.

For both half-inch and one-inch Large Sheet Series (LSS) a standard sheet size of 27 by 18 inches (68.61 by 45.73 cm) within the neat line was adopted; this was 'about the largest size which will fold conveniently'.[45] The first half-inch 'large' sheets appeared in July 1906 (Hi.36.A.1), and the first 'large' one-inch sheet 17, *Isle of Man*, appeared in December 1906, after some 84 Third Edition 'small' sheets (SSS) had been published in colour.[46] As no further new half-inch SSS

---

[41] C.F. Close, 'The ideal topographical map', *Geographical Journal* XXV (1905), 633-647. T.S.G.S. itself was a renaming of the Intelligence Department, War Office, in 1904, following the creation of a General Staff and consequent reorganisation of War Office departments.

[42] Copy, War Office to Board of Agriculture, 17 April 1905, papers in group 9263/05 in file 14847 in PRO T1/10667A.

[43] Copy, War Office to Board of Agriculture, 17 April 1905, papers in group 9263/05; Elliott to Murray, 6 March 1906, papers in group 3165/06: both in file 14847 in PRO T1/10667A.

[44] *Report of the progress of the Ordnance Survey to the 31st March 1907.* BPP (HC) 1907 [Cd. 3668], LXVIII, 439, 5.

[45] Copy, Agriculture & Fisheries to War Office, 8 January 1906: papers in group 672/06, in file 14847 in PRO T1/10667A.

[46] As will be seen from the detailed lists which follow this essay, there is some doubt when some of the 'small' coloured sheets were issued: I have assumed that all those dated 1906 and 1907 were issued in those years.

sheets appeared after July 1906, it might have been expected that the coloured one-inch would behave similarly, but no: between January and August 1907 eleven further SSS sheets were published, whereas no further LSS sheets appeared until June 1907. At first, this is puzzling, but it might be explained partly by the need to install increased printing capacity at the OS, including more machines capable of handling the larger plates and stones necessitated by the larger sheet size of the LSS.[47]

Printing capacity apart, the Scottish one-inch had been produced in *de facto* 'large' sheets from the start, and coloured sheets with a map area substantially larger than 18 by 12 inches were being produced by the OS from 1896 onwards, notably the Aldershot one-inch manoeuvre map of that year which can be regarded as the first 'production' coloured sheet (Hi.5.3). In 1900 several combined 'inland' sheets in the south-west were produced as 'two-up' combined sheets, with a mapped area of 18 by 24 inches; it is not known why this was done but, if it was an experiment, any benefits were evidently outweighed by the drawbacks. Earlier, in 1899 two of the original combined sheets of east Kent were replaced by a single sheet, 18 by 24 inches, and in 1903 the Lleyn peninsula was covered by a combined sheet 26 by 18 inches which looks like a prototype 'large' sheet, but isn't. In 1904 another comparatively large sheet provided Third Edition coloured cover of the Isle of Wight.

It is possible that production of the one-inch LSS was held up whilst sheet lines were finalised. They were evidently sufficiently settled for the Isle of Man sheet to be issued in December 1906, but the issue of a Lleyn peninsula sheet in March 1907 with small sheet numbers, rather than as LSS 49, is puzzling; this sheet was later converted to the LSS by overprinting the new number on existing stock. Possibly retention of the old numbers was justified by all its neighbours being SSS, and by this area not being the highest priority for conversion to LSS form; conversion took place in 1909-10, and indeed sheets 92.93 and 105.118pt were the last Third Edition SSS to be replaced, in September 1910. In 1906-7 there was extensive reprinting of one-inch and half-inch SSS: this looks like a deliberate policy of building up stock sufficient until the LSS could be published, and perhaps also to provide a small SSS stock for any residual demand for the format after the LSS was published.[48] There is some evidence of a similar policy for the one-inch coloured map of Ireland, as republication of the Irish one-inch in LSS form was considered in 1906, 1909 and 1913.[49] Only one Third Edition SSS, 286, was reprinted after this, in 1909, presumably to replenish stocks six months before LSS cover was published, though perhaps mention should be made of sheet 348, which nominally remained based on the revision of 1894, but which was reprinted in 1909 with extensive additions from Third Edition revision.[50]

Two other combined SSS, each with a map area 28 by 18 inches (and thus slightly larger than a standard SSS) were published in June 1906 covering east Kent, perhaps before the LSS scheme had been finalised; both were reused in the LSS, as sheets 118 and 128. Their inclusion in the LSS scheme may have been a matter of production convenience, but it is noteworthy that the 'large' combined East Kent sheet of 1899 was reprinted in April 1907, and that when the LSS sheet lines were modified around 1913 for the mapping to be based on the resumed third national revision, 118 and 128 were replaced by a single sheet, 117, covering nearly the same area as the 1899 sheet. Functioning in the SSS, 118 and 128 did not overlap any sheets; as LSS, they overlapped onto 117, 127 and 138. However, these overlaps were modest compared with those in south Devon, where the function of LSS 149 seems to have been partly to fill a gap of about four miles between LSS 141 and 150, and partly to give convenient coverage to the hinterland of

---

[47] There is a reference to increased capacity being provided at the OS in 1906 in Treasury to War Office, 12 February 1910, papers in 2127/10 in file 4071 in PRO T1/11391.

[48] Tim Nicholson, *The birth of the modern Ordnance Survey small-scale map*. London: Charles Close Society, 2002, 39: in June 1914 152 sheets of the revised coloured edition and seventy coloured Third Edition small sheets were still available, but all had been withdrawn by April 1915.

[49] J.H. Andrews, *A paper landscape: the Ordnance Survey in nineteenth-century Ireland*. Oxford University Press, 1975, 294, citing OS of Ireland files OSL 10559, 12186 and 15253.

[50] Tim Nicholson, *The birth of the modern Ordnance Survey small-scale map*. London: Charles Close Society, 2002, 32.

Torquay. Given that the OS could easily produce LSS sheets 22 inches south to north, as exemplified by half-inch LSS 35, this arrangement seems rather ill thought-out, and it is noticeable that in the rearrangement of about 1913, the fifteen original one-inch LSS in the south-west were reduced to eleven.

Coverage and overlaps apart, the one-inch LSS presented another problem. In principle, groups of four LSS were formed by nine SSS: of the nine, four would be included in a single LSS, another four would split between two LSS, and the sheet in the middle of the group would be split between all four LSS. As the names had been engraved on the SSS without thought of this cutting and joining, it follows that many names were cut by the new sheet lines: either the names had to be moved, or a break was necessary in the neat line. The latter was no doubt easier in the short term, but it is noticeable that on many of the earlier sheets there was extensive repositioning of names when they were reprinted. There was much less of this on later sheets, perhaps because the problem had been appreciated, but possibly also because there was less pressure on the litho draughtsmen, as the backlog of publication had been cleared off.[51]

Otherwise, the style of the LSS was similar to that of the later SSS: there was the same narrow (0.25-inch) border and the same style of conventional signs and footnotes; though there was no longer any need to save space by so doing, the references to tracks and footpaths were still omitted from the rights-of-way disclaimer. Scale bars were added in the west and east margins. The ratio of mapped area to total printed area was further improved, to 1:1.12. (This contrasts with 1:1.33 for the modern OS 1:50,000.) One loss was the ability to inspect the whole of a standard sheet without opening it completely: now only two-thirds would be visible without opening right out and refolding, and the advantage of the 'concertina' fold on the SSS would be lost to OS users until the advent of the Michelin fold in the 1920s (mostly used for quarter-inch maps) and the Bender fold from 1938. In 1909 railway station symbols were introduced in place of description to the engraved SSS, and they appeared on the LSS and coloured map of Scotland from early in 1910; they were very discreet. On sheets such as 58 and 66 which were made up from a mix of SSS with and without symbols, the symbols were added where necessary.[52]

The progress of Third Edition coloured publication
The replacement of the original coloured one-inch of England and Wales by the Third Edition was not a straightforward progression, reflecting outline publication and field revision. In those parts of south-east England which were of particular military interest the coloured Third Edition SSS seems to have been produced as soon as practicable, without much regard to the stock position of the earlier coloured map (though a reprint of 100 copies of the Aldershot sheet, 285, in 1904 suggests 'tiding over' until the Third Edition was ready). Elsewhere, the Third Edition SSS only seems to have been produced to replace stock. For example sheet 220, *Leighton Buzzard*, was only published in colour in July 1906, over eighteen months after it had been published in outline. However, production of new coloured one-inch sheets in 1905 may have been delayed by demands for coloured maps from other Government departments.[53] In northern England, only seven SSS were published, and the scatter, taken in conjunction with the reprinting pattern of the older coloured one-inch, suggests that this was to replenish stock rather than to provide the public with more up-to-date mapping. Nonetheless, it is interesting that Third Edition SSS 63 was published in December 1906, whilst its neighbour to the north, 53, was reprinted the following month from old material.

---

[51] Guy Messenger, *The Ordnance Survey one-inch map of England and Wales Third Edition (Large Sheet Series)*. London: Charles Close Society, 1988, 2.

[52] Station symbols appear on Scotland sheets 83-85, 94, 95, 101-103, 107-110, 113-116 and those for Orkney and Shetland. They are also used on the Glasgow district sheet of 1914. Their earliest appearance on the one-inch is in the legend of SSS coloured sheet 286, printing 6.09, where they were included in error, as they are not shown on the map.

[53] *Report of the progress of the Ordnance Survey to the 31st March 1906.* BPP (HC) 1906 [Cd. 3064], XCVIII, 649, 3.

The initial priority for LSS publication was those areas for which the Third Edition had only been published in outline, and this explains the early concentration on northern England. Much of the earlier publication, in 1907-9, was clearing the backlog; replacement of the SSS cover of southern England, mostly in the later part of 1909, was a lower priority, and replacement of the substantial block of SSS mapping in north Wales was the lowest priority of all, with the last LSS – 41 – being published in September 1910. From 1909-10 publication of the LSS followed completion of the engraved outline map fairly closely. The publication of Third Edition coloured mapping is summarised in the table below.

	England SSS	England LSS	Scotland	District
1903	2	-	-	-
1904	20	-	-	1
1905	29	-	11	3
1906	33	1	16	2
1907	11	26	13	3
1908	-	40	3	0
1909	-	28	19	0
1910	-	23	16	3
1911	-	9	7	3
1912	-	7	0	15
1913	-	11	14	6
1914	-	-	-	5

Note: 'District' maps includes manoeuvre and similar military maps produced for sale.

These figures suggest that in 1907-9 the coloured mapping of England and Wales was a much higher priority than that of Scotland, although the position is complicated by other colour-printing work in hand at the same time, such as the half-inch map, reprints of published one-inch sheets, and mapping of north-western Europe which was being stockpiled in the event of mobilisation.

Cover of England and Wales in the LSS was more comprehensive than in the original coloured map of 1897-1904 in that it included the Isle of Man and the Isles of Scilly. Cover of Ireland in 1902-6 was also comprehensive. However, there seems to have been a definite policy of restricting cover of Scotland to those sheets covering the mainland and some of the adjacent islands: the indexes which started to appear on the back covers of the one-inch of Scotland from about late 1907 or early 1908 onwards show only the mainland sheets, although there would have been room to show those of the islands as well. Cover of the mainland was completed in 1913, and at the end of the year coloured cover of Orkney and Shetland was published: each archipelago was covered by two large sheets, a striking contrast to the three for Orkney and four for Shetland of subsequent one-inch and 1:50,000 series. Was there some thought at this time of extending cover to the Outer Hebrides as well? It is perhaps notable that the half-inch mapping of Orkney, Shetland and the Outer Hebrides was published only in the hill-shaded form, suggesting that these areas were seen as of relatively little military or civil cartographic importance. Presumably most of the probably limited topographical mapping demand for these islands was met by Bartholomew. At any rate, no coloured Third Edition mapping was published of the Hebrides. However, at least two sheets were printed, presumably sometime between 1914 and 1918, with outline in black and hachures in brown, and issued in integral covers, suggesting an improvisation for military use.[54]

The superseding of the Third Edition
The last of the coloured Third Edition series sheets were published in December 1913. By that time they were stylistically obsolescent, and experiments to develop a markedly different-looking map were well advanced. Close's particular objections to the style of the coloured one-inch as he

---

[54] Sheets 88 and 89: listed in Roger Hellyer, *Ordnance Survey small-scale maps indexes: 1801-1998*. Kerry: David Archer, 1999, 49, section 15.4.

found it in 1911 were the road classification, which was inadequate for contemporary conditions, the inadequate depiction of relief, and the presence of parish boundaries.[55] In his annual report for 1913-14, signed on 28 April 1914, Close expected that the first sheets of the new series mapping would be published that summer.[56] Several are known to have been at proof stage around this time, and a pair of district sheets, *Aldershot (North)* and *Aldershot (South)*, were printed, but all the stock appears to have been used for military purposes, rather than placed on sale. Relief was shown by hachures, contours, layers and hill-shading. The first series sheets based on the one-inch revision begun in 1912 were printed in 1918 and a large group were published in June 1919, as the first instalment of the 'Popular Edition'. There may still have been some thought of publishing an alternative version in the 'Aldershot' style: successive editions of the official *Description* of OS small-scale maps referred to the Third Edition of England and Wales as the 'Fully Coloured' or 'Fully Coloured Edition or Large Sheet Series', implying that the Popular Edition was somehow a less than fully coloured interim stage. (The Third Edition coloured cover of Scotland was simply 'Coloured Edition'). Although the Popular Edition was completed for England and Wales in 1926 and Scotland in 1932, the remaining stocks of the Third Edition coloured mapping remained on sale for some time, and continued to be mentioned in the small scale *Description* up to 1930.[57] They may have been officially withdrawn once the Popular of Scotland was complete in the summer of 1932.

Although after 1913 the ordinary Third Edition coloured sheets were obsolescent, district sheets based on Third Edition material continued to be published up to 1921, and some at least remained on sale into the late 1940s.[58] This includes seven of eight new sheets in Scotland published in 1920-2, but nominally the last of the group, *The Cairngorms,* was really the first sheet of something different: it anticipated the Popular of Scotland, in that it was based on post-war revision and was wholly redrawn, for heliozincographic production. A possibly tendentious example of 'new publication' is the re-publication in 1917 of the three cross-border LSS sheets, 1, 3 and 5, with the Scottish portion filled in. Close was interested in reducing the number of meridians and consequent sheet-line systems used by the OS; the Popular of Scotland was redrawn using the Delamere meridian of the New Series, and the re-publication of these three sheets in 1917 can be interpreted as a first instalment of this. Possibly the need for reprints was the occasion of the change.[59]

Also first published when the Third Edition was obsolescent was the Black Outline Edition. In 1904 Close thought that there was no future for the engraved outline map, and in 1913 the thinking was that in the long term the one-inch would be offered in two forms, both printed by lithographic means: 'fully coloured', as exemplified by the Aldershot sheets of 1914, and an outline edition, with outline in black, contours in red or brown, and water in blue.[60] In the early years of World War I the engraved outline maps of both England and Wales and of Scotland continued to be printed direct from copper. Lithographic printing of the English sheets seems to have been adopted as an alternative, but in 1918-19 there was a more radical departure: a new, lithographed, 'Black Outline Edition' was issued. In Scotland this was based on the engraved map,

[55] *Report of the Departmental Committee on the sale of small-scale Ordnance Survey maps,* [1914], report, 30. [Chairman Sir S. Olivier. Copy PRO OS 1/6/5].

[56] *Report of the progress of the Ordnance Survey to the 31st March 1914.* BPP (HC) 1914 [Cd. 7424], XLIV, 1, 9-10.

[57] *A description of the Ordnance Survey small scale maps.* Southampton: Ordnance Survey, editions 1-7 [1919]-1930; the one-inch Third Edition coloured map was last illustrated in the Fifth Edition, 1925.

[58] Ordnance Survey to C.L. Wykes, 10 June 1947, document 133A in PRO OS 1/111. There is in a copy of *Cambridge* in a private collection, issued (on the evidence of the cover) before 1931, which bears a price alteration sticker of 1st September 1945, but this was perhaps added by a retailer to 'old stock', rather than by the OS.

[59] However, the authors have been unable to find a 1917 printing of sheet 5, and it may be that, though the plates were prepared in 1917, the 'reprint' of this sheet in 1921 was in fact its first printing.

[60] See Instructions of 6 March 1913, original in PRO OS 1/4/3, and printed in Yolande Hodson, *Popular maps.* London: Charles Close Society, 1999, 220-3.

and can be regarded as a variant on it: at least 76 (of 132) sheets were issued. In England and Wales the outline, water and contour plates of the Large Sheet Series were used, printed in black: as derivatives of the coloured mapping, they fall within the scope of this book, and are duly listed.[61]

Although the Black Outline Edition is explicable as a long-term measure in the light of Close's policy in 1913-14, the distribution pattern of the 57 sheets known to have been printed is strange. Was it determined by exhaustion of stocks of the engraved SSS? Most of the known Black Outline sheets were listed in the OS publication reports, which suggest that publication was abandoned in 1919. Why? Did printing the engraved SSS from zinc prove more cost-effective after all? Or was it found better to revert to printing directly from copper, as was the practice into the 1930s? Is it significant that, apparently in 1919, a black outline version of Popular Edition sheet 96 was printed, which is the only known example of its kind, and was presumably made for consultation purposes? Did the reaction to sheet 96 prompt wholesale reconsideration of large-sheet outline edition policy? When the first production outline derivatives of the Popular Edition appeared, late in 1921, they combined black outline and water with coloured contours: within two years, the water was being printed in colour as well. However, the engraved SSS continued on sale, although from about 1936 they were once more printed from zinc.[62] If LSS Black Outlines were only printed to replace exhausted SSS stocks, then considerable confusion might reign because of different sheet numbers and sheet lines. Whatever the explanation, after 1920 Third Edition outline edition mapping was once again printed from copper.

Whereas the Black Outline editions at least merited a mention in the publication reports, no contemporary mention is known of outline, water and contour printings of the LSS, of which a few have been found. It is not known when or why they were made, and whether they were related in anyway to the outline-water-and-contours format on the one-inch envisaged in 1913-14.[63]

District maps
Starting with *London and its Environs* in 1857, the OS published a few engraved district maps in the later nineteenth century; except for *London* they are rarely met with, and were perhaps not very good sellers. In 1899 the OS began issuing cheap lithographically or zincographically-printed one-inch district maps, with roads infilled sienna, in covers. Fifty of England and Wales, and more of Scotland and Ireland, were published in 1899-1904 based on the revision of 1893-1901, and from 1904 onwards some of these were republished based on Third Edition material.[64] Reprinting and republication suggest that there was some public demand for them; there was little commercial competition at this scale, apart from a few offerings of 'honeypot' areas such as the Lake District and the Isle of Wight. The Lake District sheets differed from the standard style in that the lakes

---

[61] Black Outline editions known: in England and Wales: sheets 1, 2, 3, 4, 6, 8, 13, 14, 15, 16, 17, 18, 19, 20, 21, 22, 27, 28, 36, 37, 38, 42, 43, 44, 45, 46, 48, 52, 53, 59, 66, 68, 73, 78, 79, 86, 93, 94, 95, 96, 98, 99, 103, 104, 105, 106, 107, 108, 111, 112, 114, 115, 116, 124, 125, 126, 150 (total of 57 sheets: sheets 38 and 48 were omitted from the OS publication reports); in Scotland: 1, 2, 8, 11, 14, 17, 18, 19, 21, 22, 23, 24, 25, 27, 29, 30, 31, 32, 33, 34, 35, 36, 37, 38, 39, 40, 41, 42.50, 43, 44, 45, 46, 47, 48, 49, 51, 55, 56, 57, 57A, 58, 59, 60, 63, 64, 66, 67, 68, 70, 72, 73, 75, 76, 77, 79, 85, 87, 91, 92, 94, 95, 96, 97, 98, 100, 102, 103, 104, 105, 106, 107, 108, 109, 110, 111, 113, 114 (total of 78 sheets in 77; sheets 35, 58, 66, 67, 68, 76, 79, 100, 111 were omitted from the OS publication reports; sheet 26 was published, but used Fourth Edition material). Several of these have only come to light since Roger Hellyer, *Ordnance Survey small-scale maps indexes: 1801-1998*. Kerry: David Archer, 1999, was published, and more may yet be found.
[62] Yolande Hodson, *Popular maps*. London: Charles Close Society, 1999, 29-32. The black outline printing of sheet 96 is in the OS 'Specimen Drawer' in the Royal Geographical Society map room. There are some examples of late zincographic printings of outline SSS sheets, complete with print codes, in the Messenger Collection in Cambridge University Library map library: they include an example of SSS 42 printed as late as 1942.
[63] Sheets known to the authors: 11, 15, 21, 30, 31, 97, 124. They are evidently not all contemporary: sheet 31 has the 2/6 mounted-in-sections price, whereas sheet 30 is 3/-. There were two printings of sheet 124 in this form, as base maps for OTC examinations, for November 1919 (with code 6.12) and March 1920 (no code).
[64] T. Nicholson, 'Buried gold: the Ordnance Survey one inch/mile black outline, coloured roads district map 1899-193?', *Cartographic Journal* 31 (1994), 123-131.

were infilled blue. At least one of the sheets seems to have been popular enough to be printed in a run of at least 2000 copies, which was large by contemporary OS standards.[65]

These outline-and-coloured-roads sheets were intended purely for the civil market. Military users of district maps had a more sophisticated product, usually in the style of the 'fully coloured' one-inch. Sheets covering the Aldershot, Salisbury Plain and Wareham districts were published in 1896-8 based on the revision of 1893-8, and from 1905 onwards these were republished.[66] The pair of Aldershot sheets, published in 1905 and reprinted several times before 1914, recalled the early, obsolescent OS coloured one-inch in that they omitted wood infill; however, overprints showing military training and out-of-bounds areas increased the number of printings needed. The Salisbury Plain sheet of 1906 was the last Third Edition coloured sheet of England to be reprinted, in 1927, albeit apparently 'For Official Use Only', and with some limited revision.[67]

The first move away from this pattern of coloured roads primarily for civilians and 'fully coloured' primarily for the military came in 1907, when *Loch Lomond District* was issued, in the same seven-colour style as series Scottish coloured one-inch maps.[68] In England, further outline-and-roads sheets were issued in 1909, but in 1910 *Winchester* was published, in the same style and colouring as the LSS; twenty more were published by the end of 1913. Some were replacements for earlier outline-and-coloured-roads sheets: others had no predecessors.

Some were to non-standard specifications. Two of the earliest were *Cambridge* and *Oxford:* some covers for these sheets carried notes associating them with the Officers Training Corps (OTC) of those universities, though the maps presumably appealed at least equally to leisure and educational users. They differed from the usual LSS style in that latitude and longitude were indicated in the borders, there was two-inch squaring drawn across the face of the map, and there were two magnetic variation diagrams. Two-inch squaring on the map face also appeared on *London (North)* and *London (South)*, both published in 1912. The numbers of constituent one-inch series sheets were given up to 1912; thereafter they were omitted. Two sheets published in 1911 (later *Ipswich and Felixstowe* and *Weston-super-Mare*) were at first identified on the map face only by the numbers of the corresponding LSS sheets (as a result of which the British Museum filed its copies with the standard numbered LSS), and by name only on the covers: this would seem to be related to the omitting of sheet names generally in 1911-12, which is discussed later. *Weston super Mare* is also encountered with the title *Clevedon* on the cover. The most obviously military sheet of this family was *Windsor and Neighbourhood*, produced for Eton College Rifle Volunteer Corps in 1907, and reissued in 1913 for Eton College OTC on different sheet lines, which was however not on sale.[69] Its sheet lines seem to have been laid out so as to facilitate the journeyings, or marches, of Etonians to and from Aldershot. Most of the others can be explained by their covering holiday resorts: *Worcester and Malvern* could be explained thus, but *Rugby* seems a strange subject. Did Rugby School and Malvern College OTCs have something to do with them?

Pwllheli and Criccieth (which covered a similar area to LSS 49 and cannot have helped its sales) and *Folkestone*, both of 1913, were in seven printings: the sea was shown with vignetted tint, as on standard Scottish coloured sheets. Other sheets conformed fairly closely to the standard LSS model, except that they usually covered a slightly larger area. The basis for selecting areas is unknown, but could be the result of suggestions from retailers, perhaps relayed by travellers

---

[65] *Report of the Departmental Committee on the sale of small-scale Ordnance Survey maps,* [1914], minutes of evidence, 24, q.537. [Chairman Sir S. Olivier. Copy PRO OS 1/6/5]; cf print-runs cited in Tim Nicholson, *The birth of the modern Ordnance Survey small-scale map.* London: Charles Close Society, 2002.

[66] Tim Nicholson, 'The Ordnance Survey and smaller scale military maps of Britain 1854-1914', *Cartographic Journal* 25 (1988), 109-27.

[67] [Tim Nicholson], 'Two inter-war oddities', *Sheetlines* 33 (1992), 60.

[68] Many of these district and 'tourist' sheets included '*District*' in their titles, but these are sometimes omitted in what follows, in the interests of brevity.

[69] Notwithstanding which, copies of the 1913 version seem to be encountered second-hand rather more readily than in the case of some sheets which did go on sale.

employed by T. Fisher Unwin, who was the agent for OS small-scale maps from 1906 onwards.[70] A variation on the district map is represented by copies of LSS 42, which bear 'Colwyn Bay District' or 'Penmaenmawr District', but no number, on the cover: how many other instances there were of this is unknown.

Cambridge, Oxford, Folkestone and *Pwllheli* all represent conservative variations on the standard specification, but that could hardly be said of *Killarney,* issued in the summer of 1913, and replacing an outline-with-coloured-roads predecessor of 1902. This was the first published fruit of Close's redesign of the one-inch, put in hand in 1912, and at least partly inspired by the 'Type 1900' 1:50,000 mapping of France. For the first time in OS practice two colours, red and yellow, were used for road infills; yet more striking was the relief, which combined contours, hachures, hill-shading and layers. The red and yellow mimicked in a general way the effect intended for mapping based on the revision of the one-inch which had recommenced in 1912 though, as all red roads were first class and all yellow ones were second class, no more basic information was available than was given on the parent engraved outline maps. Further district sheets, in a broadly similar style, were issued between April and July 1914: *Glasgow, Dorking and Leith Hill,* and *Ilkley*. Detail differences compared with *Killarney* were the solid greyish (rather than black dotted) contours and solid and chequered symbols for double and single track railways; the use of a solid line and the annotation '*(SINGLE TRACK)*' on *Killarney* and a few contemporary Irish half-inch sheets was evidently found unsatisfactory. (It would have made for 'clutter' on many sheets in the more developed or closely detailed parts of Britain.) Common to all four of these 1913-14 sheets was a redesigned border, which was an intelligent compromise between the minimalism of the standard Third Edition coloured sheets and the elaboration of the 'keyboard' style of the engraved SSS.[71]

The accepted view of these four sheets, together with a small specimen of Keswick and Derwentwater included in a new edition of the official *Textbook of topographical surveying,* written by Close and republished late in 1913, is that they were steps on the way to working out a definitive colour specification for the series mapping of Britain based on the revision that had begun in 1912. In 1936 H.StJ.L. Winterbotham, who had been in charge of triangulation and levelling at the OS in 1913-14, wrote that 'before minds were made up the Great War was upon us'. However, he rather spoilt the effect by referring to a map of Somerset which can be identified with a printing of sheet 120 of 1916, and which can be interpreted as a nine-colour compromise between the twelve-colour 'Killarney' style on the one hand and the six-colour coloured Third Edition or the Popular Edition on the other.[72] Common to all the 1913-14 published 'experimental' sheets based on Third Edition material (except the Keswick specimen) and the 'production' sheets based on post-1912 revision which were printed in 1914 is the changing of layer colours at 300, 600 and 900 feet; it may be suggested that the design was in fact settled by mid-1914, but was almost immediately called into question by economies implied following the outbreak of war in August. *Dorking and Leith Hill* has a substantial overlap with the two Aldershot sheets, and it is to be suspected that this sheet was not expected to have a very long life in its Third Edition-derived form: in the event it was reprinted several times and was only replaced in 1929. The two Aldershot

---

[70] *Report of the Departmental Committee on the sale of small-scale Ordnance Survey maps,* [1914], minutes of evidence, 10. [Chairman Sir S. Olivier. Copy PRO OS 1/6/5].

[71] The new border was not a completely new invention. An outer frame with thin-thick-thin lines and an inner diced band for latitude and longitude, was used on the quarter-inch from at least the time of its publication in the 1880s, and possibly from its inception in 1859. (See Richard Oliver, 'The origins of Ordnance Survey quarter-inch mapping in Great Britain, 1837-72', *Sheetlines* 15 (1986), 9-14.) This was similar in width to the border of *Killarney*. A narrower version of this style was used on the half-inch of Great Britain from 1903 onwards, with alpha-numeric indications, but no divisions, added from 1910. The half-inch of Ireland initially used a border similar to *Killarney; Killarney* and the later 'experimental' sheets of 1914, together with the new small-scale series introduced from 1918 onwards, added two-inch divisions in the border for the alpha-numeric referencing, as used on all the coloured one-inch maps from 1897 onwards.

[72] H.StJ.L. Winterbotham, *A key to maps.* London & Glasgow: Blackie, 1936, 75.

sheets were the first 'production' one-inch sheets to be contoured throughout at 50 feet vertical intervals: a delayed fulfilment of the War Office's request in 1892.

If the district sheets of 1913-14 were experimental, then those of 1919-22, which bore the description 'Tourist map', have some claim to be considered 'provisional', in that Third Edition base material was used because third national revision material was not yet available. Also, contours were taken from the Third Edition, with its standard intervals of 100 and 250 ft, rather than using 50 ft interval contours as on the Popular Edition. Although the areas covered presumably reflect commercial considerations, the actual style of the maps was apparently the outcome of a reaction by some OS officers, led by Colonel W.J. Johnston, to what they felt to be the 'puritanism' of the Popular Edition.[73] Perhaps they felt the style to be uncomfortably close to that of some Western Front mapping. The first sheet, exhibited at the Royal Geographical Society in December 1919, and published early in 1920, was *Snowdon*; it was followed by *Lake District* and seven others of districts in Scotland. The earlier sheets had woods with green infill; the later ones anticipated the usual style of inter-war tourist maps and omitted the infill. The general effect suggested a dilution of the 'Killarney' style, without the hill-shading, and with rather less subtle layer-tints; there was a similar loss of quality when *Glasgow, Dorking and Leith Hill,* and *Ilkley* were reprinted.

By and large most of the Scottish Third Edition 'tourist' sheets do not appear to have been particularly successful; none were reprinted and, as noted above, stocks of several were still available in the late 1940s. *Loch Lomond* and *Oban* were replaced in 1930 and 1936 respectively. *Snowdon* and *Lake District* were more successful; the latter was reprinted in 1924 – uniquely for a Third Edition sheet, railway names were revised to take account of the 'grouping' of 1923 – and both were replaced in 1925.

This brings us to two curious sheets published in 1919 and 1920. The latter, another *Lake District,* combined outline, coloured water and red and orange roads; it was perhaps issued in a limited run as a stopgap for the 1920 summer season pending the publication of the Tourist map a few months later. It is possible that it represents the style contemplated by Close in 1914 for cheap district maps, which would have embodied the new road classification, though it is unclear from the exiguous evidence whether other colours would have been used.[74] Yolande Hodson points to the use of coloured contours and water in the new standard 'outline' mapping contemplated in 1913: except for the wood infill, this is the colour scheme of the Popular Edition.[75] Equally strange was a 'Provisional Popular Edition' sheet of York of 1919; this combined Third Edition base material, including 'ladder' and 'chequer' railways, with the contemporary Popular Edition colour scheme and relief treatment, though without the additional 50 ft contours. It is unclear whether it was an experiment or a makeshift: the title suggests the latter.

The district sheets mostly outlived the regular numbered series sheets: some were replaced by Popular Edition-derived successors, but the Cambridge, Pwllheli, Staffordshire Potteries, Winchester, Ipswich and Rugby sheets were all still listed in the eighth edition (1935) of the official *Description* of small-scale maps, and all but the last two, plus all those Scottish tourist maps which had not been replaced, were still listed in the ninth edition (1937). It may be suspected that some, such as *Cambridge*, sold very slowly because the Popular Edition series sheets offered an acceptable alternative.

[73] H.S.L.W. [i.e Winterbotham], 'Sidelights: being notes on Ordnance Survey matters…' [sometimes referred to as Winterbotham's 'handover notes'], unpublished manuscript in Ordnance Survey Library, 106.

[74] *Report of the Departmental Committee on the sale of small-scale Ordnance Survey maps,* [1914], minutes of evidence, 34, qq 773-4. [Chairman Sir S. Olivier. Copy PRO OS 1/6/5]; Yolande Hodson, *Popular maps.* London: Charles Close Society, 1999, 23-4, 30.

[75] Yolande Hodson, *Popular maps.* London: Charles Close Society, 1999, 29-30.

Ireland

The Third Edition coloured mapping of Ireland is both exiguous and disproportionately complicated.

As has been noted above, a coloured one-inch SSS of Ireland was completed in 1906, similar in general style to contemporary mapping of Britain except that it lacked contours.[76] The possibility of an Irish LSS (Hi.26) was discussed in 1906 and in 1906-7 there was extensive reprinting of the coloured SSS, contemporary with the similar reprinting in quantity of the one-inch and half-inch SSS for England and Wales; perhaps there was a like intention of building up sufficient stocks to last until a LSS could be published. Indeed, the stocks of most sheets were sufficient to last into the 1940s and beyond; this was perhaps one reason why the start of Irish Third Edition publication in engraved outline in 1909 was not followed by any coloured publication. From 1911 onwards demand for the Irish one-inch, and a justification for a LSS, may have been eroded by the publication of the OS half-inch (Hi.39). It is perhaps symptomatic of the lack of real interest in an Irish LSS that a standard feature of the half-inch, from its inception to 1911 to its demise ninety-odd years later, was a diagram in the bottom margin indicating constituent one-inch SSS sheets.

The contouring of Ireland, abandoned in 1857, was resumed after 1890 following the decision to resurvey most of the country at 1:2500. After 1900 contours were added to the one-inch plates and the one-inch Third Edition was contoured from the start. It was therefore possible for the OS to publish a proto-LSS sheet of Belfast in 1912 in the style of that across the water, complete with contours: only the revision date of 1901-2 and the lack of 'Third Edition' spoilt the effect. Although apparently not published until after 1918 a LSS index for Ireland was evidently in being, as *Belfast* corresponds closely to Irish LSS 17, but of course lacks any sheet number.[77]

The first proper Irish Third Edition coloured sheet to appear seems to have been SSS 129 *Baltinglass*, in 1913 (Hi.24.A.3). It was presumably prepared and published because of the stone for the earlier SSS printings needed replacing, and this perhaps explains sheet 36 *Belfast* of 1919, which represented a 'minimalist' adaptation: the latitude and longitude indications in the border and the engraved style of legend were both retained. Both 36 and 129 lacked contours, and were thus in harmony with their Irish coloured SSS companions. Sheet 60.61pt was issued in 1932; how far it is an organic part of the 'Third Edition' will not be discussed here.[78]

Killarney, published at about the same time as sheet 129, has already been discussed. At this time, all Irish colour-printing was carried out at Southampton; *Killarney* was chosen because of its possibilities for dramatic relief treatment, and the first that the officer in charge at Dublin knew about it was when copies appeared on sale.[79]

There was seemingly a final flurry of Irish Third Edition publication in 1918-19, with the appearance of LSS *Belfast, Dublin* and *Cork*. Stylistically, all three bore a closer relationship to the post-1919 tourist maps of Britain than they did to *Killarney*, in that the hill-shading was omitted. Though dated 1918 the Cork sheet was only announced in September 1919; the other two do not

---

[76] For a list of known printings see Roger Hellyer, 'A cartobibliography of the one-inch map of Ireland, in colour, 1901-1956', *Sheetlines* 63 (2002), 12-38.

[77] The correspondence does not appear to be exact: measurement indicates that the west sheet line of the 1912 district map is about 9.5 inches east of the west sheet line of sheet 36, whereas in theory it should be 9.0 inches, but distortions in lithographic transfer and the subsequent vicissitudes of individual printed copies suggest that these figures should be accepted with caution.

[78] A number of possible Third Edition coloured sheets were issued from 1945 onwards by the Ordnance Survey of Ireland: the authors have not been able to check their content to ascertain whether they are indeed Third Editions. Sheets 174, 187 and 200.205 had Third Edition headings, but 200.205 retained an 1899 revision date; sheets 1.5, 70. 101, 131, 140.141, 142, 143, 147, 148, 150.151, 153, 160.171, 162, 164, 166, 168.179, 169.170.180.181, 173, 184, 185, 191.197.198pt, 192 and 201.202 were issued with third edition revision dates, but without 'Third Edition' headings.

[79] W.J. Johnston, 'The new one-inch and quarter-inch maps of the Ordnance Survey', *Geographical Journal* LV (1920), 192-200, 199; J.H. Andrews, *A paper landscape: the Ordnance Survey in nineteenth-century Ireland.* Oxford University Press, 1975, 294, citing file OSL 15010.

seem to have been officially announced at all. (Does this explain why SSS 36 was reprinted in 1919? Or was it issued to maintain uniformity?)

These sheets are puzzling, in that they were apparently produced in 1918, at a time when the 'Killarney' style was out of favour, certainly for series mapping; and unlike the experimental sheets of 1913-14 these were series maps rather than district maps. *Belfast* and *Cork* carried LSS numbers; *Cork* was LSS 80, *Belfast* was '16 & 17', and was extended three inches north for good measure. *Dublin*, which was based on a predecessor of 1904, did not quite fit the LSS scheme: it overlapped sheet 45 to the north by five inches, but there was a gap of about one inch between its bottom and the top of sheet 57. The integral cover on copies issued for military purposes strongly implied that it was a substitute for LSS 51; it bore both a Third Edition heading, and a revision date of 1898. Perhaps its inclusion of a small part of sheet 101 justified its being called 'Third Edition'.

Though all three are dated 1918, there are subtle indications that all three were prepared in 1914. It is well known that some sheets of what became the Popular Edition of England had been prepared in 1914, but their printing was delayed by the war: a particularly good indication is on the first printing of sheet 119, where the magnetic variation date has been obviously altered from 1915 to 1918. No such interference has been detected on the three Irish sheets but it still seems strange that, if they were indeed prepared *ab initio* in 1918, they were printed in a much more elaborate colour scheme than was being used at the same time for the Popular Edition of England and Wales.

A further suggestion that these three sheets were prepared well before 1918 is contained in Col Johnston's paper to the Royal Geographical Society, delivered in December 1919, where he observes of the 'Killarney' style: 'The few maps published on this system were four in Ireland, including Killarney, and one in Scotland (Glasgow)…'.[80] It is noticeable that Johnston refers neither to *Dorking and Leith Hill* nor to *Ilkley*, but 'four in Ireland' does otherwise take some explaining away.

So far as is known, these Irish LSS sheets were prepared in the same way as were the LSS of England and Wales, by taking transfers from copper and assembling them on stone, rather than as for the Popular Edition, where duplicates of the copper plates were cut and reassembled on the new sheet lines. The borders followed the style of *Killarney* and the Popular Edition; sheet names were in sans-serif rather than the 'shaded' style used on the Popular Edition and the post-war tourist sheets. The marginalia included 'compact' revision and publication notes (both the Popular Edition and the post-war tourist maps were much more detailed), and on 16.17 and 80, there were not only adjoining sheet diagrams but also diagrams of constituent six-inch sheets, which were conspicuously absent from the Popular Edition and its associates. Their retention on the Third Edition coloured one-inch of Scotland can be explained by inertia; their retention in Ireland is puzzling.

The demise of the Third Edition in colour
The basis of the Third Edition coloured maps was engraving on copper. However, the actual printing was from stone or zinc; the tension between these two has been explored by Yolande Hodson in *Popular maps*. The disadvantages of the method were certainly recognised almost as soon as the Popular Edition began to replace the LSS, and by 1921 the OS had decided to abandon engraving in favour of photo-lithographic methods. These were used for most of the quarter-inch Third Edition and for the Popular of Scotland with great success, and there was the possibility that this method might also be used for the northern English sheets of the Popular Edition, though in the event engraving was retained.[81] However, the combination of engraving and lithography held sway up to 1914, and at that time Close contemplated replacing the photo-etched plates for the

[80] W.J. Johnston, 'The new one-inch and quarter-inch maps of the Ordnance Survey', *Geographical Journal* LV (1920), 192-200, 194.

[81] *Report of the Departmental Committee on the sale of small-scale Ordnance Survey maps,* [1914]. [Chairman Sir S. Olivier. Copy PRO OS 1/6/5]; E.M. Jack, 'Report on engraving…', [March 1923], in PRO OS 1/9/5.

half-inch of Britain with conventional engraved ones, though this project was a victim of the war.[82] However, conventional engraving was used as the basis for the half-inch of Ireland, which was completed in 1918.

Though the problems of reconciling engraving with colour-printing by lithography lay at the heart of the case for replacing both the Third Edition coloured mapping and the Popular Edition of England and Wales (that the intended replacement of the latter by the photo-lithographic one-inch Fifth Edition ran into difficulties is something which need not concern us here), there is one marked difference, and that is in the relative permanency of the materials. The LSS and the district and tourist sheets had to be made up on stone from small sheet engraved plates: this introduced problems of fit. One way round this was to avoid making up on stone by having the engraved sheet lines correspond to those of the litho-printed coloured map, and so for the Popular Edition duplicates of the SSS copper plates were cut up and reassembled on the new 'large' sheet lines. This would also enable permanent contour and water plates to be prepared and avoid 'scraping the transfer' in order to prepare the outline.

One question to which it seems there is no answer is as to what was intended for the one-inch of Scotland in 1913-14. Did Close contemplate then what he put in hand in 1921, and carry the English sheet lines across the border? If so, did he contemplate retaining the existing Scottish engraved material by a similar process of cutting and joining electrotype duplicates as was employed in England? Would the combination of Scottish plates on the Ben Laws meridian with English ones on the meridian of Delamere have been too great an obstacle? It is worth remembering that 1:31,680 enlargements from the old engraved material were used as drawing-keys for the new heliozincographed Popular Edition, which was put in hand before Close's retirement in 1922.[83]

The fragments of the Fourth Edition SSS suggest that a Fourth Edition LSS would have been practically indistinguishable in style and content from its predecessor. No-one could have mistaken either the 'Killarney' style or that of the Popular for anything in the Third Edition.

Part II – Some matters of detail

Producing the map: revision, engraving and lithography[84]
As for the previous revision of 1893-1901, field revision for the Third Edition was undertaken by issuing the revisers with copies of the latest-available six-inch mapping, to which they added any subsequent changes on the ground which came within the one-inch specification, and noted any apparent errors on the current one-inch. The detailed instructions for this fieldwork are reprinted, with comments, in Part III below. Once complete, the six-inch field sheets were passed to draughtsmen for the revision data to be fair-drawn. The drawing would probably have been made on two sheets: a 'deletion model', indicating obsolete or incorrect detail which was to be deleted, and another drawing, indicating new detail to be engraved.

The copper plates used for the Third Edition had originally been engraved between about 1846 and 1902. There were two ways in which this material could be revised. One was to delete old detail by 'hammering up' the copper plate from behind so that the area to be corrected stood slightly proud, burnish away the unwanted detail, and engrave the new. This method had the advantage that the equipment necessary was very simple but the disadvantage that, were

[82] *Report of the progress of the Ordnance Survey to the 31st March 1914.* BPP (HC) 1914 [Cd. 7424], XLIV, 1, 10.

[83] Richard Oliver, *A guide to the Ordnance Survey one-inch Popular Edition of Scotland.* London: Charles Close Society, 2000, 12.

[84] Most of this section is based on Duncan A. Johnston [ed], *Account of the methods and processes adopted for the production of the maps of the Ordnance Survey of the United Kingdom,* revised edition. London: HMSO, 1902, 185-7, and *Methods and processes used by the Ordnance Survey for map reproduction by photo-lithography.* [Southampton: Ordnance Survey], 1928.

corrections extensive, the plate would tend to buckle: this would be disadvantageous both for intaglio printing, as it would be more difficult to obtain an even impression, and for destroying the dimensional stability which was an important advantage of using copper. It is unlikely that the OS used this method for more than limited correction of engraved plates after the mid-nineteenth century, but it was still being used by Bartholomew's of Edinburgh up to the late 1960s for the copper plates which were the back-up material for their half-inch map, with the associated penalty of an uneven surface.[85]

A variation on this was to cut away those portions of the plate where alterations were extensive, and solder or weld new metal. This method was certainly used in the 1830s and 1840s for revision of the Old Series and may have been used to revise some of the Irish revised one-inch copperplates for the Third Edition.[86] It immediately becomes understandable why there were cogent metallic reasons for the field revisers to be restrained in the amount of change which they recorded, particularly detail which involved deletion.

The other method used by the OS was much more elaborate, and that was electrotyping, which involved electrolysis, large batteries, noxious chemicals and special tanks.[87] This method was certainly used for the revision of 1893-1901 and for the Third Edition in England and Wales. Either hammering-up or soldering was used for the Third Edition in Ireland, but it is unclear what procedure was used for the Third Edition of Scotland: as in Ireland, the later revision often produced very little in the way of change which required deletion, and for many sheets hammering-up or cutting-and-replacing may have been more cost-effective than electrotyping. From the 1850s onwards the usual procedure for the one-inch map was to print sales copies from electrotype duplicates rather than from the original copper plates, so that for each sheet there was, in theory anyway, an original, which was not normally printed from, an electrotype matrix, and a duplicate which was used for printing sales copies and which, when it showed signs of wear, could be replaced by a new duplicate from the matrix. 'Intermediate' revision, discussed later, could be carried out on both the original plate and on the duplicate.

Revising using electrotyping exploited the attribute that on the matrix the lines cut into the original plate would appear in relief; unwanted detail could be scraped away, and a new electrotype positive made, on which the areas scraped on the matrix would appear as smooth plain copper, ready to be cut into. From the point of view of the engravers this was the best solution, as they had a smooth surface to work on, but it had the disadvantage that it needed elaborate equipment. Comparison of the image-quality of the mapping of England and Wales based on the revision of the 1890s with that of the Third Edition shows a very slight deterioration, and repeated electrotyping would tend to degrade the image over time. It is an inexorable rule of analogue map production that duplication means degradation.

Once the revision was engraved, further electrotyping produced a duplicate plate for printing sales copies. However, there were still several more processes necessary to produce a coloured sheet. By the time that the Third Edition SSS was started, in 1903, the OS had evolved a method of colour-printing which used a mixture of lithographic stones and zinc plates. Litho stones yielded better-quality linework, but they were heavy (one for a standard LSS sheet would have weighed somewhere around 350 lbs or 160 kilos), and seem to have been reserved for outline, hachures and water; the other colours were printed from zinc, where the plates were much lighter and the quality of line was not so crucial. Images on zinc were more liable to deteriorate over time in storage than were those on stone.[88] In principle, prints were taken from the copper

---

[85] These copper plates are now in the Bartholomew Archive in the National Library of Scotland.

[86] Cutting-and-soldering certainly appeared to have been used on the plate for Irish Third Edition sheet 168 when the writer examined it at Phoenix Park in 1984. Most of the Irish copper plates covering the '26 counties' are now in the National Archives of Ireland, but of those for the 'six counties' all, save a couple of specimens, went for scrap in about 1968: see PRO OS 1/648.

[87] See Duncan A. Johnston [ed], *Account of the methods and processes adopted for the production of the maps of the Ordnance Survey of the United Kingdom*, revised edition. London: HMSO, 1902, 220-3, 225-6.

[88] Tim Nicholson, *The birth of the modern Ordnance Survey small-scale map*. London: Charles Close Society, 2002, 19. *Account of the methods and processes adopted for the production of the maps of the Ordnance Survey of*

plates in lithographic ink; it is not known whether this was from the 'original' or from the 'printing duplicate', though as the whole point of making the duplicate was that it could be readily replaced if it showed signs of wear, perhaps the original was used. Then again, it might depend on whether the duplicate was fresh enough to yield satisfactory pulls. It would seem that, for the Third Edition in colour, two prints were taken in lithographic ink on 'transfer paper': one would be used for the outline and one for the water. The transfer for the outline had the contours and water scraped away with a fine penknife and it was then transferred to zinc; the transfer was laid face down on the stone, which was then passed through a rolling press several times to ensure that the lithographic ink moved from the transfer paper to the stone, and the transfer paper, now theoretically ink-free, could be peeled away. Disadvantages of 'scraping the transfer' were that during the process the transfer was liable to become 'dead' and to need a good deal of touching up, it was liable to distort, and overall the method was costly.[89] Standard marginalia, such as legends, footnotes and scales, could be supplied by transfer from copper; marginalia individual to the sheet, such as sheet titles and numbers, would have had to be written or typed on the transfer. (Marginalia were less of a problem on the Scottish Third coloured than on the England and Wales counterparts, as much was already in position on the parent copper plate.) It is not known whether this was undertaken on the transfer before laying down onto stone, or directly onto the stone: the ragged style of writing some dates in publication notes suggest that these, at least, were written on the stone.

The water plate was prepared in a similar manner to the outline, except that everything but the water detail was scraped away, and there was very little in the way of marginalia.

The third important element, the contours, could in theory have been prepared as for the outline and water, but in practice they, like the road and wood infills, were redrawn anew. One way of doing this would have been to take a print from the engraved plates in a colour other than black, and use it as a 'drawing key' to redraw the contours in lithographic ink: they could then be transferred to stone as for the transfers for outline and water. Another method, certainly used for the road and wood infill plates, was to take an 'offset' from the outline stone onto a zinc plate, in powder, which could serve as a key for drawing in lithographic ink; when drawing was completed the powder could be cleaned off. This method could also be used to draw layer and water-tint plates. This method was considered to give the best register, but, as the contours had been removed from the outline, it is difficult to see how they could have been supplied on zinc. From a comparison of the outline and coloured versions of Scotland sheet 29 Guy Messenger noted that the correspondence between the engraved and redrawn coloured contours was not exact, and that elsewhere traces of imperfectly-deleted contours might remain on the black plate.[90] On the 1914 reprint of LSS 18 the contours were redrawn over part of the sheet.

The standard interval for contours was 50 feet, 100 feet and then at 100 feet intervals to 1000 feet, based on precise survey, and at 250 feet intervals above 1000 feet, based on water-levelling, a much looser method.[91] Additionally, in Lancashire, Yorkshire and Lincolnshire the 25 feet contour was surveyed and was usually included on the New Series one-inch and hence on Third Edition coloured mapping. There are occasional exceptions: the 25 feet contour was omitted from SSS 63, and was also omitted from LSS 27, making for a strange effect in the Derwent valley at Kexby.[92] There was also a rather odd effect on LSS 47 where the 25 feet contour meandered across the sinuous Lincolnshire-Nottinghamshire border, and so appeared in the former county, but not the latter.

---

the United Kingdom. London: HMSO, 1875, 195, quotes about 450 lb for a standard 1:2500 sheet, so 350 lb for a somewhat smaller LSS stone seems reasonable.

[89] W.J. Johnston, 'The new one-inch and quarter-inch maps of the Ordnance Survey', *Geographical Journal* LV (1920), 192-200, 193.

[90] Guy Messenger, *A guide to the Ordnance Survey one-inch map of Scotland Third Edition in colour.* London: Charles Close Society, 1991, 6.

[91] See Heloise Collier, 'A short history of Ordnance Survey contouring with particular reference to Scotland', *Cartographic Journal* 9 (1972), 55-8.

[92] This contour was completed on Provisional Popular Edition *York District,* 1919.

The hachures were easiest to transfer as all that was necessary was to take a print of them in lithographic ink from the separate engraved hachure plate and to lay the print down on stone or zinc immediately.

The combined sheets in the SSS and Scottish Third Edition, and all the LSS, district and tourist sheets involved joining transfers together. It may be surmised that the transfers were laid down on the stone as each was ready, with no doubt some pulling and squeezing to overcome paper distortion and ensure that the internal joins were smooth, and that the completed assembly was therefore produced by several series of passes through the press.

Once a complete set of stones and zinc plates had been made up, they were ready for printing. This could either be direct from the stone or indirect by offset methods. Direct printing from the original stones and zinc plates was probably the usual method up to 1914: it would ensure the sharpest image. An alternative was to print from zinc plates. These could be prepared by a variation of the method used to make the initial transfer from copper: a print from the litho stone or zinc offset was taken in lithographic ink onto transfer paper, and in turn the image on the transfer paper was passed through a press several times with the zinc plate that was to receive the image. It is not known when this method was introduced to OS work, but it is possible that the noticeably inferior quality of many post-1914 printings is due to the use of duplicate plates, rather than lowered production standards.[93]

Post-publication revision could be carried out in theory either by re-transferring from copper that part which had been revised, or by redrawing separately on the stones or zinc plates. Comparison of Immingham Dock and the associated railways on LSS 33 with the engraved counterparts, which was amongst the most extensive alterations on published Third Edition mapping, shows clearly that redrawing was used in that instance.

Post-publication revision
This was investigated in detail by Guy Messenger for the LSS, but no comparable study has been made for the SSS or the Scottish sheets, or for the parent engraved maps.[94] Much of what follows therefore draws on the work on the LSS. The scope for post-publication alterations is indicated by a total of 149 dated reprints of 110 LSS sheets in 1909-14, as compared with 250 reprints of 169 revised coloured SSS sheets in 1900-1910, and 43 reprints of 35 Third coloured SSS between 1905 and 1909.[95] In contrast, only 35 Scottish sheets were reprinted between 1908/9 and 1914. There was thus much more scope for change to the LSS than to the other series, though on the other hand the interval between publication of the engraved SSS and the coloured LSS sometimes means that the latter included 'intermediate' revision made after first publication of the engraved parent. Intermediate revision of the coloured map on reprint started with the early reprints of the revised coloured map, but was abandoned after December 1914 for all OS small-scale maps as a wartime security measure, and it was presumably not revived afterwards on grounds of economy. The revision of railway names on the 1924 reprint of the *Lake District* tourist map therefore seems anomalous, but might be explained by a lithographic draughtsman having a little time to spare.

'Minor corrections' notes started to appear on OS small-scale maps during 1909, though such alterations had been made to published maps for many years past; the appearance of the note indicates a change in what was disclosed to users rather than a change in revision practice. 'Minor corrections' would appear to have been intended to apply to any alterations other than railway

[93] Guy Messenger, *The Ordnance Survey one-inch map of England and Wales Third Edition (Large Sheet Series)*. London: Charles Close Society, 1988, 2, suggests that lithographic material prepared for the revised coloured map may have been reused for the LSS, but the processes described here make that inherently unlikely.
[94] Guy Messenger, *A guide to the Ordnance Survey one-inch map of Scotland Third Edition in colour*. London: Charles Close Society, 1991, 8, states that post-publication revision has only been noted on one Scotland coloured sheet (30, *Glasgow*), but as these maps were not investigated as thoroughly as those of England and Wales this statement must be accepted with considerable caution.
[95] Tim Nicholson, *The birth of the modern Ordnance Survey small-scale map*. London: Charles Close Society, 2002, 38.

revision. There appears to be a fairly good correlation between a 'minor corrections' note in the footnotes and non-railway revision to the map.

Railways

It is a commonplace that from about 1863 onwards the only significant revision to the one-inch Old Series was the addition of new railways. A similar policy was pursued for the New Series and Scottish mapping, leavened by a few instances of new dock and harbour works, for example at Tilbury on New Series sheet 271 in the late 1880s. After the fifteen-year revision policy was introduced in 1892-3 new railways continued to be added to the one-inch as they were opened. Other revision was limited: access roads to new railway stations were added, but not those associated with new suburbs. Railway alterations, which could include new stations as well as new routes (and occasional deletions[96]), were usually signalled by a 'Railways inserted' note on both the engraved and colour-printed forms of the one-inch up to 1905/6. Thereafter there was a change of policy: in principle, 'Railways inserted' continued to be used on the engraved maps as before, but 'Railways revised' appeared on coloured printings. (Odd examples thereafter of 'Railways inserted' on coloured printings are probably aberrations.) 'Railways revised' seems to denote a change of policy for small-scale coloured reprints, whereby there was an indication to the user that the railway information had been checked at the stated date (month-year), but it does not necessarily indicate that there has been any change to the railway information since the previous printing. Further, usually the check seems to have been confined to passenger railways.[97] It was unusual for new non-passenger lines to be added to either the engraved or the coloured maps; those on LSS 33 (SSS 81.82) are a unusual exception, and are probably a by-product of adding the new dock at Immingham and its associated passenger lines. A freight-only line was brought into use for construction traffic between the site of the new dock and Grimsby in May 1906, probably just after the revision was made for both the one-inch and the large scales, but this was only added to the SSS copper plates and LSS stones after advertised passenger services over it began on 3 January 1910. It thus neatly missed the reprinting of LSS 39 in that month.[98]

Railway additions seem to have been made to the copper plates as soon as the lines or stations were opened (the OS were advised of openings by the Board of Trade), but were only added to the stones for the coloured maps as part of the reprinting procedure. As a result a few lines which were opened after the last pre-war printing of the coloured map never appeared on it, though they were recorded on the engraved map. Two notable examples, both opened in 1913, are the Kirkstead and Little Steeping line added to SSS 115 but not to LSS 48 and the Elsenham and Thaxted Light Railway, added to SSS 222 but not to LSS 97.

Guy Messenger noted railway alterations on 40 LSS sheets; these included the addition of wholly new lines to 20 sheets and of new stations to existing lines on 20 sheets.[99] Apart from the

---

[96] See, for example, on LSS 108, '7.14', where three stations are deleted on the 'Turkey Street' line (4C, 4D: more formally known as the Churchbury Loop), although they had closed to passengers on 1 October 1909: see C.R. Clinker, *Clinker's register of closed passenger stations and goods depots in England, Scotland and Wales 1830-1977*. Weston-super-Mare: Avon-AngliA, 1988, and M.E. Quick, *Railway passenger stations in England, Scotland and Wales : a chronology*. Richmond, Surrey: Railway & Canal Historical Society, 2002.

[97] For example, the High Dyke branch of the Great Northern Railway, opened in 1909, is omitted from sheet 55, 4.12, squares 8H, 8J.

[98] George Dow, *Great Central*, III. London: Locomotive Publishing Co./Ian Allan, 1965, 234.

[99] Railway revision notes appear on LSS sheets 6, 7, 8, 9, 10, 12, 14, 15, 16, 18, 19, 20, 21, 22 (twice), 23, 27, 28, 32, 33 (twice), 37, 38, 39 (twice), 41, 42 (twice), 43, 44 (twice), 45 (twice), 46, 47, 48 (twice), 50, 51, 52, 53 (twice), 54, 55, 56, 57, 58, 61, 62 (twice), 63, 64, 65, 66, 67, 68, 71, 72, 73, 74 (thrice), 75, 76, 77, 81, 82, 83, 84, 85 (thrice), 86 (twice), 87 (twice), 88 (twice), 89, 90, 91, 92, 94 (thrice), 95 (twice), 96 (twice), 98, 99 (twice), 103 (twice), 105 (twice), 106 (thrice), 107 (twice), 108 (thrice), 109, 110, 111, 112 (twice), 113 (twice), 114, 115, 116, 117, 118 (twice), 119, 120, 121, 122, 123 (twice), 124, 125 (twice), 126 (twice), 127, 128, 129, 133 (twice), 134 (twice), 135 (twice), 136, 137, 138, 142, 144 (twice), 145, 146, 151, 152, and on the following district sheets: *Cambridge*, *Ipswich and Felixstowe*, *Lands End and Lizard*, *Maidenhead, Windsor and Henley*, *Oxford*, and *Sidmouth, Budleigh Salterton and Exmouth*: a total of 109 LSS and 6 district sheets. (The phrase 'Railways inserted' is used on sheets 45 and 106.) Railway alterations have only been noted on 39 LSS and 1 district sheet, as follows: new lines added: sheets 20, 21, 32, 33, 37, 39, 45, 49, 53, 61, 95, 96, 98, 103, 107, 108, 110, 112, 113,

railways associated with Immingham Dock, one of the most substantial additions, in aggregate, was the Great Western Railway's Ashendon-Aynho line, opened in July 1910, and added to LSS 95 and 96.

Docks

The only additions of new docks on the LSS were at Immingham, already discussed; there were also revisions to the harbour at Pwllheli on the 1913 printing of LSS 49.[100]

Postal facilities

Revision of postal information has been noted on 104 LSS sheets.[101] Changes can vary from a single one to a dozen or more, and the necessary information could have been obtained readily from the annual official Post Office guide; similar changes can be found on contemporary half-inch maps. The changes are usually upgrading, either from post office (P) to telegraph office (T), or else the provision of either of these at a place where previously there had been none. A few examples of such changes have been noted on earlier SSS coloured sheets, but sufficiently few to suggest that the alterations were not systematic.[102] What does seem to be clear, however, is that postal changes were not made to the engraved sheets. Thus a change from P to T at Amcotts and Broomfleet appear on LSS 32, code 7.12, with minor corrections to March 1910, but not on SSS 80 with railways revised to March 1914. Once the coloured one-inch was complete in 1904 the engraved SSS must have lost whatever military justification it had hitherto had.

Roads

Although there may have been a policy of adding important new roads,[103] in practice no such roads were added to the Third Edition: this no doubt reflects the effective standstill in significant road construction, other than that to serve suburban development, between about 1840 and 1920. The only new roads noted on the LSS are short access roads to new railway stations.

There are a few instances of changes to colour infills on LSS reprints; it is unclear why this was done. The only changes noted to roads on the coloured map of Scotland were those due to new railways.[104]

Some minor changes on the *Folkestone and Dover* district sheet seem to have been the result of revision made for the Fourth Edition.

---

116 (total 20); stations added to existing passenger lines: sheets 37, 52, 53, 54, 62, 77, 81, 83, 90, 98, 99, 103, 107, 108, 110, 113, 118, 126, 127, 136, and *Maidenhead...* (total 20 LSS and 1 district sheet); alterations of existing lines (usually non-passenger to passenger, sometimes also with the addition of stations): sheets 5, 12, 16, 61, 112, 126 (total 6: that on sheet 5 was effected on the republication of 1917, without a 'railways revised' note); with changes of name to stations or lines: sheets 1, 3, 16, 27, 41, 53, 61, 84, 86, 95, 96, 107, 116, 134, 135 (total 15; those on sheets 1 and 3 were effected on the republications of 1917, without 'railways revised' notes); stations or lines deleted: sheets 39, 62, 86, 103, 108 (total 5).

[100] The new King George V dock across the Humber at Hull, opened ceremonially on 26 June 1914 and to traffic on 1 August (K. Hoole (ed), *The Hull & Barnsley Railway*, I. Newton Abbot: David & Charles, 1972, 125), was not recorded on the version of LSS 33 prepared a couple of months later, but as this would have involved some ground survey it may have been an early victim of the outbreak of war.

[101] Changes to post and telegraph information have been noted on LSS sheets 3, 6, 7, 8, 9, 10, 11, 12, 14, 15, 16, 17, 18, 19, 20, 21, 22, 23, 27, 28, 32, 33, 37, 38, 39, 42, 43, 44, 45, 46, 47, 48, 49, 50, 51, 52, 53, 54, 55, 57, 58, 61, 62, 63, 64, 65, 66, 67, 68, 72, 73, 74, 76, 77, 81, 82, 83, 84, 85, 86, 87, 88, 89, 90, 91, 94, 95, 96, 98, 99, 103, 105, 106, 107, 108, 110, 111, 112, 113, 114, 115, 116, 117, 118, 120, 121, 122, 123, 124, 125, 126, 127, 128, 129, 131, 133, 134, 135, 136, 137, 142, 143, 146, 142 and on the *Cambridge* and *Sidmouth, Budleigh Salterton & Exmouth* district sheets: a total of 104 LSS and 2 district sheets.

[102] Tim Nicholson, *The birth of the modern Ordnance Survey small-scale map*. London: Charles Close Society, 2002, 32, cites two examples.

[103] Lt Col Brooker, in *Report of the Departmental Committee on the sale of small-scale Ordnance Survey maps*, [1914], minutes of evidence, 31, qq 695-6. [Chairman Sir S. Olivier. Copy PRO OS 1/6/5]; his statement that only roads and railways were corrected on reprints is at odds with the evidence offered by the maps themselves.

[104] Guy Messenger, *A guide to the Ordnance Survey one-inch map of Scotland Third Edition in colour*. London: Charles Close Society, 1991, 8.

Reservoirs

As with docks, new reservoirs were regarded as important enough in principle to add to the one-inch without waiting for cyclic revision, but only two such additions to the LSS have been noted, on sheets 3 and 108.

Other 'minor corrections'

As mentioned above, there was considerable rewriting of names cut by sheet lines on earlier LSS sheets when they came to be reprinted, but such changes are purely cosmetic; they do not indicate change on the ground. There are a few examples of changes to names, e.g. 'Rivaulx' to 'Rievaulx' on LSS 22 and 'Broadhall' to 'Broadhill' on sheet 44, and a marked repositioning of 'Vale of White Horse on LSS 105 and 106. Other examples have been noted on LSS sheets 3 and 108.

There was extensive redrawing of contours in 1914 on part of LSS 18; this was presumably to rectify faulty compilation in 1907. Odd traces of incompletely deleted black contours have been noted on some Scottish coloured sheets.[105] Solitary examples have been noted of changes to a lightship (on LSS 39: this could have been taken from Admiralty *Notices to mariners*), and a new bridge over a tidal channel (LSS 18), an electric tramway (LSS 107) and a tumulus (LSS 27, in square 14A). One difference between SSS and LSS sheets, resulting from a change in security policy in 1907, was the restoration to civil sales editions of various defence establishments such as Woolwich Arsenal (on LSS 108 and 116).[106] A 'Wireless Tel. Sta.' was deleted from LSS 152. A river widened on LSS 133 seems to have been to facilitate edge-matching, rather than reflecting change on the ground.

Whereas boundary changes were extensive on both the engraved and the coloured revised New Series, none have been noted on Third Edition coloured mapping. Parish boundaries were disliked by military users; those deleted in making the water plates for the experimental district sheets of 1914 were not restored, and they were omitted from the tourist maps prepared in 1919-21.

No revision of urban areas was made to Third Edition coloured maps. Given the comparatively short interval between the first large-scale revision and that for the Third Edition, and the generally very moderate rate of suburban expansion, this need not be expected under normal circumstances, but the extensive 1:2500 revision in 1911-12 for land valuation generated a considerable volume of urban revision. The only use of this for small-scale revision seems to be the addition of the new garden city at Letchworth to engraved SSS 221: the corresponding coloured LSS sheet 97, only received its first reprint after intermediate revision of the one-inch had been stopped after December 1914.

Magnetic variation, headings, footnotes and other marginalia

In principle, sheets covering only English territory carried 'ORDNANCE SURVEY OF ENGLAND' top left; those including Welsh territory (which excluded Monmouthshire at this time) had 'ORDNANCE SURVEY OF ENGLAND AND WALES'. When LSS 1, 3 and 5 were republished in 1917 they were headed 'ORDNANCE SURVEY OF ENGLAND AND SCOTLAND'. On Scottish sheets 'ORDNANCE SURVEY OF SCOTLAND' appeared top centre. On Irish SSS sheets 'ORDNANCE SURVEY OF IRELAND' was top centre; on LSS sheets it was top left. *'(Third Edition)'* invariably appeared top left, to the right of 'ORDNANCE SURVEY OF ...' , if present, and otherwise by itself.

Sheet names, when present, appeared top centre on maps of England and Wales and on Irish LSS, and top right, to the left of the sheet number, on Scottish sheets and Irish SSS. Until 1911 they were repeated on the cover of folded copies. They were omitted from one-inch and half-inch coloured sheets which were either newly published or were reprinted between about June 1911 and May 1912. They were restored on later new publications and corrected reprints, but

---

[105] Guy Messenger, *A guide to the Ordnance Survey one-inch map of Scotland Third Edition in colour*. London: Charles Close Society, 1991, 6.

[106] Other changes to defence establishments are found on LSS 107, 111, 118, 128, 137, 145 and 151.

never did appear on a few sheets first published in 1912 but not given a corrected reprint before 1915; sheet names for these are only known, if at all, from the cover of post-war issues. The omitting of sheet names may have been brought about by the introduction, earlier in 1911, of a new cover style with a sketch-map on the front naming the principal places included in the map: perhaps it was felt that sheet names were superfluous but, if so, this policy did not last long. It had the curious consequence, already noted, that two district sheets issued in 1911, covering Ipswich, Harwich and Felixstowe and Weston-super-Mare and Clevedon, were identified on the map only by the numbers of the constituent LSS sheets. It should be noted that the sheet names on the map and on the cover on post-war issues sometimes differ.

As published, SSS and Scottish sheets used the same names as their engraved parents; these were usually either the largest town on the sheet, or the largest town closest to the centre. For example SSS 220 was *Leighton Buzzard,* which was close to the centre of the sheet, but Luton, in the south-east corner, was twice or thrice as large. For both the half-inch and one-inch LSS the policy at first was to name the sheet after the town closest to the centre, which avoided the problem of several rival claimants for the honour, but could result in unaccustomed prominence. After sheet naming resumed in 1912 the names on both LSS and Scottish sheets were often altered or wholly changed, so that LSS 48, named *Spilsby* (population about 1400) when published in 1909, became *Horncastle & Skegness* (populations about 3900 and 3800 respectively) when reprinted in 1912. However, it was only after 1918 that sheet names returned to series map covers; presumably the cover sketch-maps were meant to be adequate to booksellers' displays, and titles such as *Melton Mowbray, Oakham & Stamford* lurked out of sight until the map was opened up.

Top right was the sheet number. To the left on Scottish and Irish SSS sheets was the sheet name; to the right on LSS sheets (except on a few post-war reprints) was *(Large Sheet Series)*; this was omitted from the half-inch SSS after 1909, once the small sheets had been superseded, but presumably was retained on the one-inch LSS because of the continuance of the engraved SSS.

Magnetic variation was shown either by a diagram near the top of the right-hand margin, and cutting into the border, or, where possible, in a sea area. As remarked above, the *Cambridge* and *Oxford* district sheets were singular in that two such diagrams were given, in the left-hand and right-hand margins. Magnetic variation diagrams had been a standard feature of coloured small-scale maps since their inception, presumably at military behest, though they had been suggested as long ago as 1851 by Alexander Keith Johnston, the Edinburgh map publisher.[107] The design of those on Scottish sheets was modified in 1906, to reflect the redesign a little earlier on the England and Wales maps for the 'compact' style.[108] Up to the end of 1914 magnetic values were corrected on reprint.[109]

A curiosity of folded and mounted-in-sections copies of one-inch and half-inch LSS up to the abandoning of hinged covers during World War I was that the trimming of the map was often so close that the actual figures for magnetic variation were lost, which would seem to defeat the whole object of compiling and printing the information in the first place. However, it may have been of somewhat questionable value anyway: it was compiled from tables by Rucker and Thorpe, which had been published in 1896 following observations in 1892, but which by 1907 were known to be not wholly reliable. A reasonable assumption might be that the magnetic value given was applicable to the whole sheet and that, as the value varied across the sheet, it was an average applicable to the centre of the sheet. In 1907 it came to notice that on Irish coloured one-inch sheets the value quoted was that applicable to the east sheet line: it is not known if this also applied to pre-1907 British sheets as well.[110]

---

[107] *Report from the Select Committee on Ordnance Survey (Scotland).* BPP (HC) 1851 (519), XX, 359, evidence, q.725: Johnston's suggestions that latitude and longitude values be added to the one-inch was accepted immediately, but that for a legend was only partially realised from 1886 onwards.

[108] Guy Messenger, *A guide to the Ordnance Survey one-inch map of Scotland Third Edition in colour.* London: Charles Close Society, 1991, 7.

[109] Magnetic variation on half-inch reprints were still being corrected in 1915.

[110] Correspondence on magnetic declination, 1907 in PRO OS 1/8/4.

In the left and right margins of LSS sheets, but not of the others, were scale-bars of miles: they may have been provided for the convenience of users when the map was partly folded, with the bottom margin tucked out of sight.

Bottom left was the conventional sign panel or legend. On Scottish sheets this was taken directly from the engraved parent; on those of England and Wales it was redrawn. On Scottish and early English SSS sheets the legend was so designed that the post and telegraph indications 'P' and 'T' were an afterthought which, as on the engraved maps, were either inserted in the space occupied by marine symbols on coastal sheets, or else were outside the legend, to the right. The engraved parent made no provision for woodland, and this was shown, unframed, to the right on Scottish and early English SSS sheets.[111] Tree symbols were omitted from the woodland example on the SSS and Scottish coloured sheets until 1910, when they were added on reprint and to new publications. Common to all the designs of legend was the lack of any land-use or foreshore symbols (apart from woodland), which did appear on separate sheets of conventional signs and writing, but which were probably never seen by the great majority of map-users. Detail variations between conventional sign panels over the years include the depiction of streams passing under railways.[112]

The 'compact' legend introduced in 1905 was so designed that 'P' and 'T' and woodland symbols were part of the standard layout, and an extra panel for marine symbols was added to the right if needed, though occasionally this was included or excluded in error. From 1910 railway station symbols were included though these, too, are sometimes included or excluded in error.[113] The worst anomaly is on an undated post-1918 printing of LSS 29, which carries a legend appropriate to an Irish revised coloured sheet, complete with specimen trigonometrical height and 'pond insect' lightship symbol. On post-1919 tourist and district sheets a modified form of Popular Edition legend was used. In principle, on inland sheets two red contours were shown in the legend and on coastal sheets one land and one marine contour were shown, but in practice this was not always so.

On all Third Edition coloured reprints up to 1922 a month-year code appears bottom left, not always very legibly, so that, for example '2' might be misread for '7' and '3' for '8'. We interpret this to indicate the date when the plate or stone was ready for printing, after the inclusion of corrected magnetic data and any 'intermediate revision', rather than the actual date of printing. From about August 1904 until December 1914 alterations to plates were normally indicated by this month-year code: thus 5.13 denotes May 1913. In the past this has been interpreted as a 'reprint code', but, if so, one has to explain why these codes cease between December 1914 and January 1920, after which time they do indeed seem to denote a reprint rather than alterations to the stones or plates. Up to December 1914 it was probably normal practice to correct the stones and plates in advance of a reprint, and so the date code would be amended, but evidence that the date code does not necessarily indicate either the date of reprinting or the date stock was placed on sale is provided by the two East Kent sheets which were renumbered from SSS to LSS. 118 was nominally reprinted in November 1910, but only announced in March 1911, whilst 128 was nominally reprinted in July 1912 but only announced four months later. Both sheets had been republished in 1909, but were not announced for sale, and copies are rarely encountered; were most of the stocks taken by the military, and civil sales met by releasing quantities of SSS stock which had been stored against possible War Office requisition?

On a few Scottish sheets, 'Expansion' between a double-headed arrow appears, either to the left end or below the legend: the meaning of this is unknown. They all seem to be on printings first made in 1907-9.

---

[111] There was considerable variation in the shape of the woodland symbol, but it is doubtful if this signifies anything; the subject is discussed in Guy Messenger, *A guide to the Ordnance Survey one-inch map of Scotland Third Edition in colour.* London: Charles Close Society, 1991, 7.

[112] These are discussed in detail in Guy Messenger, *The Ordnance Survey one-inch map of England and Wales Third Edition (Large Sheet Series).* London: Charles Close Society, 1988, 16.

[113] Their earliest appearance is on the 6.09 printing of SSS 286, where they are unquestionably included in error.

Bottom centre in theory, though in practice offset somewhat to the right in order to reduce any imbalance of blank space, were a scale-bar, graduated in miles and furlongs, a note as to land altitudes, a copyright note, a price note and, where appropriate, a note that marine contours had been taken from Admiralty surveys. The copyright note was usually placed below the price note on SSS sheets. Up to the autumn of 1912 the copyright wording was 'All rights of reproduction reserved'; on 30 September 1912 it was ordered that 'Crown Copyright Reserved' (CCR) was to be used, and thereafter it was used on all new publications and most reprints. However, the first use of the CCR wording is on the '5.12' printing of LSS 77: either this anticipates the later instruction, or is a later alteration, but it supports the idea that the date-month code is to be associated with changes to the plate rather than with any printing date.[114] At first the lettering was comparatively bold, being evidently the result of writing or rewriting on the stone; from the '5.13' printing of LSS 45 onwards the usual style is much smaller and neater, and evidently derived from an engraved original. For sheets published up to late 1907 the date of Admiralty survey was cited; this was omitted from sheets first published later, but was not usually deleted from reprints. Prices on the earliest SSS sheets, published in 1903-5, were 1/- for a standard sheet and 1/6 for a combined sheet; from September 1905 they were 1/- and 1/6 respectively for paper and 1/6 and 2/- respectively for mounted copies; from July 1906 a price – 2/- or 2/6 – for mounted in sections was added. Scottish sheets were at first 2/- for cloth; from November 1905 they also quoted 1/6 for paper and from September 1906 they added 2/6 for mounted in sections. 'Net' was added to the prices printed on the maps from about December 1906 onwards. LSS sheets were 1/6, 2/- and 2/6 from the start; sometime in 1916 the price for the mounted style was increased to 3/-, and after January 1920 the price note was omitted.

On Scottish sheets the adjoining sheet diagram was placed to the left of the scale, etc; on SSS and LSS sheets it was to the right. On Scottish and SSS sheets combined sheets were indicated by thickened lines, which may have been graphic, but was not very elegant. To the right of the scale on Scottish sheets was a diagram of component six-inch sheets; these were usually, but not always, suitably extended on combined sheets.

Bottom right was the publication note. On Scottish sheets this was usually taken directly from the engraved parent, to which was added a date of 'printing' for the coloured version, which might be a year or more after the nominal date of publication. (Scotland sheet 19+ was unique in having a 'compact' publication note.) On Scottish and earlier SSS sheets the name of the DGOS nominally responsible was given. The 'compact' marginalia introduced in 1905 omitted this and used a standard wording evidently transferred, like the other marginalia, from an engraved master, with the dates of revision and publication added: the latter were not always ideally legible, particularly as insufficient space was left for revision dates across a span of years. Below the revision and publication notes, which on Scottish sheets included the dates of original survey and outline publication, were the railway revision and minor correction notes (if any), and the rights-of-way disclaimer note: the order of these varies, but the most common arrangement was railways – minor corrections – rights of way. As noted above, from 1902 onwards the rights-of-way note on colour-printed one-inch maps of England and Wales omitted 'track or footpath'. This may have had some logic on the half-inch map, which did not show footpaths at this time, but it seems a strange omission from the one-inch, which did. The omitted words were sometimes restored in post-1918 reprints. From late 1922 reprints were indicated by a note bottom right in quantity/year style: thus 1000/23 indicated a run of (nominally) 1000 copies made in 1923.

Up to the end of 1907 first-class roads leading off the map were annotated in the border as leading 'To' or 'From' a town; the rationale as to which was used is unclear. Thereafter distances in miles were given, and LSS and Scottish sheets were amended as necessary on reprint. The borders also had the numbers (top and bottom, running left to right) and letters (from A to whatever was necessary, down the sides) for the reference system: these divisions were nominally at two-inch intervals, though on LSS sheet 12 as originally printed the easternmost division was a three-inch one. On the 1918 *Dublin* sheet the topmost letter was X, followed by A: this seems to

---

[114] Circular by [Col] A.D.M[eeres], 30 September 1912, in 'Southampton Circulars', Book 2.

reflect a similar arrangement on a manoeuvre map predecessor, which was an extended version of a coloured district sheet issued in 1904.

The *Cambridge* and *Oxford* district sheets were unique in that their borders were diced for latitude and longitude, at one-second intervals.

Squaring and reference systems

The division of margins to provide a simple alpha-numeric reference system and the publication of the *Cambridge* and *Oxford* district sheets with two-inch squaring across the map face has been noted above. The development of more elaborate reference systems has been described elsewhere, and for the most part does not affect Third Edition coloured mapping, but there are a few exceptions.[115]

The 1912 printing of sheet 135 (*Portsmouth*) is known in a version overprinted with squares of 2000 yard sides, subdivided into 400-yard sides. The numbering of the squaring in the top and bottom margins suggests that sheet 145 may have been similarly treated.[116] During World War I, probably early on, the 'Western Front' squaring system was overprinted on a few sheets, presumably for training purposes: known examples are LSS 107, 115 (at least two printings) and 124, and Scotland 22.[117] There may be a few other examples waiting to be discovered, but it is most likely that, from early 1915 onwards, any training in the use of the squaring was carried out on the 1:20,000 training maps, GSGS 2748, as they became available. (See figures 2 and 6.)

Print runs and reprint patterns

The print-runs for the revised coloured one-inch of 1897-1904 have been investigated by Tim Nicholson. Data in OS annual reports and in reprint codes on the maps themselves indicated that initial print-runs were 400 to 500 copies and reprints could be anything from 100 to 1000 copies, though probably usually no more than 500.[118] Unfortunately, by the time that the first Third Edition sheets were reprinted the quantity/year reprint codes had been replaced by the month-year system, discussed above under marginalia, which seems to indicate when the plate or stone was prepared for printing. The quantity/year system was adopted once more late in 1922, but by that time there was little Third Edition reprinting left to do. A further difficulty is that the Third Edition coloured mapping was, in modern parlance, a joint civil-military product, and was produced at a time when reorganisation and re-equipping of the army might have been expected to lead to an increase in military consumption of maps, but also when the military was making extensive use of the half-inch. A single print-run could thus serve both civil sales at trade discount and military purchases at cost price. There are two documentary sources for Third Edition coloured print-runs between 1909 and 1922: one is a file dealing with prices for WO map purchases, and the other is an investigation into OS map retailing in 1914.

In 1909 the average run for a coloured OS one-inch sheet was reckoned to be 750 copies and for a half-inch 2000 copies; in 1914 figures of 1000 and 2500 respectively were quoted, but may have applied to sales rather than printings, and the main customer for the half-inch was the War Office. It was 'the principal military map of Great Britain'. The annual sale of LSS sheets in 1909 was reckoned to be 533, but this included those taken by the WO at cost price: thus a printing of 1500 would last for three years. In 1909 the average annual sale of coloured one-inches of Scotland was reckoned at 360 sheets, with a run of 1000 copies to last for three years.[119] From

<hr>

[115] Richard Oliver, 'The evolution of the Ordnance Survey National Grid', *Sheetlines* 43 (1995), 25-45.

[116] This copy is in a private collection, and only came to light after I had written my article in 1995.

[117] The *Aldershot (North)* and *Aldershot (South)* non-relief sheets of 1914 are also known with overprinted squaring: they, too, seem to date from early in the war. All known examples of overprinted sheets are in private collections.

[118] Tim Nicholson, *The birth of the modern Ordnance Survey small-scale map.* London: Charles Close Society, 2002, 33-36.

[119] Memoranda by Col Hedley in PRO OS 1/270; *Report of the Departmental Committee on the sale of small-scale Ordnance Survey maps,* [1914], report, 30 (comment by Col C.F. Close), minutes of evidence, qq 691, 713 (from Col Brooker). [Chairman Sir S. Olivier. Copy PRO OS 1/6/5]. In 1897-8 annual sales of 250 copies of each

1906 a policy was in force of building up 'a reserve of maps of certain portions of the United Kingdom' for the War Office, but it is unknown which sheets at which scales were needed. They remained in OS custody until requested by the WO: 164,000 had been accumulated in Southampton and Dublin by January 1910. A statement that 'the supply is constantly being brought up to date' could be taken as implying that, when civil sales stocks were close to exhaustion, a reprint was put in hand, and that, once complete, reprinted stock was allocated for WO purposes and the superseded WO stock was transferred to ordinary sales stock.[120]

By themselves these figures do not help very much, and they are called into question by the pattern of reprints. It seems curious, for example, that LSS sheet 39, *Grimsby and Louth,* was reprinted in January 1910, only fifteen months after it had been published. Was there a run on stocks for some reason, or was the initial print-run much less than average? The same applies to LSS 88 and 109, both reprinted a few months after initial publication, though here it might be argued that growing military interest in the possibility of an invasion along this coast, which took more concrete form shortly afterwards with the inception of a secret 1:25,344 series of East Anglia, was responsible for further printing. A rough estimate of peacetime consumption can be gauged from what is known of print runs of the civil and military versions of the Popular Edition, but the pattern of printing tended to be fragmentary, at any rate away from areas of population or tourist or military interest, and a further complication is that there was a substantial increase in the numbers of OS small-scale maps sold after 1918. But then, in 1914 it was noted that a 'map habit' had grown since 1906.[121] What is known for the Popular Edition suggests that one-inch sheets for the south-east of England outsold those for the far north by about five to one; thus if the pattern of consumption before 1914 was broadly similar to that after 1918 the average print-run for a south-eastern sheet published in 1908-9 and reprinted twice in the next six years would be about two or three times that of a northern sheet published in 1907-8 and first reprinted in 1913-14.[122] Guy Messenger's suggestion that probably no sheet was printed in more than 10,000 copies in total for civil purposes seems reasonable.[123]

The question of quantities printed is intimately connected to that of reprinting. Our surmise that the month-year coding used from 1904 to 1914 relates to the date when the plate was ready for printing, rather than when the printing was undertaken, has been discussed above, under marginalia. 1912 was a remarkable year for LSS reprints, or at any rate of adding date-codes to the stones: there were 62 of them, plus the Oxford and Cambridge district sheets, mostly in the south and east: one wonders if the explanation lies in the War Office building up mobilisation stocks following the Agadir incident the previous summer. Otherwise, it seems odd that sheets affected should all need reprinting within a few months of each other, despite having first been published anything from less than eighteen months (in Norfolk) to nearly five years (in Yorkshire) before. Distribution and timing make reaction to a run-down of stocks through sales implausible for many of these sheets.[124]

There is at present no evidence for undated and uncorrected 'facsimile' reprints of Third Edition maps before 1915, though a few instances are known when reprint codes were omitted

---

sheet of the engraved New Series were apparently regarded as reasonable: Tim Nicholson, *The birth of the modern Ordnance Survey small-scale map.* London: Charles Close Society, 2002, 21.

[120] Correspondence between War Office and Treasury, 28 January, 12 February and 26 February 1910, in file 2127/10 in PRO T1/11391.

[121] *Report of the Departmental Committee on the sale of small-scale Ordnance Survey maps,* [1914], report, 5. [Chairman Sir S. Olivier. Copy PRO OS 1/6/5].

[122] These figures derive from the data in Yolande Hodson, *Popular maps.* London: Charles Close Society, 1999, 283-366.

[123] Guy Messenger, *The Ordnance Survey one-inch map of England and Wales Third Edition (Large Sheet Series).* London: Charles Close Society, 1988, 6.

[124] The sheets are, by month (total in brackets): January: 42, 96 (2); February: 7, 53, 73 (3); March: 50, 64, 65 (3); April: 55, 56, 58, 66, 67, 68, 72, 84 (8); May: 54, 57, 74, 77, 95, 106, 114, 116, 127, 135 (10); June: 22, 47, 48, 51, 63, 76, 81, 82, 87, 94, 99, 107, 113, 123, 124, 136, 145, *Oxford,* (18); July: 28, 32, 39, 86, 103, 128, 137, 138 (8); August: 27, 37, 46 (3); September: 105, 108, 120, 144 (4); October: 33, 85, 129 (3); November: 38 (1); December: *Cambridge* (1).

(notably LSS 69 in 1913): such facsimile reprints might be detectable by variations in shades of colour, but these might also be the result of long-term chemical reaction between ink, paper and mounting material. After December 1914 a positive indication of a reprint is the increase in the price of the mounted in sections style to 3/-, which seems to have taken place some time in 1916. Month-year codes first reappear on Third Edition printings in January 1920, and price statements seem to have been removed from the plates almost immediately afterwards, following the price increases of 26 January 1920. A considerable number of coloured Third Edition and half-inch sheets lack both reprint code and price note: the assumption is that they date from 1920. After December 1914 post-publication revision and correction on reprint ceased, and this may explain why existing month-year codes, where present, were left unchanged when further, nominally 'facsimile', reprints were undertaken thereafter. Sometimes a 1914-16 reprint can be identified by a marked change in colour, which goes far beyond what can be explained away by minor variations during printing or post-printing chemical changes.

A further complication is that whereas up to June 1904 the coloured one-inch was offered only mounted on cloth, and was printed solely on linen-backed paper, thereafter it was available unmounted, and from 1905 it was offered mounted in sections. The paper and sectioned forms necessitated printing on unmounted instead of linen-backed paper, and so, in theory at least, from 1905-6 each printing was made partly onto linen-backed paper and partly onto unmounted paper.[125]

Covers can also provide a guide. Before the war military issues were in hinged covers, as for civil issues.[126] Mobilisation stocks of maps of north-west Europe printed from about 1909 onwards and the 1:25,344 mapping of eastern England printed in August-September 1914 were provided with simple paper labels pasted to the exposed part of the map when folded. Even this was luxurious compared with, for example, 'England 1″ sheet 23', and nothing else, printed or stamped directly onto the cloth, but this is probably indicative of a printing in the early months of the war. By October 1915 a directly-printed cover, adapted from the pre-war hinged style, was in use: these would appear to have been printed onto the back of the map as an integral part of the production process, rather than added subsequently.[127]

It is reasonably certain that most coloured Third Edition sheets were reprinted in 1914-15 to provide stocks for both home defence and for training the rapidly expanding army. Whereas a considerable number of LSS are known with the post-1916 3/- mounted-in-sections price, far fewer Scottish sheets are known thus: the presumption is that sheets not reprinted after 1916 proved sufficient both for war-time needs and for civil sales thereafter, until superseded by the Popular Edition. Although the half-inch may have enjoyed greater military favour up to 1914, and indeed was issued just after the outbreak of war in a mass-produced three-colour 'Training Map' form, thereafter the one-inch seems to have been used for training, notwithstanding the progressive introduction of a 1:20,000 training series, GSGS 2748, which more closely resembled the sort of mapping likely to be encountered on the Western Front. However, the half-inch, rather than the one-inch, remained the officially-favoured small-scale map until 1923.[128] Though the number of surviving copies cannot be used even to suggest a ratio of relative consumption, it is noticeable that whereas relatively large numbers of military-issue coloured Third Editions survive, very few examples of GSGS 2748 are known.

---

[125] Tim Nicholson, *The birth of the modern Ordnance Survey small-scale map.* London: Charles Close Society, 2002, 46, citing *Report of the Departmental Committee on the sale of small-scale Ordnance Survey maps,* [1914], minutes of evidence, 30, q.688. [Chairman Sir S. Olivier. Copy PRO OS 1/6/5].

[126] It is unclear whether military issues were still being put into hinged covers in the summer of 1914, or whether these had been discontinued by then.

[127] The dating rests on an example of LSS 72, with '21/10/15' added in manuscript to an official stamp, in the University of Exeter geography collection.

[128] Yolande Hodson, *Popular maps.* London: Charles Close Society, 1999, 76-7.

Map covers

These were discussed at some length by Guy Messenger, and those interested in the use of particular cover designs on particular sheets are referred to his studies of the LSS and of the Scottish coloured map. It is has not been possible to re-investigate covers exhaustively for the present work; what follows is based largely on his work and of that by Tim Nicholson on the revised coloured map. A central argument of the Nicholson study was that map and cover were a 'package' and it is possible to carry this thesis forward to the Third Edition, at any rate up to 1914: what has been dubbed here the 'compact' style, introduced in 1905, does suggest a conscious integration of map, marginalia and folding.

In theory, each printing of a sheet can be expected to appear in every style of cover and mounting in use during its currency; how far this was actually so is uncertain. In the following description cover designs are referred to by the numbers used by Roger Hellyer in his list in John Paddy Browne's *Map cover art.*[129]

The first cover to be seen on Third Edition coloured mapping was used in 1903-5. It is red, measures about 102 mm wide by 156 mm tall, is in a single piece pasted book-like to the back of the map, which for a standard sheet is folded 6 by 3, and only appears on the earliest SSS sheets (H.3.1.a). On the back are 'Rules for ordering'; pasted inside is a list, with prices, of OS map series. Like other covers used up to the First World War, it projected slightly when the map was folded up.

This style was replaced in the winter of 1904-5 by a taller and narrower version, H.3.2.a.1, which continued in use until at least March 1906.[130] It measures about 95 by 183 mm, and is attached to the map by a hinge formed by trimming the map so as to leave projections. These hinges were effective on cloth-backed sheets, but the weight of the cover sometimes proved too much on paper sheets, and was liable to detach itself after a certain amount of usage, not always rough. The covers were made from superseded mapping (usually six-inch or 1:2500) with the fabric pasted on top. The back outside cover was blank: the list of OS scales and formats was pasted inside the front and the 'Rules for ordering' (even for a more formal age this seems distinctly offputting) inside the back. Dated inserts can be found between January and March 1905. Other clues to when covers were made up are: mention of the ten-mile coloured map from February 1904, the reduction in price of the Scottish outline edition from 1s.9d to 1s.6d in January 1905, the arrival of the Scottish coloured one-inch and the publication of the 1:1 million map in March 1905, the start of the Third Edition Large Sheet Series in December 1906 and the ending of sales via post offices in March 1907.[131]

It is uncertain whether the practice was followed for earlier cover styles, but those of H.3.2.a.1 were certainly issued in pale buff protective envelopes, on which was printed the same design, including sheet name and number, as on the cover proper. These protective envelopes do not often survive, but then they were not meant to. Some had dealers' names printed on them.

As was noted above, the red dye used for the fabric outer cover material was wont to run when wetted, and the War Office requested a replacement. Accordingly, from March or April 1906 a 'colourless' material was substituted, which present-day students and collectors invariably seem to refer to as 'white'. The cover design was otherwise unchanged (H.3.2.b.1). At about this time a reversion to book-mounting was tried, but it is not known if any Third Edition sheets appeared in this style (H.3.2.b.3). The front cover remained unchanged until the winter of 1910-11. This style was designated by Guy Messenger OS/A (sheet name in serifed lettering) and OS/B (sheet name in sans-serif); OS/B was usually used, OS/A usually being reserved for sheets with longer titles. A standard LSS or Scottish sheet in this cover-style was folded 8 by 3.

Standard SSS sheets issued in H.3 covers were folded outwards, so that the whole of the map could be inspected without having to be unfolded right out: with standard Scottish and LSS

---

[129] John Paddy Browne, *Map cover art.* Southampton: Ordnance Survey, 1991, 122-144.

[130] It has been noted on a copy of SSS 120, issued in March 1906.

[131] Tim Nicholson, *The birth of the modern Ordnance Survey small-scale map.* London: Charles Close Society, 2002, 30, 49.

coloured sheets it was only possible to inspect two-thirds of the sheet without refolding. As remarked above, this perhaps explains the introduction of scale-bars in the left and right margins of LSS sheets.

Dissected or 'mounted in sections' sheets seem to have been introduced, initially to special order only, at some time in 1905, but were perhaps a standard offering from mid-1906, when the price of this style began to be printed on the maps themselves.[132] The covers (H.3.2.b.4) were pasted directly onto the map backing, which made for compactness, though usually at the expense of cropping the magnetic data. Pasting the cover onto the backing necessitated 'inward' folding. The folding and cover-size of the folded map differed somewhat from of that the paper and mounted styles: initially, standard Scottish sheets were folded 6 by 3, with a cover 110 by 175 mm, and standard LSS sheets were folded 7 by 3, with a cover size of about 102 by 178 mm. 7 by 3 folding was later adopted for the Scottish sheets. District sheets were sometimes folded 7 by 3, sometimes 8 by 3: *Oxford,* and possibly others, was issued 7 by 3, but with a cover 106 by 180 mm, thereby avoiding cropping of the magnetic data. Dissected sheets carried back-cover indexes when these were introduced, but not the letterpress which was pasted inside the covers of the other folded styles.

As well as requesting a change from red the War Office also asked for back cover indexes. These were never used on the SSS or on district and tourist sheets, but seem to have been used on the half-inch LSS from their inception in 1906, and on the one-inch LSS by June 1907.[133] However, they were only introduced to Scottish sheets in or after late 1907. The index on the back of the Scottish sheets showed the whole of the mainland, including combined sheets. Three were used on the LSS: a northern portrait-shaped one, which reached down to the row 69-74, a central landscape-shaped one, covering sheets 18-99, and a southern landscape-shaped one, covering sheets 78-152. They derived from a common parent, which showed LSS 34 as originally planned as a standard-sized sheet, and 89 as overlapping sheets 78 and 90, and broken names, etc, were not made good.

Letterpress insets continued to be used inside the front and back covers: in 1907 the notes on OS scales inside the front were simplified to omit mention of alternative formats, and Guy Messenger noted minor variations in wording dateable to 1909. 'Net' was added to front covers from 1909: it seems to have been added retrospectively to stock which had not yet been issued to retailers.[134]

In or shortly before March 1911 a new cover style was adopted, characterised by a location map (H.4.1 in its hinged style; H.4.2 on dissected maps: Guy Messenger's OS/C), although a solitary use of the H.3 style on a coloured Third LSS has been noted as late as October 1912.[135] Except necessarily on district maps, the sheet was identified on the cover only by its number. Although adopted some nine or ten month's into George V's reign, it continued to use Edward VII's arms (about 46 by 24 mm). Earlier issues of H.4 retained the 'Rules for ordering' inside the back cover: from later in 1911 these were omitted, and the inside back cover was left blank. George V's arms (about 25 by 30 mm) were adopted in or after July 1913 (Guy Messenger's cover

---

[132] Tim Nicholson, *The birth of the modern Ordnance Survey small-scale map.* London: Charles Close Society, 2002, 46. Combined and sectioned LSS sheets might also be produced to order: there is in a private collection an example of LSS 25, 26, 30 and 31, mounted together and folded in sections, with inner margins trimmed, folded 14 by 6, in H.3.2.b.4 cover with "England & Wales (Large Sheet Series) Sheets 25, 26, 30, 31", and cover price ten shillings. It is possible that a limited stock was prepared for a retailer in one of the West Riding towns: it may not be coincidence that the area covered resembles the *Ilkley District* sheet of 1914. The *East Kent (North)* and *(South)* sheets were sold, similarly dissected and mounted together. The cover name was *East Kent* and the price of the package 5/-. A copy is recorded in a private collection.

[133] They were apparently not part of the initial one-inch LSS 'package': LSS 17 was initially issued with a blank back cover.

[134] Circular, 19 July 1909, in 'Southampton Circulars', Book 2 (formerly in Ordnance Survey Office, Dublin; now in National Archives of Ireland, Dublin; photocopy in Ordnance Survey library, Southampton). 'Net' had been used on the maps themselves from about 1906 onwards: the effect of this circular seems to have been to tidy up practice in this regard.

[135] By Guy Messenger on LSS 89. The H.3 style continued to be used on Irish SSS sheets until after 1918.

style OS/D), and at about the same time stiffening using cut-up pieces of superseded OS maps ceased.[136] This basic style continued in use until 1919-20, but at some time during World War I hinged covers and outward folding were abandoned in favour of pasting the cover directly to the map (H.4.2) and inward folding; this may be associated with the introduction of a direct-print version of the cover, without price, for military issues (H.4.3) some time in or before October 1915. (Before August 1914 the standard military issue was cloth folded in covers: the same finished stock therefore sufficed for both military and civil use.) As has been noted above, some military issues, probably in the early months of the war, were made with a bald statement such as '1″ ENGLAND. SHEET 23.', printed directly onto the map when folded (H.5). Some Scottish sheets were issued for military use with an extract from an index diagram on the front (H.6): these may also date from earlier in the war, as the H.4.3 style was also used, and seems to be particularly associated with printings bearing a 3/- mounted in sections price in the map footnotes. Military issues lacked back cover indexes.

The use of directly-printed covers can be seen as contributing to the idea of map and cover as a 'package', but the change in cover mounting and cover styles showed that the 'package' was not immutable. Both the style of the maps and their covers received some attention when OS map retailing was considered by Sir Sydney Olivier's committee in the summer of 1914. Although the white covers did not run, they did soil easily, and this mattered when the maps were being offered to the public in shops, whatever use they might be put to subsequently. Maps which were inspected but not bought acquired undesirable signs of handling, and their 'protective' envelopes soon became tatty and torn. These points were made forcefully to the Committee.[137] The OS was able to respond that a new cover design was in hand, and displayed one. The description in the Olivier Committee's report suggests a light background with red printing; a design of this sort was used on the two-inch map of Jersey, issued about this time (H.71), and it is just possible that this was indeed what was displayed. A witness before the Committee thought it attractive (if it looked anything like the Jersey cover it certainly compared well with offerings from contemporary commercial publishers), but still liable to soil.[138] The OS evidently tried again, and produced a design in black on an aquamarine ground: an example is known, attached in bookfold style to the June 1914 printing of LSS 126 (H.9 – see figure 9).[139] It seems to be incomplete, in that there is no location map, and the sheet name and number, in red, look like an improvisation. The back cover is blank, and an index to sheets 78-152 is pasted inside the front cover. The bookfold style, allied with 'inside' folding, the colour and the index inside, are irresistibly suggestive of the contemporary Bartholomew half-inch, though bookfolding was also used by other firms, notably G.W. Bacon, who also sometimes included indexes on the inside.[140]

---

[136] LSS 26, issued July 1913, is known in a cover with Edward VII's arms.

[137] *Report of the Departmental Committee on the sale of small-scale Ordnance Survey maps,* [1914], report, 9. [Chairman Sir S. Olivier. Copy PRO OS 1/6/5].

[138] Tim Nicholson, *The birth of the modern Ordnance Survey small-scale map.* London: Charles Close Society, 2002, 46.

[139] The original is in a private collection, and is understood to have been found in a Southampton bookshop: a possible explanation is that a few copies were produced and made available to OS staff.

[140] The H.9 design may have been the result of a suggestion by an OS staff member: see Ian Mumford, note in *Sheetlines* 35 (1993), 44-5, citing Southampton Circular, 29 October 1913, which announces Treasury approval of the OS staff suggestion scheme [original in 'Southampton Circulars', Book 2 (formerly in Ordnance Survey Office, Dublin; now in National Archives of Ireland, Dublin; photocopy in Ordnance Survey library, Southampton)], and a circular of February 1915 [location uncertain], announcing an award to Civil Assistant C.J. Lawrence for one-inch and half-inch map cover designs. (In commenting on this in *Sheetlines* 35, 45, I assumed, perhaps too readily, that the H.9 and 'Lawrence' designs were the same: it is of course possible that the H.9 design is indeed Lawrence's work and differs from that displayed at the Olivier Committee proceedings only in colour and material, and not in basic design.) Dr Mumford suggests that the H.9 design was rejected as 'the design statement "Ordnance Survey of England and Wales" was deemed to offend the Scots and Irish, whose national shields provide two of the four corners of the panel frame'; I am not wholly convinced.

During or just after World War I a few sheets were issued in a cover with a slightly more modern-looking typeface (H.7.1.a), sometimes on buff card (H.7.2.a).[141]

No further work on 'decorative' cover design is known to have been undertaken until 1918 or 1919, when the OS employed Ellis Martin, a commercial artist who had served during the war in the Royal Engineers, to design covers in quantity. Although he formally joined on 9 May 1919, it is unclear exactly when Martin started working for the OS, and under what circumstances, and it is therefore difficult to say when he prepared his first designs, but it may be significant that he designed a Christmas card for the OS in 1918.[142] It is possible that he was seconded to the OS before being discharged formally from the army. What is certain is that his design (H.11.1) was in use for the one-inch Popular in time to appear on the first issues in June 1919, and it seems reasonable to assume that a similar design, dominated in its upper half by a large lion and unicorn and used on other one-inch coloured mapping, was introduced at the same time (H.10.1; Guy Messenger's OS/E). In its original form this was black, on buff card, with the sheet name in red, and in a single piece, attached to the back of the top left-hand panel of the map when folded. Inside the front cover were a brief note on the various scales of OS map available.

This did not last long, possibly both because the buff was liable to appear soiled and the bookfold wrap-round cover was liable to tear easily.[143] (This last difficulty would not have arisen had stiffened textile been used, as was standard by Bartholomew between the early 1890s and about 1918, and as was standard for the OS up to some time during the war, including the experimental cover of 1914.) The first measure was to cut the existing stock into front and back halves, and revert to pasting both front and back halves directly onto the cover.[144] As a result, covers of this type can be found with the letterpress obscured by the pasting-down; this style is found widely. The second was to redesign the cover so that the black was now dark brown, and there was a red band all round (H.10.2: Guy Messenger's cover style OS/F). This doubtless helped to counter soiling, but it also helped distinguish between the scales at a glance: red was the code for one-inch, green for half-inch and blue for quarter-inch. Such colour-coding had been suggested to the Olivier Committee by Messrs Cornish of Birmingham.[145] The back cover index diagrams were reprinted in dark brown to match, but there seem to have been large stocks of the earlier style, and H.10.2 front covers coupled with back cover indexes originally intended for pairing with H.10.1 are sometimes encountered. As before, LSS sheets were given northern, central or southern diagrams, now amended to show LSS 34 as published; Scottish sheets had indexes showing sheets 117-131, but as for the engraved parents, rather than in the radical combinations actually used. The Irish LSS and district sheets were issued with H.10.2 front covers and blank back covers.[146] A minor innovation, only made after the first stocks of H.10.2 had been printed, was to add the sheet number top right. As the Popular Edition equivalent of H.10.2 (H.11.2) was certainly ready by December 1919, probably H.10.2 was also in use by then.[147] 'Inward' folding was retained for both paper and mounted and folded and for dissected sheets: standard LSS sheets were folded 8 by 3

---

[141] It is possible that H.7 was adopted very late in the war, and was superseded almost immediately by the Ellis Martin style, H.10, discussed below.

[142] John Paddy Browne, *Map cover art.* Southampton: Ordnance Survey, 1991, 64, 66; Yolande Hodson, *Popular maps.* London: Charles Close Society, 1999, 196-7.

[143] A few LSS sheets in the number range 95 to 125 have been reported in this style (see figure 10, footnote 173, and Guy Messenger, *The Ordnance Survey one-inch map of England and Wales Third Edition (Large Sheet Series).* London: Charles Close Society, 1988, 27); it is also found on a few early Popular Edition sheets.

[144] The bookfold style was also used briefly on the half-inch map, with all red lettering instead of a mixture of black and red.

[145] *Report of the Departmental Committee on the sale of small-scale Ordnance Survey maps,* [1914], report, 33. [Chairman Sir S. Olivier. Copy PRO OS 1/6/5].

[146] H.10.2 covers were also used on post-war issues of Irish coloured one-inch maps based on the revision of 1898-1901.

[147] W.J. Johnston, 'The new one-inch and quarter-inch maps of the Ordnance Survey', *Geographical Journal* LV (1920), 192-200, 199.

and standard Scottish coloured sheets were still folded 7 by 3, and the covers were a similar size to those used pre-war, but the cropping of the maps was less drastic and the magnetic information was consistently left intact. H.10.1 was apparently only used on the LSS, whereas H.10.2 was used on the Scottish and Irish Third Editions as well. H.10.2 covers were sometimes pasted over hinged H.3 or H.4 covers, especially in Scotland and Ireland, and both H.10.1 and H.10.2 are often met with pasted over direct-print H.4.3 covers. Presumably there was a period in 1919-20 when Scottish and Irish sheets were still being issued in H.4 or H.7.1.a covers; the latter was used on the curious *Lake District* 'roads' sheet of 1920.[148] District sheets were at first issued in H.10.2 covers, except for *York*, which was issued in Popular covers (H.11.2) but, possibly in 1922, a special 'district map' cover, designed by Arthur Palmer, was introduced (H.29). From their introduction in 1920 the tourist maps were issued either in a generic Ellis Martin cover, showing three people having an animated discussion in a car (H.28), or in individual covers.[149] The longer-lived district maps also appeared in later generic cover-styles: a plain one used from the late 1920s (H.8.1), and a full-colour one of a rambler with a pub and bus-stop in the background (H.30) introduced in 1932 or 1933.

Although in principle one would not expect to find post-1918 covers on stock nominally superseded before December 1914, and indeed a H.10 cover may be a subtle indicator of a mediocre post-1914 printing inside, nonetheless the OS had on its hands after 1918 some unissued stocks which it took the opportunity to dispose of. Thus copies of LSS 107 printed in 1912 are found in H.10.2 covers, notwithstanding that this sheet had been reprinted in 1914. In this case and any parallel ones the anomaly can perhaps be explained by stocks of the 1914 reprint being stacked on top of the remaining flat stocks of the 1912 printing; the latter would only have come to notice again as the 1914 stock was exhausted. Titles on H.10 covers sometimes differ noticeably from those on the maps inside, and the same sheet may appear with alternatives, sometimes provided by a sticker, and no doubt with a view to encouraging local sales. The price rise of January 1920 often results in the earlier prices being amended with stickers, including some for the 'Popular Edition'.

Retailer's covers
Although not strictly part of OS history, enough Third Edition coloured sheets are encountered in covers supplied by retailers to warrant a brief mention: again, this was explored in more detail by Guy Messenger.[150] Third Edition coloured SSS sheets do not seem to be encountered at all in retailer's covers (and their revised coloured predecessors very rarely are), Scottish coloured sheets seem to be encountered very rarely, and then in W. & A.K. Johnston covers, and so retailer's covers are largely associated with the LSS.[151] The most commonly met with are those of Edward Stanford. It is unclear why this firm should have undertaken the sectioning and covering of OS small-scale maps once the OS began offering them as a standard product from 1906 onwards, particularly as by Stanford's own admission the financial return was poor; but they did.[152] Perhaps it was a logical extension of their undertaking this work for OS engraved and large-scale maps which, a few trivial exceptions apart, were available from the OS only in paper-flat form. A considerable number of LSS are also found in T. Fisher Unwin covers. This firm was appointed agent for OS small scales in 1906, apparently because they had no other map-producing interests,

---

[148] Irish SSS sheets were issued in H.10.2 covers after the first world war; before that they are only known in H.3 or H.7 types.

[149] These were: H.32 (*Snowdon District*), H.36 (*Deeside*), H.37 (*The Lake District*), H.38 (*Oban*), H.39 (*The Trossachs & Loch Lomond*), H.40 (*Scott's Country*), H.41 (*Burns' Country*), H.42 (*Lower Strath Spey*), and H.47 (*Rothesay & Firth of Clyde*).

[150] Guy Messenger, *The Ordnance Survey one-inch map of England and Wales Third Edition (Large Sheet Series)*. London: Charles Close Society, 1988, 33-7.

[151] Tim Nicholson, *The birth of the modern Ordnance Survey small-scale map*. London: Charles Close Society, 2002, 52-3; Guy Messenger, *A guide to the Ordnance Survey one-inch map of Scotland Third Edition in colour*. London: Charles Close Society, 1991, 3, 10.

[152] *Report of the Departmental Committee on the sale of small-scale Ordnance Survey maps*, [1914], minutes of evidence, 12-13, qq 222-51. [Chairman Sir S. Olivier. Copy PRO OS 1/6/5].

unlike such OS retailers as Stanford or Philip.[153] It is notable that, with a couple of exceptions which might be explained (like the 1912 printing of LSS 107 in its H.10.2 cover) by the issuing of leftover stock, Fisher Unwin covers appear on printings current after December 1914, and indeed often pasted on top of directly-printed H.4.3 covers. This suggests that Fisher Unwin was relieving the OS of some of the burden of providing covers for civil sale copies during and just after World War I. Some other retailers' covers seem to date quite definitely from before the war.[154]

Part III – The field revision instructions of 1901

Although the revision of Great Britain for the Third Edition took nearly twice as long as that for its predecessor, this was probably due almost entirely to the relative lack of urgency and corresponding reduced allocation of manpower as to any unforeseen problems. The revision of 1893-8 had been of mapping up to half a century out of date: once it was completed, the rate of work was that determined by the policy of revising every sheet once every fifteen years, and, as was recounted above, there was a period in 1909-10 when the cycle was extended to twenty years.

The earliest known surviving instructions for one-inch revision are those of 1896. These were published in *Sheetlines* 66 in 2003, but, as was observed there, it is highly likely that there was a predecessor of 1893. However, if the relative elaboration of the 1901 instructions as compared with those of 1896 is any guide, the putative ones of 1893 may have differed somewhat from those of 1896.[155] For the second revision of the one-inch fresh instructions were issued: some sections follow those of 1896 word-for-word, others differ markedly, and the arrangement is alphabetical rather than thematic. As with the 1896 instructions, several sections (11, 15, 17, 25) enjoin the collection of information which was not published. It must be supposed that this was collected for military purposes. The six-inch sheets on which the one-inch revision was plotted are not known to survive – they were either destroyed by enemy action in World War II or were intentionally discarded earlier – and so this unpublished information is no longer extant.

The text of the 1901 instructions follows below: editorial comments are added in *italic* as necessary after the section or group of sections to which they apply.[156]

---

[153] Tim Nicholson, *The birth of the modern Ordnance Survey small-scale map.* London: Charles Close Society, 2002, 38.

[154] Guy Messenger noted LSS and district sheets in covers issued by: G.E. Arundel; Cornish Bros.; Forster Groom; A.W. Gamage; Henry Good & Son; Andrew Iredale & Son; George Philip; Sifton Praed & Co.; Edward Stanford; Thompson; T. Fisher Unwin; Alfred Wilson. The Arundel [Exmouth] and Iredale [Torquay] covers were on maps of Exmouth and Torquay respectively, and are unlikely to be found on maps covering areas very far away from Devon, and no doubt the same could be said of maps encountered in other 'local' retailers' covers. It is noticeable that Wilson [London] covers have only been reported on maps of south-east England.

[155] Richard Oliver, 'The one-inch revision instructions of 1896', *Sheetlines* 66 (2003), 11-25.

[156] The text is taken from a photocopy in the British Library Map Library, Maps 207.d.14.

Ordnance Survey
Instructions to one-inch field revisers

Colonel Duncan A. Johnston, R.E.
Director-General of Ordnance Surveys
1901

[Table of contents omitted]

SECTION I.

Instructions for the 2nd revision of the 1-inch map in the field.

The United Kingdom.

General Rules.

1. The object of the 2nd Revision is to supply detail that has come into existence since the sheets of the map were last revised, to remove obsolete or unnecessary detail, to correct errors, to secure uniformity by a systematic classification of new roads, &c.

2. The Revision will be made on 6-inch impressions so as to admit of the alterations being made with accuracy; but no time should be wasted in correcting or inserting detail, which, from its minuteness, cannot be re-produced on the 1-inch scale.

3. It should be impressed on the Reviser that before making any alteration or addition he is to consider its effect on the 1-inch scale.

4. All detail which appears on the 6-inch and which is considered of sufficient importance to *add* to the 1-inch Map is to be encircled or underlined in blue, the remark "Insert on 1-inch" being added.

5. With the 6-inch cards the Reviser will send in a 1-inch impression, to be called the "Reviser's Fair Sheet", on which he will show additions and alterations to and erasures of names. The new classification of roads, of which the classification has been altered by the Reviser, should be coloured up on this sheet, which will enable the Reviser and the Officer to see at a glance the extent of the alterations.

6. The Reviser's Fair Sheet will be complete as to names which are to appear on the revised 1-inch map. Names include Ch., P.T., L.B., altitudes, road levels, but not F.P., B.R., M.C.D., &c.

7. Special instructions will be given in cases in which the 1-inch map is of more recent date than the 6-inch scale.
Unfortunately, these 'special instructions', which would certainly have been needed in west Cornwall and much of Lincolnshire, are not known to survive.

8. The following detailed instructions are to be strictly carried out, but it must be understood that the Reviser must discriminate between the different Countries, *i.e.,* Scotch sheets would differ somewhat from the English or Irish.
This passage strikes this commentator as obscure.

Antiquities.

9. If a Reviser or Examiner thinks that Antiquities such as Castles, Roman Roads, Tumuli, Sites of Battles, Monuments, which do not appear on the 6-inch should be shown on the 1-inch he should draw attention to the apparent omission by letter to his Officer, who will decide whether the Antiquity is to be shown on the 1-inch.

One wonders how revisers were to find out about these 'invisible' antiquities, for surely if there were anything visible it would already have been recorded on the six-inch?

10. Should it be desirable to insert an Antiquity on the 1-inch which already appears on 6-inch it will suffice to underline in red on 6-inch and insert on Reviser's Fair Sheet.

Boundaries
The one feature appearing on published Third Edition mapping which is not mentioned in the Instructions printed here are public administrative boundaries: no doubt the subject would have been covering in the corresponding drawing instructions, which are not known to survive.

County and civil parish boundaries were shown in Great Britain; only county boundaries were shown in Ireland. Whereas in the revision of 1893-1901 county boroughs had not been distinguished, being treated as civil parishes, on the Third Edition they were shown by the county boundary symbol. Parish boundaries were not liked by the military, but there were civil pressures to retain them, and they were presumably too much trouble to remove entirely.[157] It is perhaps symptomatic of the pressure to retain them on the one hand and reprographic complications on the other that parish boundaries running along the centres of double-line streams were shown in blue: presumably scraping them off the water transfer and making them good on the outline was too much trouble. On some of the 1914 experimental district sheets (e.g. Dorking & Leith Hill*) parish boundaries running along streams were omitted altogether.*

Bridges.
11. Bridges *over* roads or railways are to be distinguished from *those* under roads or railways, thus:-

[Bridge symbols over and under stylised depictions of single-track and double-track drawn in six-inch style are illustrated at this point in the original.]

and the Revisers are to ascertain whether they are correctly shown on the 6-inch map. All bridges, both old and new, are to be further shown as (M) masonry, (W) wood, (I) iron, and (S) suspension. If a Bridge is carried by an iron girder or girders it should be described as "I" (iron); if by a masonry or brick arch or arches as "M"; if by a wooden structure as "W". If in a bridge of two or more spans, one span is I and one is M, the bridge will be described as I and M, and similarly in other cases.
This repeats and, by including the sentence on bridges which were a mix of 'I' and 'M', amplifies a section of the 1896 instructions. This information was presumably collected for military purposes.

Canals.
12. All locks and bridges are to be distinctly shown.

Churches and Chapels.
13. Churches with spires are to be distinguished by the symbol ♂, those with towers by the symbol ♁, those with a tower surmounted by a spire, should, as a rule, be distinguished by the symbol for spire, but when the height of the tower occupies ¾ or more of the total heights from the roof of the building to the top of the spire, and the top of the tower forms a platform and is accessible, the Church should be distinguished by the symbol for tower ♁; Churches without either tower or spire to be marked by a +. Chapels having towers or spires are to be shown as if they were

[157] Tim Nicholson, *The birth of the modern Ordnance Survey small-scale map.* London: Charles Close Society, 2002, 14; cf W.J. Johnston, 'The new one-inch and quarter-inch maps of the Ordnance Survey', *Geographical Journal* LV (1920), 192-200, 199.

Churches. In all cases a Church should be distinguished by writing "Ch." or "Church" and a Chapel by writing "Chap." or "Chapel".

14. Illustrations for guidance as to Church symbols in doubtful cases.

 A Tower when height of low spire is ¼ the height of structure from roof to top of low spire.

 A Spire when height of spire is about ⅓ of the height of structure from roof to point of spire.

 A Tower when an incomplete tower is capped with a tiled roof resting on a string course and presenting an obviously unfinished appearance.

Sections 13 and 14 were published in Sheetlines *23 with the comment: 'How is the church symbolized when the height of the spire is between ¼ and ⅓ the height of the tower?!!'[158] The distinguishing of church steeples was introduced at the behest of the Baker Committee in 1892: the object appears to have been partly to distinguish landmarks, and partly to indicate potential lookouts.*

Most interesting are the underlying social and cultural assumptions: a 'church' is evidently an established one of the Church of England, Wales or Scotland; it is to be suspected that Roman Catholic churches were not included, as on the published maps they are indicated as 'R.C.Ch.' in italic, whereas established churches, except where there was no room for the text, are usually 'Ch', in lower-case roman, though on some later Third Edition sheets (e.g. SSS 164, published 1911; included in LSS 69, 70), and on all subsequent one-inch maps, these annotations are omitted, and the symbols alone appear.

Cuttings and Embankments.
15. Cuttings and Embankments six feet and over in depth and height are to be distinctly shown on railways, and the greatest depth or height shown in figures. On roads, only very important cuttings or embankments will be shown.
The thinking here was presumably to indicate railway earthworks which could be used to conceal bodies of troops: the height and depth data were not published. Road earthworks were only shown exceptionally: the dramatic examples on the Watling Street north-west of Dunstable and near Streatley on the future A6, on SSS 220 and LSS 96, give some idea of what was 'very important'.

Docks, Piers, Lighthouses.
16. Docks, Piers, Lighthouses, not appearing on the 6-inch Map are to be inserted.
Navigation features could also be checked by reference to Admiralty lists of lights and Notices to Martiners. A 'lighthouse' might occasionally be an ordinary house which displayed a light, rather than a tower: there is such an example at Stallingborough (SSS 81.82, LSS 33).[159] A curious omission here is navigation beacons, which were sometimes shown by annotation on earlier mapping on post-1893 revised mapping by symbol. Comparison of map and ground suggests that only larger beacons are shown but, if so, what was the criteria? Were they in fact 'prominent landmarks', as covered by section 52 below?

Dykes.
17. Where districts are much cut up by Dykes, either for drainage or irrigation purposes, the Revisers should see that the most important appear on the 1-inch map.

---

[158] 'Tower or spire?', *Sheetlines* 23 (1988), 27.
[159] Richard Oliver, 'Taking to the water', *Sheetlines* 45 (1996), 9-27, 19.

But what is an 'important dyke'?!

Ferries.

18. Ferries are to be written and described thus:-
"For foot passengers only."
"For vehicular traffic."
"Steam."

The 1896 instructions (section 17) are similar. This is another example where information was collected, presumably for military interest, but not published, at any rate before the Popular Edition (where foot and vehicular ferries were indicated on the published mapping). 'Steam ferries' are sometimes indicated on Third Edition mapping, but there are some significant exceptions, e.g. whereas those along the Thames at Woolwich and elsewhere (SSS 271, LSS 116) are shown, that between Hull and New Holland (SSS 81-82, LSS 33) is just 'Ferry'.

Fords.

19. Fords in rivers and streams exceeding 15 feet in width to be written.

Gardens.

20. Gardens, Market Gardens, Allotment Gardens, and Nurseries, which do not at present appear in garden character on the 1-inch scale map will not be added to the map in that character.

21. Those which already appear on the 1-inch map will not be removed on revision unless they have ceased to exist as gardens, &c.

This in an interesting contrast to the corresponding section (29) of the 1896 instructions, where 'Enclosed gardens round villages or detached houses are to be shown.' Possibly showing areas as garden was found to serve no useful purpose, but it was considered that deleting existing garden 'ornament' was not worth the trouble. In the event, garden depiction in this residual form lasted onto those one-inch New Popular Edition sheets, published in 1945-7, which were derived from New Series material.

Gravel Pits, Quarries.

22. Only those Gravel Pits and Quarries which are deep, cover a large area, and are likely to remain as permanent features on the ground are to be shown.

But what is a 'large area'? Stipulating a minimum size would have been useful.

Greenhouses and Glasshouses.

23. Greenhouses or other Glasshouses, in or near houses, are not engraved on the 1-inch map, and should not be supplied by Field Revisers, but *large* Glasshouses if on brick or other permanent foundations, and if so far separated from houses so as to admit their appearing on the 1-inch scale, will be shown by the Field Reviser as Glasshouses on the 6-inch plots, and will be engraved on the map as houses.

A cross-hatched symbol had been used for 1:2640 and larger-scale mapping since at least the early 1850s, but was only introduced onto the six-inch with the advent of the National Grid Regular Edition in the early 1950s. The first use of cross-hatching for glazed areas noted by the writer is at Feltham and Hanworth on Popular Edition 114; it was standard on the Fifth Edition (published 1931 onwards).

Heath & Moor.

24. Heath and Moor to be shown by a band of Burnt Sienna and writing R.P. Rocky Pasture unfit for camping grounds is to be distinguished by writing "Rocky P."

25. When R.P. is cancelled on 6-inch, describe the condition of the ground as – Pasture, Arable, &c. as the case may be, and cancel boundaries of the cancelled R.P. unless they represent detail which should appear on the 1-inch scale irrespective of the Rough Pasture.

26. R.P. is not to be added to the 1-inch scale unless the area so added is Heath, Moorland, or covered with Furze.

The instruction in section 25 to note former uncultivated ground, as it might be called nowadays, as arable or pasture is extremely interesting, as this information was not only never published on the one-inch, but had not been published for the 1:2500 either since November 1879, when the publication of land-use in parish area books was discontinued. However, such information continued to be collected in conjunction with 1:2500 revision up to 1918, and so, as there was a considerable pruning of minor detail shown on the large scales after 1893, presumably recording arable and pasture fulfilled a need: a military need, perhaps?[160]

Houses.

27. All are shown and where convenient are blocked.

Inns.

28. In the open country all Inns will be shown which are of local importance, but when two Inns are close together only the more important one need be noticed. In a village, only the most important Inn will be indicated. In a town it is obvious that there must be an Inn, no reference to an Inn need be made.

29. By "Inn" is meant only a fully-licensed house where food and lodging can be obtained. In the case of an important country inn such as some of the old coaching inns, the name of which is very well known throughout the neighbourhood, the Reviser must call special attention to the name with a view to its being engraved in full on the 1-inch map.

30. Inns whose names should be written are sure to be named on the 6-inch scale.

31. It is only very exceptionally and generally in isolated positions that an Inn name should be written in full.

The 1896 instructions (section 32) define inns as 'fully licensed' houses, but make no mention of food or lodging. See also section 80, below. Irish inns are treated separately in section 94 below.

Marsh, Bog.

32. Marshes and Bogs where not clearly shown on the 6-inch map are to be distinguished by encircling them with a blue band, and writing "M" or "B" as the case may be.

Milestones, Direction Posts.

33. Milestones are to be shown, Direction Posts are not to be shown.

The object of checking milestones was for the provision of mileages along main roads on the published maps. Mileages were only shown, however, where a road was furnished with milestones or mileposts (the latter apparently any indicator made of metal, notwithstanding any superficial resemblance to a mile indicator of stone or concrete); thus many 'first class' roads are shown without mileages but, conversely, mileages are shown on a few 'second class' roads (e.g. at Sir William Hill on SSS 99, LSS 45). From 1883 the six-inch and larger scale maps only recorded the distances to the two nearest towns,[161] *although many milestones and posts also recorded the distance to London or other important places further afield. The standard practice on the one-inch New Series and the one-inch of Scotland from the early 1880s onwards was to show mileages leading from the larger of two towns to the smaller. A common practice on milestones was to quote the distance in one direction in whole miles, and in the other in miles and furlongs; on the OS six-inch the furlongs were rendered as eighths of a mile. It sometimes happened, particularly if towns changed in relative importance, that applying the principle of using the larger of two places as the*

---

[160] See J.B. Harley, *The Ordnance Survey and land-use mapping 1855-1918.* Norwich: Geo Books, 1979, 27: he was evidently not aware of this instruction of 1901.

[161] Richard Oliver, *Ordnance Survey maps: a concise guide.* London: Charles Close Society, 1993, 68, citing Southampton Circular, 31 May 1883.

starting-point could lead to mileages along roads being expressed in fractions of a mile: there are good examples of this on the future A16 on either side of Louth (SSS 90 and 103, LSS 39 and 48).

Names.

     34. Very few alterations are desired with regard to names. It must be assumed that every name on the 1-inch is correct, and no alteration will be made without strong authority, but where the 6-inch differs from the 1-inch scale enquiry should be made which is correct.

     35. Important names that have been omitted from the 1-inch will be added, and obsolete names will be struck out. It is not desirable to overcrowd the map with names.

     36. Large isolated farms should generally be named, but not small cottages, &c. unless they are landmarks in open country.

     37. In very open country sufficient names should appear (even if of minor importance) to enable a map user to easily identify any part of the country.
This might perhaps be paraphrased as: 'to give a name to any hill or mountain he may happen to notice'.

     38. It is believed that in some cases in Scotland, Hill and Forest Names, and in a few cases well known Tourist's Resorts have been omitted from the map which might with advantage appear on it.
It is unclear whether 'tourist resorts' are hotels or places of interest.

Method of showing names.

     39. Draw a single red line under those names which appear on the 6-inch and which ought to be added to 1-inch and write the name in red on the reviser's fair sheet as near the right size as possible, and in proper position.

     40. Cancel by a red line through the name on the 6-inch and reviser's fair sheet any name which should not appear on the 1-inch, and give reasons for so doing on 6-inch plot.

     41. Attention should be drawn to any name which is wrongly spelt on the 1-inch map by underlining the name in red on the 6-inch and correcting it on the reviser's fair sheet; leave as they are on the 6-inch any names as to which no action is needed on the 1-inch; this includes those names which already appear correctly on the 1-inch, and those names not on the 1-inch and which need not appear on that scale.

     42. New names which are not on the 1-inch or 6-inch, and which ought to appear on 1-inch will be written in red on the 6-inch and the reviser's fair sheet. Name Sheets to be supplied in these cases except in the case of Railway Names which can be checked in the Office with the Railway Guide.
The 'Railway Guide' is Bradshaw's monthly guide.

     43. Small alterations such as "Inholmes Wood" to "Inholmes Copse" for the purpose of assimilating to the large scale are to be avoided, unless the name on 1-inch is actually wrong. Abbreviated forms of names are usually permissible on the 1-inch, *e.g.*, Ho. for House.

Parks, Ornamental Ground, Lodges.

     44. Parks and Ornamental Grounds where not distinctly shown are to be distinguished by a light shade of neutral tint.

     45. The principal lodges are also to be shown.

     46. Very small pieces of ornamental ground, *i.e.,* those less than $1/16$ of a square mile in area should not be shown.

     47. When ornamental ground is cancelled the present state of the ground should be stated on 6-inch plots.
'Neutral tint' is grey. It is unclear why 'principal lodges' needed to be shown. The specification of $1/16$ square mile (40 acres: about 16 hectares) is in contrast with the subjectivism elsewhere (sections 22, 48). The 'present state of the ground' might be interpreted as arable or pasture: cf comments on section 25 above.

Ponds.

48. Only those ponds that are of large size and of a permanent nature should be shown.
Again: what is 'large'?!

Post and Telegraph Offices, Letter Boxes.

49. Post Offices to be distinguished on Cards by P.O., Telegraph Offices by T.O., both offices combined as P.T.O. Only one should be shown in each village; it is understood that each town has an office, so they need not be shown in towns. Letter Boxes beyond the limits of towns and villages to be shown by L.B.

50. Field revisers should note that the term "Telegraph Office" must be taken to include not only post offices where telegraph business is transacted, but all those other places where public telegraph business is transacted on behalf of the Postal Department, *e.g.,* railway stations, &c.

51. This information can be obtained from the Postal Guide which can be seen at any Post Office.
'P' and 'T' were written under village names on the published maps: the only exceptions seem to have been telegraph offices at railway or coastguard stations. The published maps showed letter-boxes, by 'L.B.', at villages with no post offices, as well as those away from villages. If the information on post offices was available from the official Post Office guide, why check it on the ground? Or was there some military need here, too? See also section 80, below.

Prominent Landmarks.

52. All objects which are prominent landmarks, such as towers, obelisks, conspicuous single trees, &c., though small on plan, should be shown by writing the word "conspicuous", and their names if any given to them. Clumps of trees of no importance should be cancelled. All features and objects of interest to tourists are to be shown by writing.
Presumably revisers were expected to acquire a feel of what might be of interest to 'tourists'.

Orchards.

53. Large orchards are to be shown by writing "Orchard" or "Or."
Once again: what is 'large'? Later instructions specified a minimum area.

Railways.

54. Single lines are to be distinguished from double by writing "single line" or "double line" as the case may be. Railways and tramways are to be distinguished thus:-
        Double line *[illustrated by solid line in the original]*
        Single line *[illustrated by pecked line in the original]*
        Mineral line and tramway *[illustrated by solid line with cross-bars in the original]*

55. This should be shown in red and an explanatory reference made on the margin.
The 1896 instructions (section 10) ordered that triple and quadruple lines should be recorded; this information, presumably of military interest, was not published, and as it would have been recorded in the course of large-scale revision, perhaps its collection was felt to be unnecessary once cyclic revision of the large scales was established. 'Tramway' might either be a colliery or quarry tramway, possibly horse-worked and pretty ramshackle, or a passenger-carrying tramway, possibly electrified, and of a quite different nature.

Not mentioned in the instructions are underground railways in London and Glasgow: those in London were shown on the New Series by a line-with-close-crossbars symbol, but that in Glasgow was omitted. The symbol was not noted in the legend on the published maps (SSS 256 and 270, LSS 108 and 115), and the unwary might assume that it indicated a feature on the ground. This might explain why the symbol was omitted from the Popular Edition, though it also added the sort of 'clutter' that Close wanted to be rid of.

Railway Stations.

56. Railway stations are to be shown on that side of the line upon which the ticket office is situated. Railway stations used for goods purposes only to be marked "Goods" on the 6-inch plots. *The usual practice was not to show goods stations explicitly on the published one-inch; users were left to infer them from patterns of lines and buildings.*

Roads.

57. The different classes of roads are to be coloured in the field as under:-

           1st Class Roads - - - Purple
           2nd Class Roads - - - Carmine
           3rd Class Roads - - - Green
           4th Class Roads - - - Yellow
           Carriage drives - - - Blue

First Class Roads.

58. First class roads, coloured purple, are main roads generally leading from town to town, metalled and kept in good repair, and the minimum width of metalled roadway, exclusive of edges or footway, must be 14 feet.

It should be noted that 'metalled' means surfaced with broken stones, with varying degrees of consolidation: it is not synonymous with 'tarred'. Although there were isolated sections of tarred road in the 1900s, it only became general in the inter-war period: some idea of road surfaces at the time of the Third Edition can be gained from the Gall and Inglis road books, published from about 1900 onwards.[162] These road books seem initially to have been aimed initially at cyclists, who were the fastest things on the road until the coming of the motor-car, but it is noticeable that these OS instructions make no mention of cyclists: 'fast' in section 59 below is fast in equestrian terms, and a 'loose' surface which might be satisfactory for horses and the iron-tyred vehicles which they drew might be very difficult to cycle on. Untarred but 'fast' roads which would correspond either to the 'first class' of the 1896 and 1901 instructions or to the 'Good and fit for fast traffic' of the Popular Edition are rarely met with today, but are sometimes found on cycle paths, and there were some lengths on the eastern side of the Derwent Valley reservoirs in Derbyshire in April 2003, but such surfaces deteriorate fairly rapidly unless carefully maintained.

Second Class Roads.

59. Second class roads, coloured carmine, are metalled roads in good repair and fit for fast traffic at all seasons, *i.e.*, it should be possible to drive carriages and light carts over them at a trot. This class will as a rule include roads between villages, or between villages and towns, or between one first class road and another, and approaches to railway stations.

For 'fast' traffic see section 58 above. It is noticeable that in 1901 Bartholomew, with the co-operation of the Cyclists Touring Club, introduced onto their half-inch map a road classification that was markedly more informative, as well as cycle-friendly, than that of the OS.[163]

Third Class Roads.

60. Third class roads, coloured green, are all other metalled roads suitable for wheel traffic. This will include all metalled roads, which from want of repair are not fit for fast traffic.

Fourth Class Roads.

61. Fourth class roads, coloured yellow, are all unmetalled roads.

---

[162] 'Very bumpy near York, then a very fair tarred road to Thirsk, after which fine to Northallerton': Harry R.G. Inglis, *The contour road book of England (northern division)*. Edinburgh: Gall & Inglis, 1915, 74.

[163] Tim Nicholson, 'Bartholomew and the half-inch layer-coloured map 1883-1903', *Cartographic Journal* 37 (2000), 123-145.

Carriage Drives.

62. Carriage drives are gravelled roads running through parks and ornamental grounds. They should be coloured blue with M.C.D. written to the main drive.

The noting of main carriage drives was presumably to assist the reviser when generalising: there is a similar section (7) in the 1896 instructions. It is noticeable that these are often shown as 'second class' on the engraved maps, but without infill on their coloured counterparts.

Cart Tracks.

63. Cart tracks, except when they are the only and main approach to a farm from a road, are not to be shown.

Private Roads.

64. Private roads are to be distinguished by letters P.R. and classed as ordinary public roads.

In the writer's experience, more questions are generated by the OS's treatment generally of roads, paths and other 'ways', and in particular of their possible indications of public rights of way, than by all other matters relating to OS maps. It cannot be emphasised too strongly that the official position of the OS is that it records only physical facts, and not 'attribute' information such as questions of ownership or of rights, and it is this writer's contention that, in any case, section 12 of the Survey Act of 1841, in providing that nothing done under the Act shall affect any property right, might be held to apply to rights of way questions as much as to questions of land ownership. There is a similar passage to this (section 6) in the 1896 instructions. It is perhaps as well that the six-inch revisers' sheets have been lost, otherwise there would no doubt be intense interest in what ways were recorded with 'P.R.', though it could be countered that though the road might be private (privately owned? privately maintained?) there might still be some sort of public right over it, on foot, or horseback, or in a vehicle of some sort. The information may have been recorded for military interest: it is noticeable that nothing is said as to the degree of rigor with which revisers were to ascertain whether a road was 'private' or not, and perhaps it was hoped that the rights-of-way disclaimer on published maps would keep queries from civil users at bay. Those using OS maps for rights of way investigations are strongly urged to consult Yolande Hodson's articles on the subject.[164]

Shooting Paths.
See Para. 78.

65. N.B. – Roads should be classified according to their general character and not with reference to their best or worst portions. A class should not be given to very short pieces of roads differing from that of the adjoining portions.

66. The classification of roads should not be changed unless an alteration is clearly necessary. No alteration should be made which can be considered a matter of opinion. After a long course of wet weather the class of a road is apt to appear lower than at other times.

67. The condition of minor roads is apt to vary from year to year.

68. As a help to revisers it may be stated that roads directly connecting towns are usually 1st class, those directly connecting important villages are seldom below 2nd class, and roads directly connecting other villages are seldom below 3rd class.

It is apparent that the classification of untarred roads was fraught with difficulty, and that those framing these revision instructions were anxious that road classification should only be changed (and electrotype matrices scraped) when absolutely necessary.

---

[164] Yolande Hodson, 'Roads on OS 1:2500 plans 1884-1912', *Rights of Way Law Review* (1999), Section 9.3:107-118; Yolande Hodson, 'Roads on OS one-inch maps 1801-1904', *Rights of Way Law Review* (2000), Section 9.3:119-27.

69. Although the classification of roads on the 1-inch scale will not necessarily be assimilated with that on the 6-inch scale, due weight may be given to the latter in doubtful cases.

70. Roads which have been laid out for building purposes should be classed 3rd, although their present condition may not be up to that standard.

There is a good example of 'roads laid out for building purposes' on SSS 290, LSS 118, in squares 13J and 13K, between Ringwould and St Margaret at Cliffe.

71. In order that the alteration may be clearly visible only alterations and additions should be coloured on the 6-inch cards and reviser's fair sheet, and an explanation given on O.S. 513 as to the need for alteration of class, stating whether the character of the road has altered, or whether the original classification was wrong, and any other information likely to assist the Division Officer to judge whether the alteration is judicious.

72. Important footpaths and bridle roads are to be distinguished by the initials F.P. or B.R. on 6-inch plots as the case may be. This will only apply where it is found necessary to add new, or to correct existing ones. Only footpaths that are habitually used by the public should be shown.

73. Unimportant footpaths need not be remarked upon on the 6-inch impressions, unless shown on the 1-inch, when they should be cancelled on the 6-inch plots and reviser's fair sheet.

74. Any path shown on the 1-inch which has ceased to exist should be similarly treated, and a remark made on the 6-inch plot, "/ No F.P. on ground. /" *[In the original, / has open circles on ends, similar to boundary change symbols on 1:2500 mapping.]*

75. The cases of footpaths required to be added to the 1-inch map will be rare, but where this is necessary, a blue dotted line should be drawn along the footpath on the 6-inch plot.

Sections 72-75 beg the question 'what is "important"'? The 1896 instructions (section 8) went into more detail; presumably by 1901 additions to the one-inch were to be conditioned by what was already shown. 'Unimportant' paths could probably be identified by comparing the one-inch with larger scales; but those concerned with rights of way will doubtless be mindful of the maxim 'Once a highway, always a highway'.

Rifle Ranges.

76. Rifle ranges are to be shown by writing "Rifle Range" when the firing range exceeds 400 yards.

Schools.

77. The word should only be written in isolated positions.

Shooting Paths.

78. Shooting paths, when open and forming a ready means of communication between roads and points, should be shown. Those wide enough to allow the passage of wheel traffic may be classed and coloured as roads and marked P.R., those wide enough for foot passengers only should be marked F.P.

79. The number of such roads and tracks at present shown on the 1-inch map may be taken generally as a guide as to the number of such tracks to be shown. Only important shooting paths should be added to the map.

This repeats the wording of the 1896 instructions (section 8).

Smithies.

80. All smithies, at which horses can be shod, not situated in villages are to be shown; in villages where there are more than one, only one is to be shown, enquiry being made as to which is the most important; smithies should not be shown in towns.

> No Inn
> No Smithy   } To be written where none exist in a village.
> No P.O.

The depiction of forges had been requested by the Baker Committee in 1892.[165] *The 1896 instructions bearing on this (section 33) are much briefer, with no mention of noting explicitly the absence of inns, smithies or post-offices.*

Sea Coast.

81. The character of the coast line is to be corrected where necessary, and distinguished as cliff, sand dunes, &c.

82. The low water mark for the 1-inch map will be taken from the 6-inch plots, unless extensive alterations to it have occurred since the 6-inch survey.

What might happen in practice was explored by the writer in an article in 1996.[166] *No instructions are given here as to what was to be done had there been 'extensive alterations': instructions for large-scale survey of low water dateable to the late 1870s indicate that this work could be damp and labour-intensive.*

Streams.

83. No streams with well defined channels should be omitted. Streams 15 feet wide and over are to be distinguished by a continuous coloured line along the stream and the approximate width in feet shown here and there. When a field reviser is in doubt whether to show a stream as over or under 15 feet he should see how it is engraved on the 1-inch. If engraved as a double stream it should be shown as 15 feet, if as a single stream show it as under 15 feet. The object in each case is to leave the original engraving unaltered.

Tram and Mineral Lines.

84. Tram and mineral lines are to be distinguished by writing "Tram" or "Mineral" line, and the gauge.

85. Termini of tram or mineral lines should always be described, *e.g.,* "Colliery", "Lead Mine", so that they may if possible be described on the 1-inch.

Wells.

86. Public wells in the open country, and villages supplied by wells, should be marked W. *Wells were shown on the published one-inch revised New Series and Third Edition on Salisbury Plain, but not elsewhere: perhaps this is another example of information collected for military purposes. Water to supply to villages was recorded on the early (1911-14) sheets of the 1:25,344 Map of East Anglia [later GSGS 3036].*

Windmills.

87. All windmills are to be shown, and the purpose for which they are used should be noted. If the windmill be permanently disused the words "Old Windmill" are written.

88. Windfan, Ontario, and other such pumps in isolated positions will be shown by 1-inch field revisers on the 6-inch plots and will be engraved on the 2nd revision of the 1-inch map.

89. They should not be shown in or close to towns and large villages where there is not room to show them properly. Should it occur exceptionally that these pumps are so numerous in a country district that all cannot be shown on the 1-inch map, the reviser will select the most important ones to show. These pumps will be indicated on the revised maps by the symbol *[illustrated in the original: similar to that used on published maps].* The reviser besides showing them on the 6-inch plots should indicate them by this symbol in position on the reviser's fair sheet. *There is here a definite change from the practice in the revision of 1893-1901, where windpumps appear to have been shown, in theory at least, by a windmill symbol without annotation. It should be noted that 'windpump' could include a wide range of structures, including brick towers which*

---

[165] *Report of Committee on a military map of the United Kingdom.* London: War Office, 1892, 10 (War Office number A.237). [Chairman Sir T.D. Baker. Copies RGS, OS Library].
[166] Richard Oliver, 'Taking to the water', *Sheetlines* 45 (1996), 9-27.

were used for drainage rather than grinding: thus the great majority of what are usually taken to be 'windmills' in the Norfolk Broads (SSS 148, 162; LSS 67, 68: a good surviving example is that at Horsey, Norfolk, TG 457222, which, as it was built as late as 1912, is not to be found in square 6C on LSS 68) were recorded on the Third Edition, and indeed up to the early Seventh Series in the 1950s, as windpumps. This distinction by function rather than appearance is an exception to the usual OS rule of concentrating on indisputable physical attributes.[167]

Woods.

90. Woods of coniferous trees and those of deciduous trees are to be distinguished by writing "Con." or "Dec." as the case may be. If a wood be made up of separate patches of deciduous and coniferous trees, these patches if large enough (say 400 yards square) to be shown distinctly on the 1-inch map, should be shown distinctly on the 6-inch by reviser. If however they are very small the wood may be shown as "mixed" by writing the word "mixed".

SECTION II.

Special instructions for Ireland.

Constabulary Barracks.

91. Constabulary Barracks to be shown in villages and open districts, but not in towns. Temporary huts will not be shown.

Limekilns.

92. Limekilns will not be shown.

Forts.

93. Forts (antiquities) will remain as now shown by symbol.
This presumably refers to the depiction of earthworks by miniature hachures.

Inns & Hotels.

94. Inns and Hotels should only appear on the 1-inch map when it applies to a place where travellers are taken in for food and lodging. In the country districts there are a number of grocer's shops, &c. which are licensed for the sale of beer, wine, and spirits, these should not be shown as "Inns" unless there is accommodation for travellers. It must be remembered that the Hotel of the average country town in Ireland would only probably rank with a wayside Inn in England, so that "Inns" are proportionately bad.
Perhaps this was written as a result of bitter experience in the one-inch revision of Ireland in 1898-1901?

Bogs.

95. Peat or moss which is often called "bog" in Ireland does not necessitate any alteration of the 1-inch maps. A "Marsh" is, speaking generally, an area which is wet at all seasons of the year, and in which peat is not cut; such an area must of course, as in the past, be described as "Marsh".

---

[167] The depiction of windmills on OS maps has been studied in William H. Bignell, *The cartographic representation of landscape features by the Ordnance Survey: a nineteenth-century perspective*, unpublished University of Exeter Ph.D. thesis, 2002.

Meeting Houses.

   96. In the north of Ireland numerous buildings are described as "Meeting House"; it should be described on the 6-inch plots to what use such places are put as "Presbyterian Church" or "Chapel", and the usual symbol shown if the building is used as a place of worship; the more important of these buildings should be described as "very large", "conspicuous", &c.

In practice these seem to have been shown by description rather than by symbol.

Woods.

   97. During the revision of Ireland the distinction between deciduous and non-deciduous trees has not been carried out on the drawings, but the field reviser should make the distinction on the 6-inch plots.

The revision referred to here is probably the one-inch revision of 1898-1901 rather than that for the 1:2500 or six-inch.

Richard Oliver

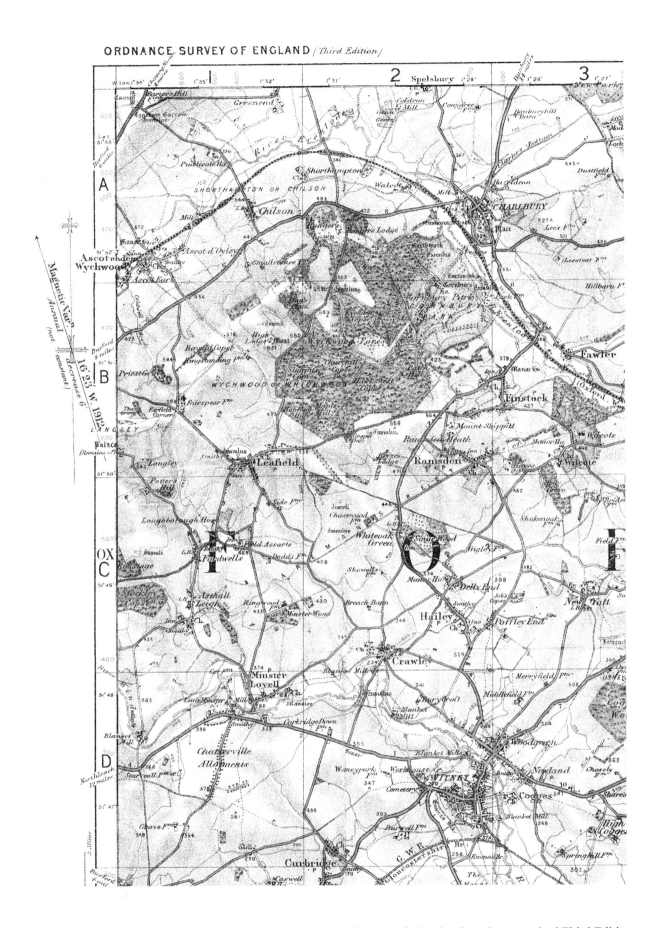

Figure 1 *Oxford and District*, 6.12 reprint. Note the special features of what is otherwise a standard Third Edition coloured map: the additional magnetic variation diagram in the left hand margin, the two-inch squaring system, and the narrow diced border with latitude and longitude values at one minute intervals.

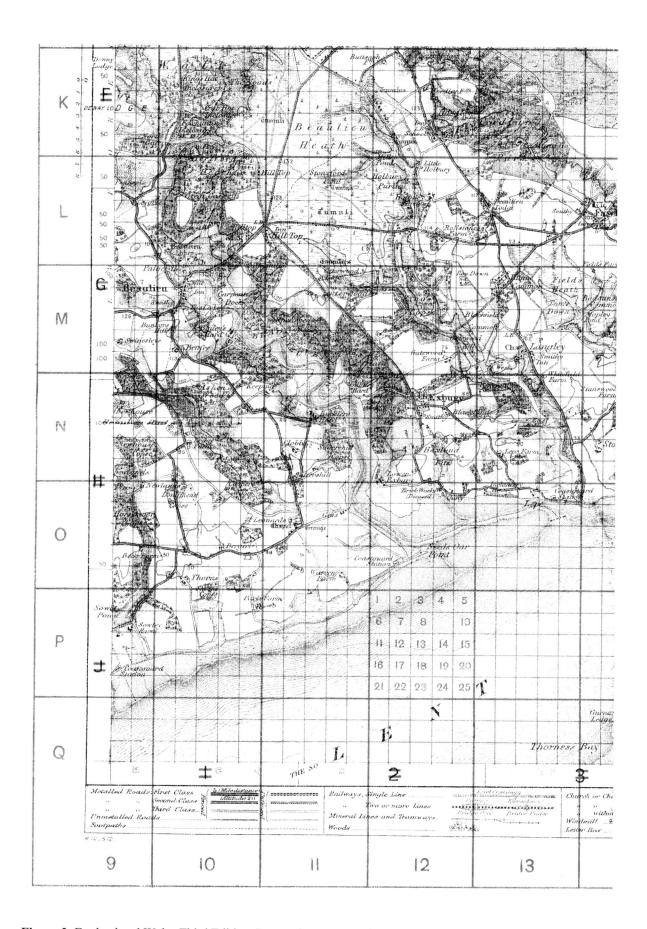

Figure 2 England and Wales Third Edition (Large Sheet Series) sheet 135, 5.12 reprint. Overprinted in red with a military squaring system. The large squares have 2000 yard sides, the subdivisions 400 yards. Note that the overprint also deletes the marginal alpha-numeric values.

55

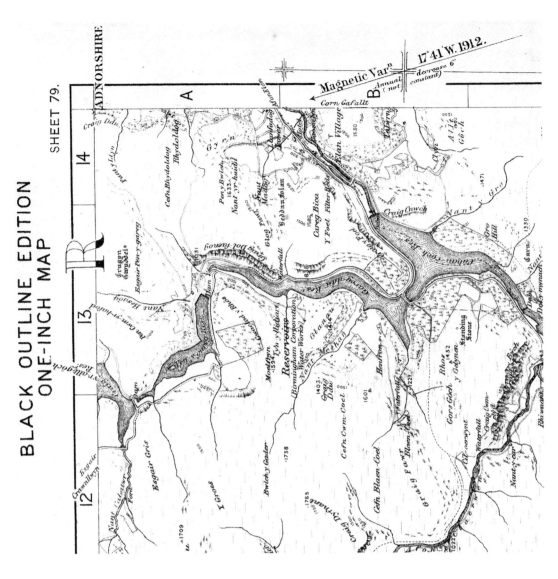

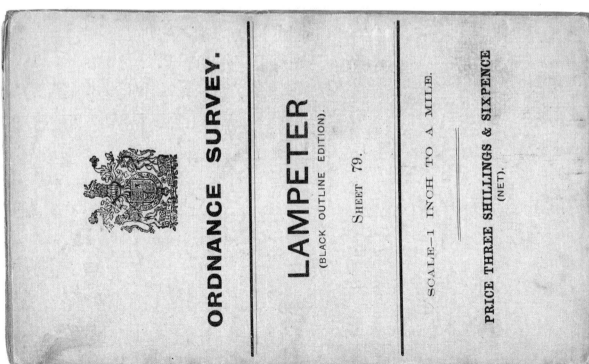

Figure 3 The *Black Outline Edition. Left:* an example of the H.7 cover design used, on white card. Examples on buff card are also recorded. *Right:* the heading, and a sample of monochrome mapping, with black waterlining and no contours. The cover is reduced to 88%.

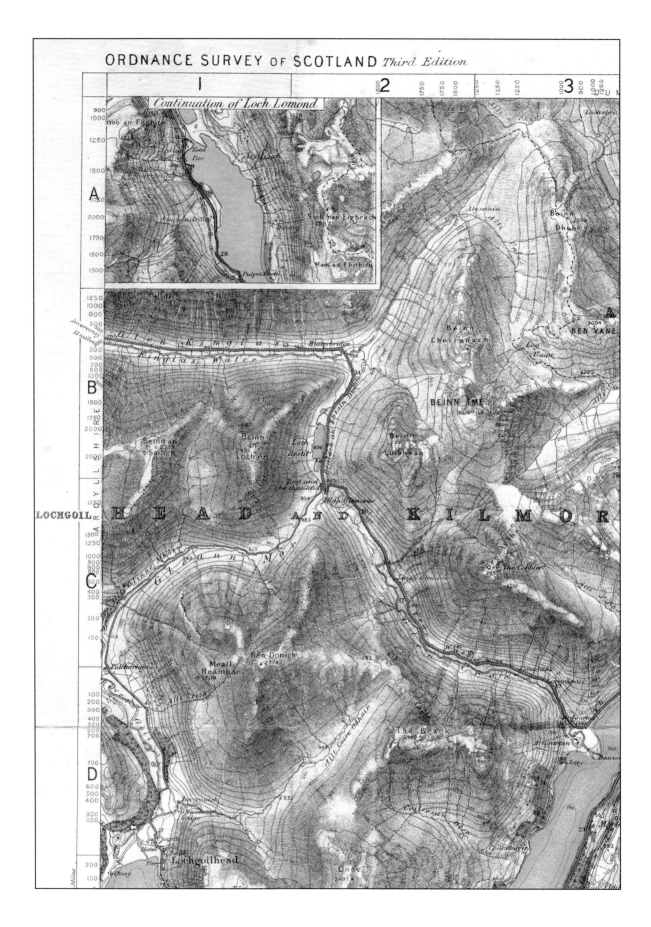

Figure 4 *Loch Lomond District*, 1908. In Scotland the third edition map shows water by a blue tint, rather than waterlining as in England and Wales. This is the one known Scottish sheet with a narrow (quarter-inch) border, which was standard on coloured one-inch mapping in England and Wales and Ireland at this time.

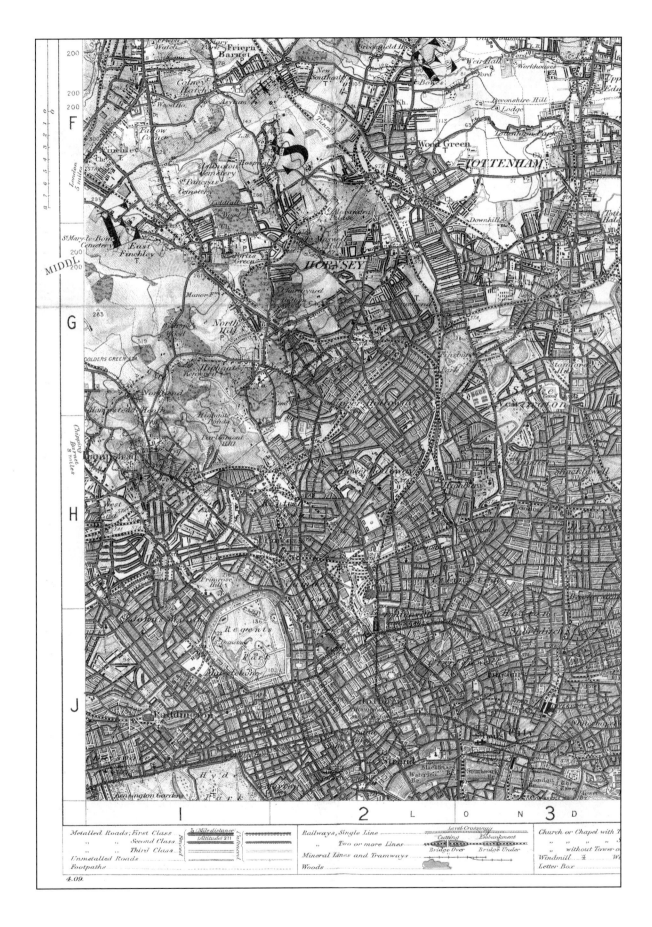

Figure 5 England and Wales Third Edition (Large Sheet Series) sheet 108, 4.09 reprint. Note the depiction of the underground railway system of London, including the deep tube lines, by the special symbol of a single line and cross bars. This did not appear in the legend.

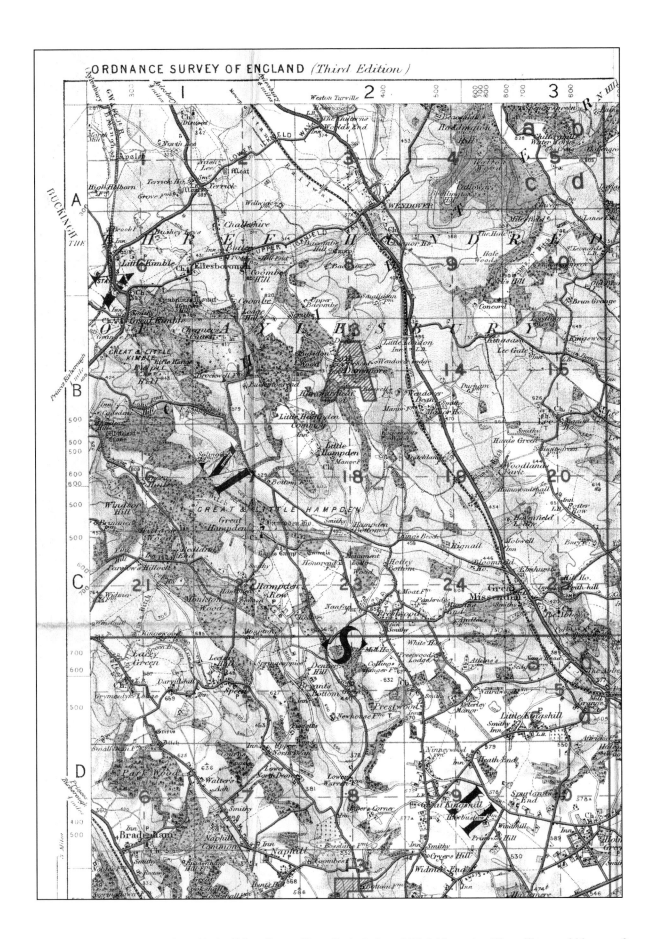

Figure 6 England and Wales Third Edition (Large Sheet Series) sheet 107, 6.12 reprint. The military grid is one of four different systems known, and has its origin in the north-west corner of the sheet. It was probably used for artillery training.

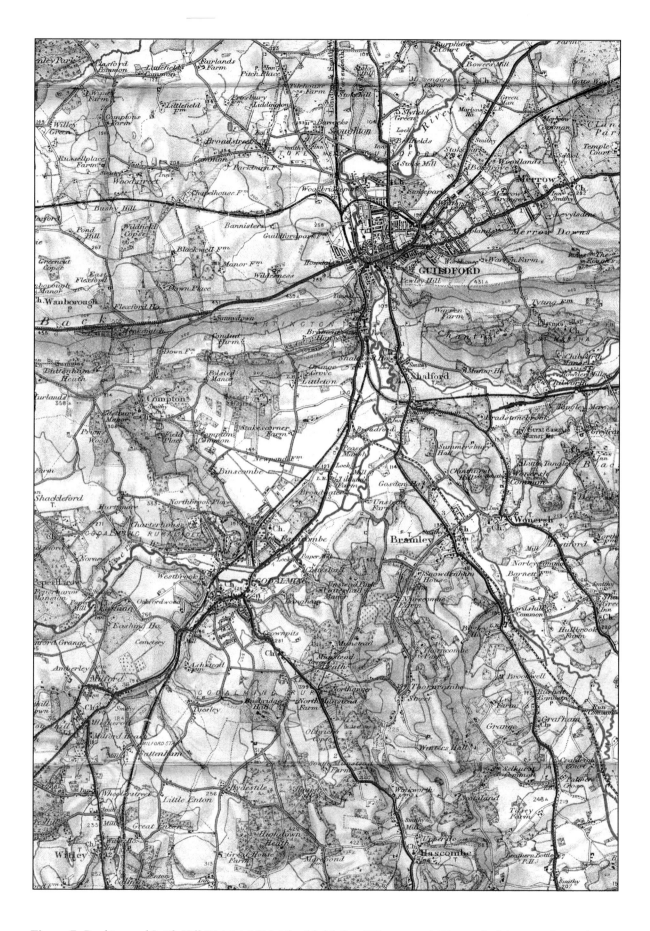

Figure 7 *Dorking and Leith Hill District*, 1914. The third (after *Killarney* and *Glasgow*) of the experimental maps published by Charles Close with enhanced colours, including hill shading. The symbols depicting double and single track railways derive from those used on coloured first revision mapping.

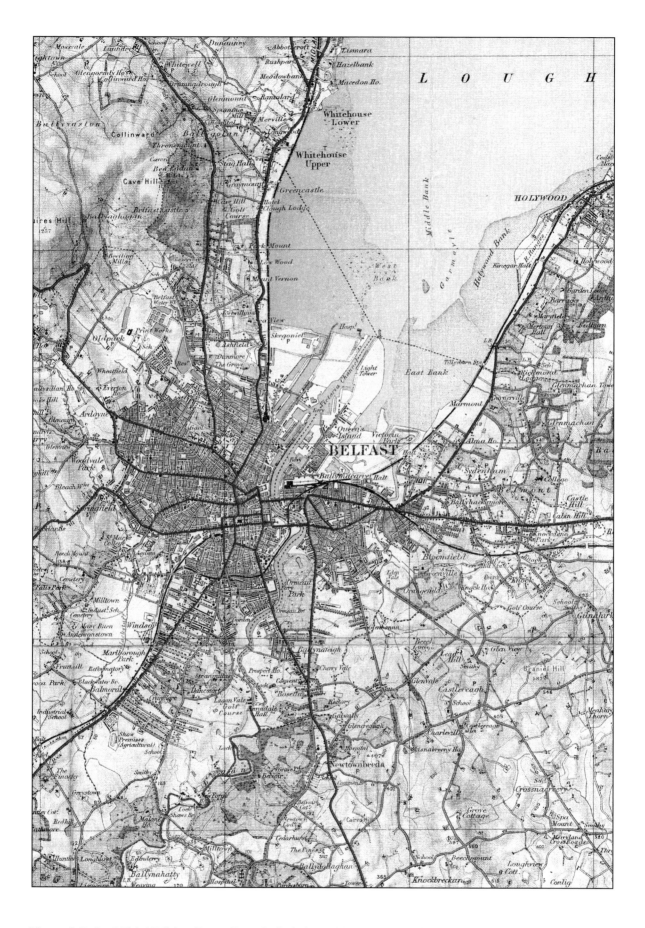

Figure 8 Ireland Third Edition (Large Sheet Series) sheets 16 & 17, 1918. The three Irish sheets published in 1918 continue in the tradition introduced by Charles Close in 1913 with *Killarney* of an enhanced depiction of relief, shown here by a combination of contours, hachures and layers, but omitting hill shading.

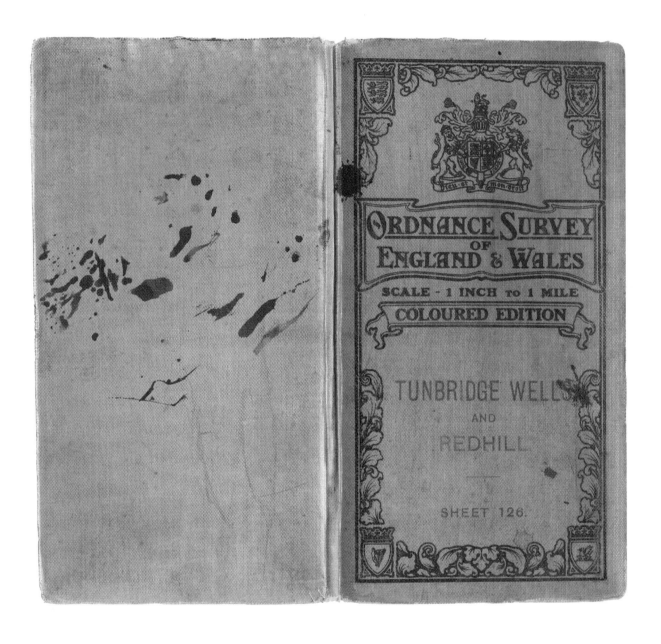

Figure 9 The only known example of what appears to be an Ordnance Survey experimental standard series cover, applied to the July 1914 printing of LSS sheet 126. It is possibly the work of Civil Assistant C.J. Lawrence (see footnote 140). Space is reserved in the lower half for sheet name and number, which are here overprinted in red. The reverse side of the bookfold cover more accurately reflects the original colour of the cover, which was at some point spattered in red ink. Reduced to 83%.

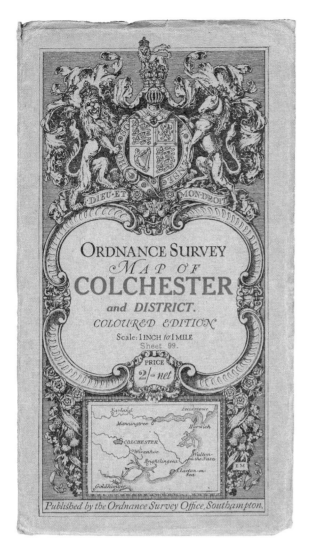

Figure 10 Ellis Martin's cover design, used on one-inch Third Edition maps after the First World War. *Left:* the first colour scheme, recorded only on the England and Wales LSS map. This is an early bookfold example, with the sheet number below the scale statement. *Right:* the standard colour scheme, which was also used on Scottish and Irish coloured maps. The sheet number is prominently positioned at the top of the index diagram, and repeated, albeit somewhat obscurely, in brown on the dark red surround, in the top right hand corner. Note the lack of Scotland mapping on the index diagram. See also footnote 173 and appendix 6. Reduced to 75%.

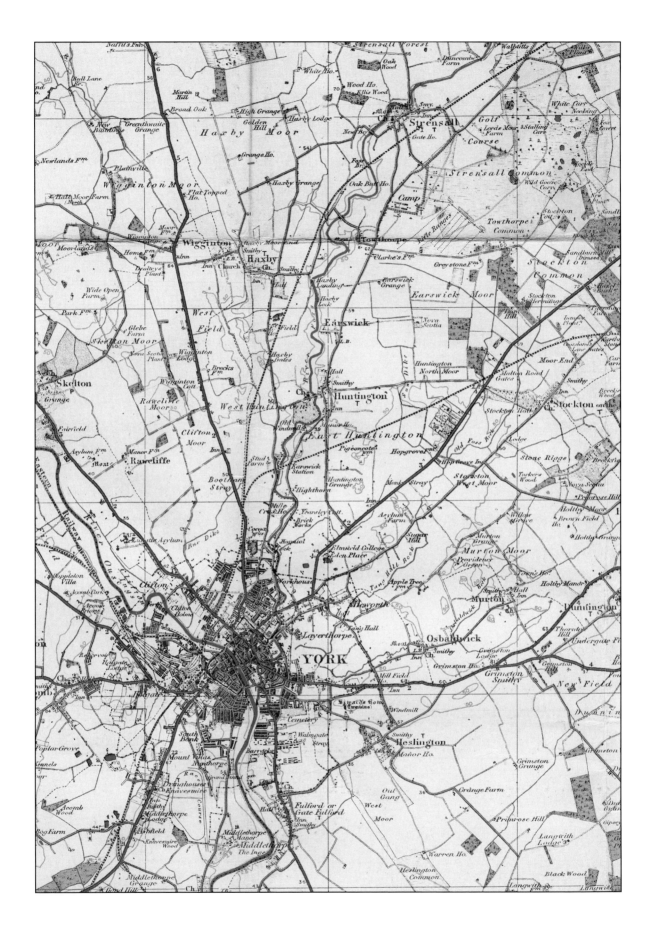

Figure 11 *York District*, 1919. A second revision map on the cusp between Third and Popular Editions, reflecting the past in the depiction of town infill and railways, and the future in its marginalia and squaring system, road colourings, and lack of hachures and parish boundaries.

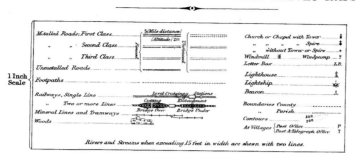

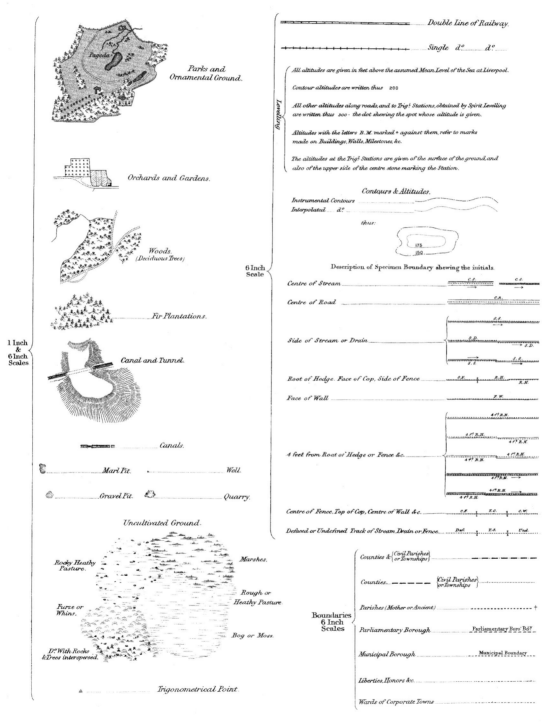

Figure 12 The characteristics used on one-inch and six-inch Ordnance Survey maps. From Colonel Charles Close, *Ordnance Survey maps of the United Kingdom. A description of their scales, characteristics, &c.* London: HMSO, reprinted 1913. Reduced to 79%; estuarine features are not displayed.

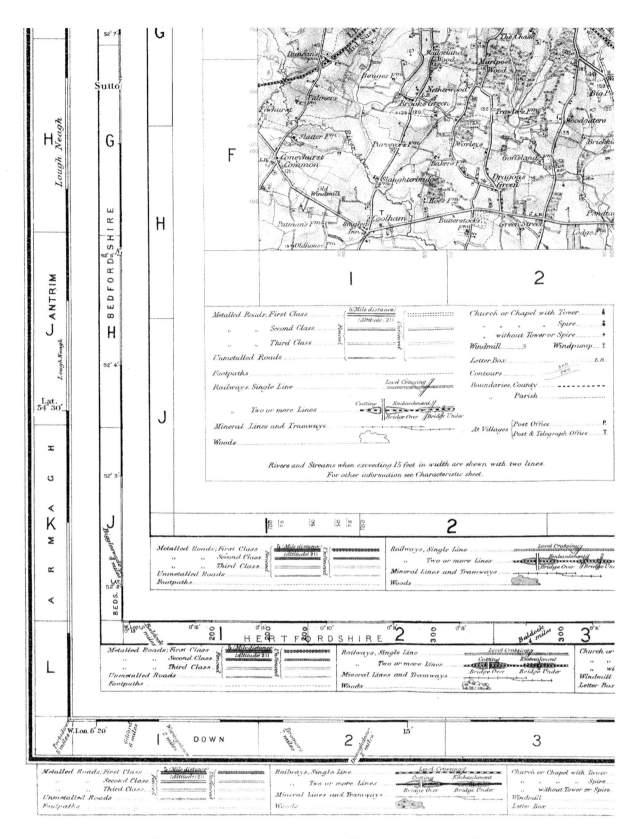

Figure 13 Borders. The four border designs typical of Third Edition coloured maps. All contain an alpha-numeric system in two-inch divisions. *Innermost:* the border is approximately a half-inch wide, and was in use on SSS sheets until about 1905. The border on Scottish sheets was somewhat narrower and was unchanged throughout. See figures 15 and 17. *Inner:* the narrow (approximately quarter-inch) border introduced in England and Wales and Ireland in 1905. *Outer:* the same border, with the addition of a narrow band showing latitude and longitude diced at one minute intervals, which was applied only to the *Oxford* and *Cambridge* district maps. *Outermost:* the new border introduced to the one-inch map with *Killarney District*, 1913, with the latitude and longitude figures more prominent, and a decorative three-lined outer band.

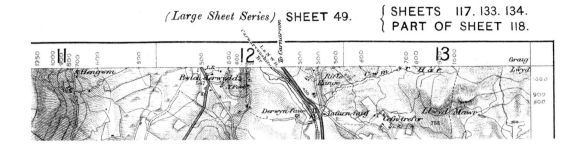

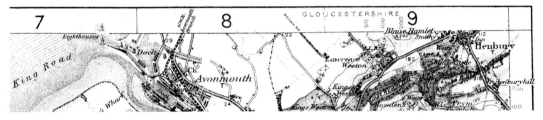

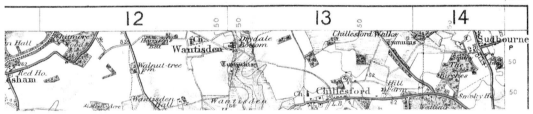

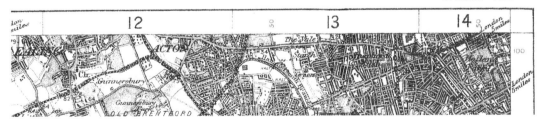

Figure 14 Large Sheet Series headings. *Top:* the supplementary LSS heading overprinted on the SSS *Pwhelli* sheet. *Upper centre:* the heading to the *Weston super Mare* district map, published in 1911 without sheet title. *Lower centre:* the heading to the *Ipswich and Felixstowe* district map, which was also published in 1911 without sheet title. *Bottom:* the heading of sheet 115 in a printing with the words *(Large Sheet Series)* deleted.

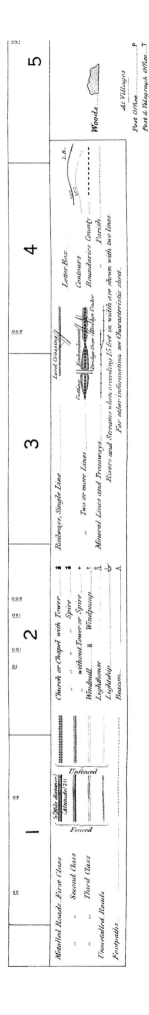

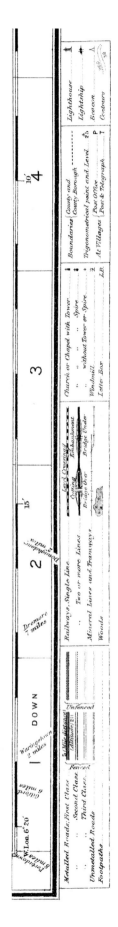

Figure 15 Legends. *Top*: a legend typical of those applied to the Scottish map. There was a similar disposition of information in the legend (in a box half as wide and twice as deep (see figure 13)) applied to SSS maps until 1905, when both border and legend were redesigned in order to save paper. *Upper centre*: the redesigned border and legend used on England and Wales SSS and LSS mapping, now divided into four boxes, with a fifth for coastal sheets. *Lower centre*: the comparable legend used on Irish mapping: the lighthouse, lightship and beacon as depicted in the final legend was present in a fifth box on coastal sheets. The 1923 reprint of England and Wales LSS 29 was erroneously supplied with such an Irish legend. *Bottom*: the legend in use on the LSS in Ireland.

68

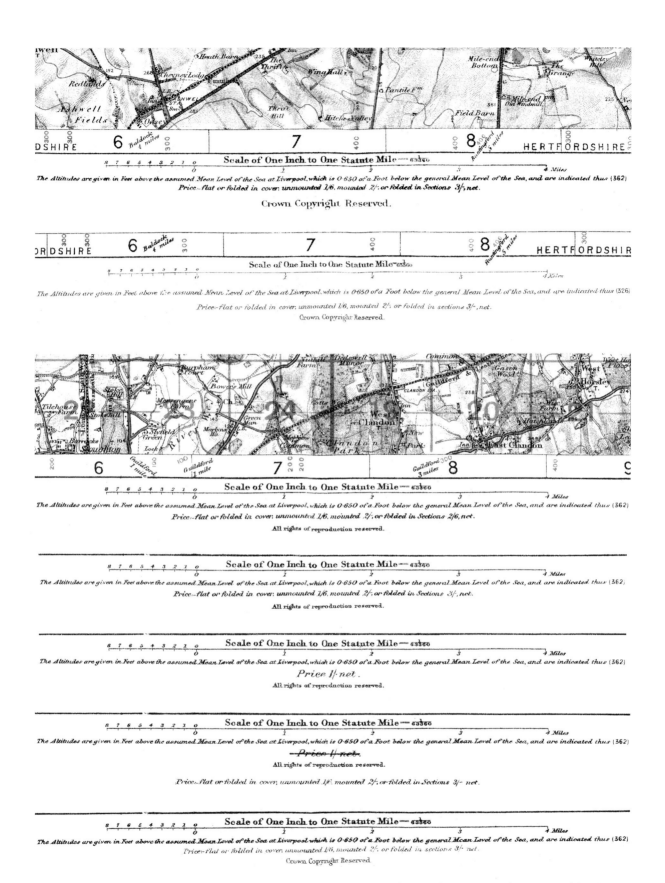

Figure 16 Price and copyright statements. *Top:* two versions of LSS sheet 85, reprint 9.14, with "Crown Copyright Reserved" and a folded in sections price of 3/-. Note the large lettering of the copyright statement in the first: this was the style adopted when the expression first came into use, in mid-1912. Note also "Sections" and "362" on the first, and "sections" and "326" on the second. *Bottom:* the five known price/copyright variants used on the 8.11 printing of sheet 115. The 1/- price is presumably an erroneous transfer from the black plate prepared for the Black Outline Edition (see also sheet 108). Reduced to 94%.

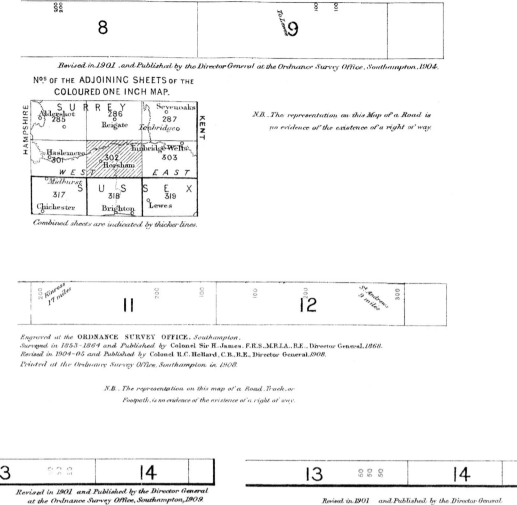

Figure 17 Imprints and rights of way statements. *Top:* the imprint layout as it first appeared on the SSS in England and Wales. With the introduction of narrower margins, it was redistributed over two lines, as in the lower centre samples below. *Upper centre:* a typical imprint of a Scottish map. The imprint of the engraved original is retained, with the "Printed....." line providing details of publication of the coloured edition. *Lower centre:* the standard LSS lettering, here as it appears on sheet 125, 5.14 reprint, and a later printing of the same state of the map, with the imprint relettered. *Bottom left:* the "Printed..." imprint on the *Wareham* district map, 1907, retained from its military original a year earlier. *Bottom right:* the apparently standard imprint on Ireland SSS 129, with the curious replacement of "Published" by "Printed".

The full rights of way statement with the expression "Road, Track or Footpath" was standard on the one-inch map until 1902. In England and Wales, and sometimes in Ireland, reference to track and footpath was then removed, though it was mostly retained on Scottish mapping. It was restored to some reprints after the First World War. Examples of both forms of wording are illustrated here.

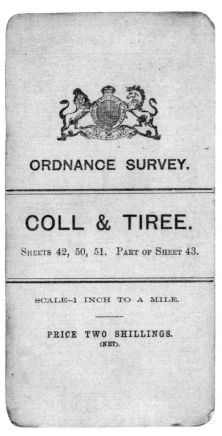

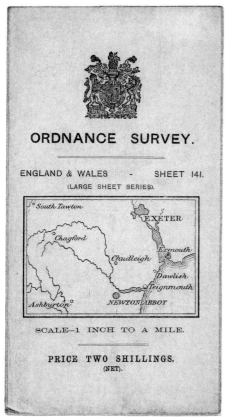

Figure 18 Ordnance Survey standard covers. *Top left:* the tall H.3 design, with sheet name on a central band, first red, then white from 1906. Edward VII coat of arms. *Top right:* the H.4 design, white, with index diagram, introduced in 1911. Edward VII coat of arms. *Bottom left:* the same design, George V coat of arms. *Bottom right:* the H.7 design, with square "Ordnance Survey" lettering. In use from about 1916, on white or buff card, usually with index diagram. With George V coat of arms. See also the OSNI cover on figure 20. Reduced to 60%.

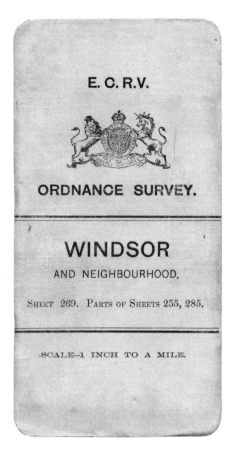

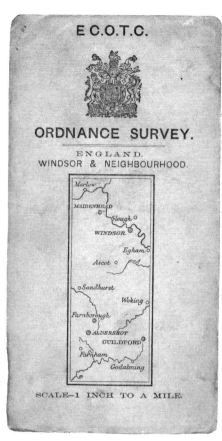

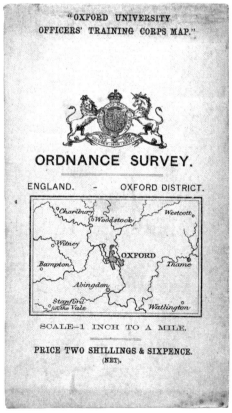

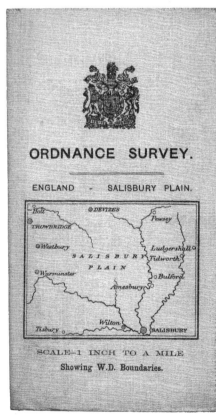

Figure 19 Ordnance Survey covers with a military training theme. *Top left:* a special map for the Eton College Rifle Volunteers, 1907. *Top right:* a special map for the Eton College Officers' Training Corps, 1913. *Bottom left:* the cover produced for the standard *Oxford* district map, 1911, apparently attached to copies intended for the Officers' Training Corps. *Cambridge* covers were similarly overprinted. *Bottom right: Salisbury Plain,* reprinted in 1914. With an overprint of the boundaries of War Department lands. Reduced to 60%.

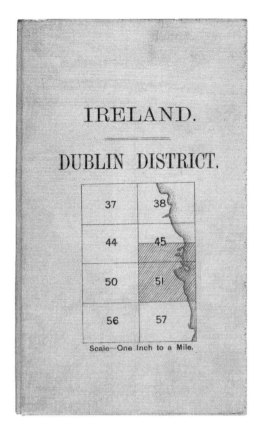

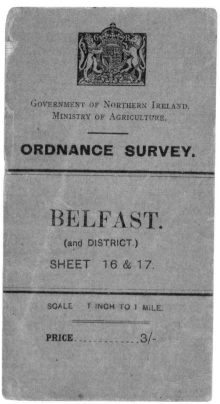

Figure 20 Irish cover designs. *Top left:* the original wartime integral cover for the *Dublin District* map of 1918. The coverage as depicted is erroneous on all four sides. *Top right:* Ordnance Survey of Northern Ireland, Belfast. Derived from the H.7 design, featuring square "Ordnance Survey" lettering. Black on buff. *Bottom row:* Ordnance Survey of Ireland, Dublin. *(left):* the Suirbhéireacht Ordonais pictorial cover. Black on pale green. *(right):* the Léarscáilíocht éireann cover. Recorded in two colour schemes, on one-inch maps, black on maroon (shown here), and red on white. Reduced to 60%.

One-inch Third Edition
map of
England and Wales
small sheet series

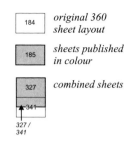

original 360
sheet layout

sheets published
in colour

combined sheets

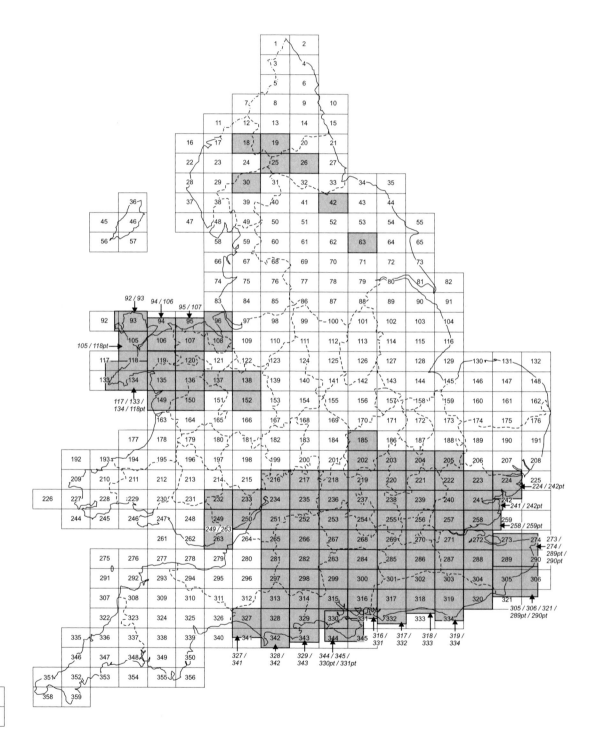

74

*One-inch Third Edition
map of
England and Wales
Large Sheet Series*

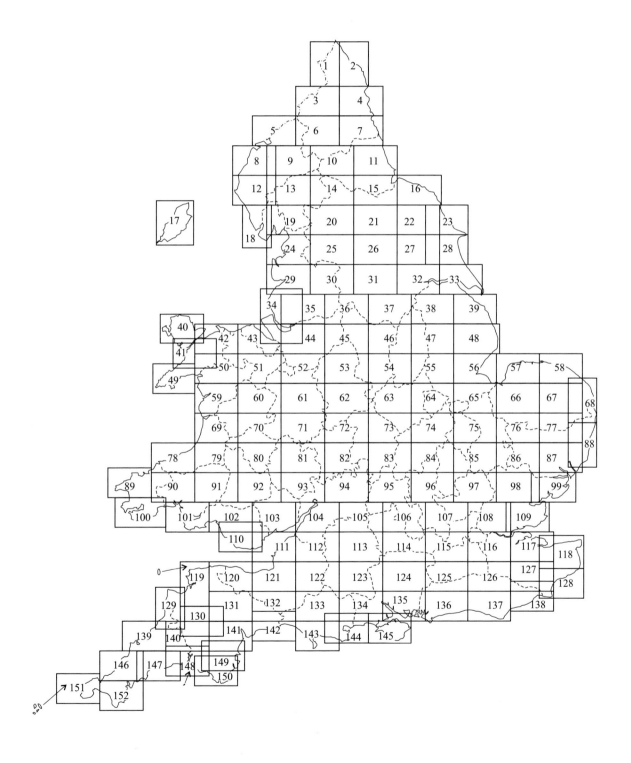

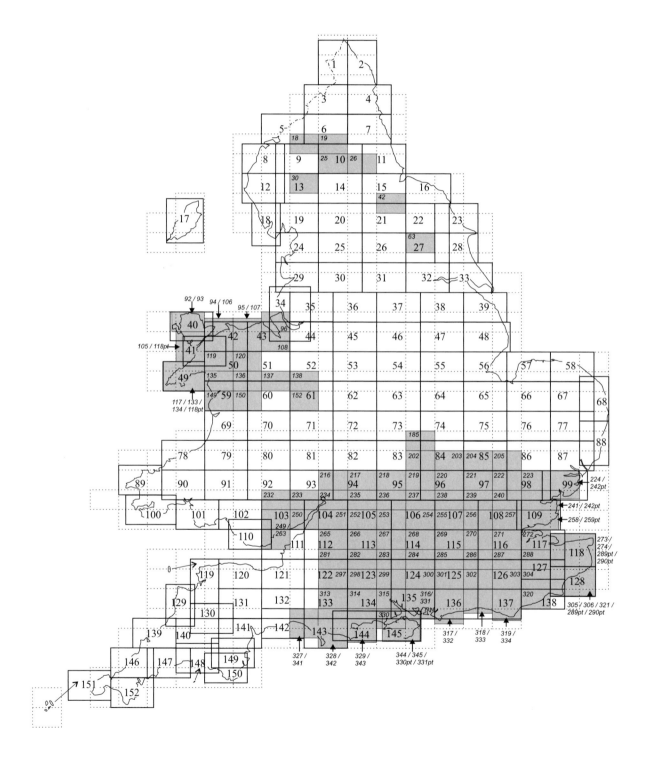

One-inch Third Edition
map of
England and Wales
in colour

One-inch Third Edition
map of Scotland

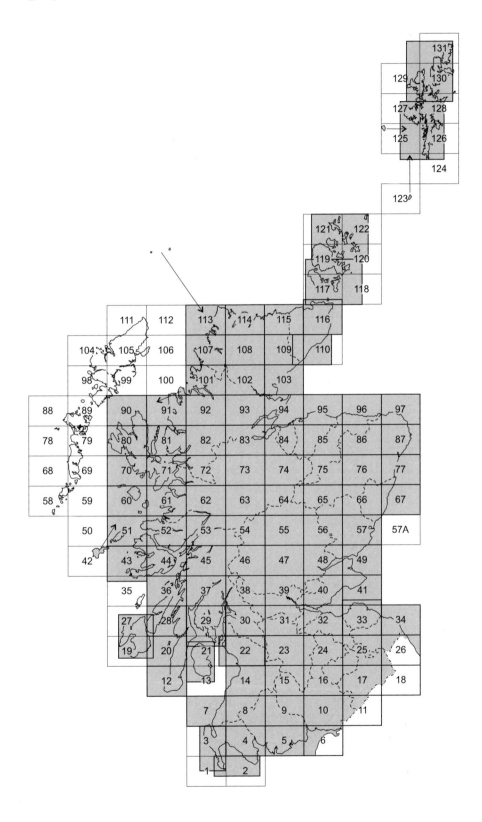

The sheets published in colour are indicated by shading

One-inch Third Edition map of Ireland small sheet series

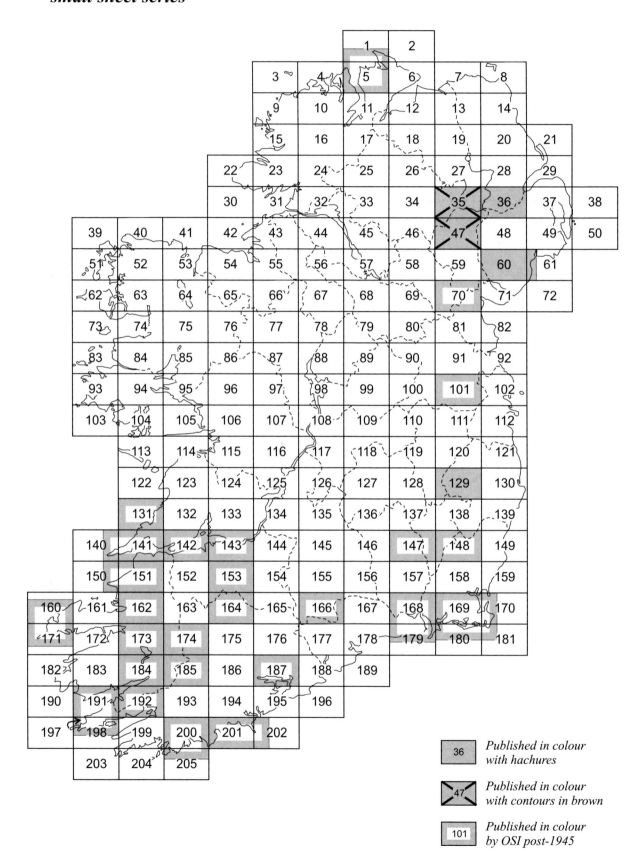

Published in colour with hachures — 36

Published in colour with contours in brown — 47

Published in colour by OSI post-1945 — 101

One-inch Third Edition
map of
Ireland
large sheet series

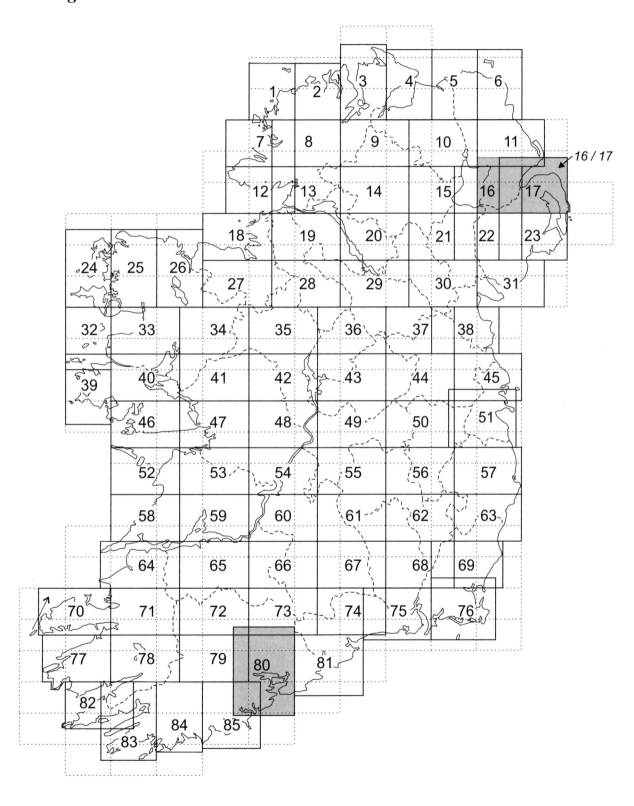

The sheets published in colour are indicated by shading

Compiler's notes

Guy Messenger's ground-breaking monograph on the One-inch Third Edition (Large Sheet Series)[168] of England and Wales has long been out of print, and the discussion about what if anything should replace it has only been little shorter. A straight reprint has been ruled out for a number of reasons. Much new information, both historical and cartobibliographical, has come to light since 1988 which it would be absurd not to include. The texts of both Guy's books, the Large Sheet Series (LSS) and the subsequent listing of the Third Edition of Scotland in colour,[169] were produced on his typewriter. Such a method would be wholly unacceptable today. And thirdly Guy's work, like anyone else's, was not wholly free from error.

The second option was to publish a revised edition of his monograph. But this was also vetoed because it would have involved rekeying his entire text; further, checking every single detail of his text for previously unidentified errors, which in its turn would mean revisiting, were it possible, every state of every map and every cover variant that he encountered (without, in some cases, knowing where he actually located copies), and finally adding into Guy's established framework all the new information that has come to light since. If only because of the second of these constraints, such a revision was discarded as wholly impractical.

What has therefore been attempted is a new cartobibliography, taking as its starting point Guy's published texts. It has been decided to abandon certain elements that he included, to illustrate others in a different way, and to add the occasional new feature. The scope of the work has been expanded to include all the coloured one-inch third edition maps of the British Isles: the series maps that Guy listed (sections 2 and 3), the incomplete small sheet series (SSS)[170] that preceded the large in England and Wales (section 1), and the fragmentary coverage in Ireland (sections 4 and 5), also the district maps associated with each of these series, and, as far as one could discover any record of them, the special maps made for military use.

How far should this new work follow Guy's precedents in the type of information to be included? In a single volume it would obviously be desirable, as far as is practicable, to follow a standard procedure throughout, even though five separate map series are described between its covers. At the outset, therefore, we are confronted with the problem that Guy's Scottish text dealt with many fewer features than did that of the LSS – details of topographical change, national grid co-ordinates, altitude ranges, superseding sheets, names of counties covered, location of sources – these and other features did not form part of the Scottish work. All this would need to be newly supplied for Scotland, and after that Ireland, if the specification of his large sheet series volume were to be followed.

For this reason, coupled with the practical requirement that all information listed should be capable of display within a single line for each map state, most of these categories of information have been excluded from the present work, together with the classification of legends and map covers. The sheets issued, and the relative areas covered by each sheet may however be ascertained by examination of the index diagrams provided (these include a comparative index showing the overlay of the SSS against the LSS in England and Wales), by the measurements of overlaps provided in footnotes, and, for the regularly positioned sheets, with absolute precision from the lists of sheet line co-ordinates provided by Brian Adams (see appendix 7 on page 145).

---

[168] Guy Messenger, *The Ordnance Survey one-inch map of England and Wales Third Edition (Large Sheet Series)*. London: Charles Close Society, 1988.

[169] Guy Messenger, *A guide to the Ordnance Survey one-inch map of Scotland Third Edition in colour.* London: Charles Close Society, 1991.

[170] The expression "small sheet series" is intended to be merely comparative, and does not appear on any coloured third edition map. It is used in this book in order to distinguish such maps of England and Wales and Ireland from those which have a legitimate claim to "large sheet series" status.

However, I suspect that the disappearance of two categories of information will cause some disappointment among owners of Guy's original volumes, it having been decided not to continue to list details of topographical change or map covers.[171] As to the first, this is largely a matter of alterations to post and telegraph facilities, railway lines and stations, and defence establishments. While undoubtedly of interest in its own right, there is no recorded instance whereby a new state of any of these maps has been identified solely by means of such topographical change; thus it is not of cartobibliographical importance such as, for instance, the record of railway revision is to identifying new states of engraved nineteenth century maps. Further, it must be added that Guy was able to accomplish this study, which anyway he only did in depth for England and Wales, because he owned a large collection of the LSS, and he was able to make the essential detailed comparison of states, necessarily side by side, over a long period of time.

As to covers, an examination of their several designs in combination with the various states of the maps to which they are attached is again a study of some importance, but one, it is suggested, that should focus upon each specific cover design in relation to *all* the maps to which it may be attached, not just those of one series or another. This seems especially true of the general purpose cover designs (H.3 to H.7)[172] in use by the Ordnance Survey until Ellis Martin entered their employment at the end of the first world war. These were indeed used on coloured third edition maps, but more on the wider spectrum of maps not covered in this volume. All that said, a few additional words about the Ellis Martin cover design usually associated with coloured third edition maps (H.10) might be appropriate. It is well known that the royal arms and mantling design was produced in two colour schemes, in black with a red sheet name, and in brown with a much deeper red sheet name and surrounding border. Both are usually on buff card.[173] The first has only been recorded on the England and Wales LSS and associated district maps, first in bookfold (on a few sheets only), then as end cards, and the second rather more widely, being used on the Scottish and Irish series sheets and district maps as well. In Ireland it is further recorded on the coloured one-inch map and district maps derived from the first revision. It is thus not specifically a third edition cover, but then, of course, its cover wording lays no claim to be so. The names offered by Martin on his covers were mostly formed from one or more of the places listed in the sheet name, usually with the addition of the words "and District". Cover names recorded that are not derived from the sheet name are noted, as are those which had to be supplied for unnamed sheets.

Another feature abandoned from Guy's layout is his union listing of collections in which he located each particular printing of a sheet, something he did for England and Wales though again not for Scotland. One attraction of that layout is that it offers an immediate impression of the rarity or otherwise of each printing, but the amount of space required to reproduce that information

---

[171] They have disappeared, at any rate, from the lists – discussion of these topics features strongly in Richard Oliver's historical essay.

[172] These numbers refer to my list of OS cover designs in John Paddy Browne, *Map cover art*. Southampton: Ordnance Survey, 1991. Samples of these are illustrated in this book in figure 18.

[173] Further, more detailed, subdivisions in the development of the design may be discerned. 1. In its earliest form it was a bookfold cover in black and red, priced 2/- (mounted on cloth), with the sheet number squeezed between scale and price statements. 2. Still bookfold, the sheet number was transferred to a convenient location on the index diagram (LSS 125, copy Cu-m). LSS 95, 96, 97, 98, 99, 106, 115, 125 are recorded in bookfold covers. 3. The cover was converted to end cards. Only LSS 3, 5, 91, 146 have yet to be recorded in these black and red formats. 4. The colour scheme was altered to brown and a much darker red. A border in dark red was added (LSS 42, 142, copies Cu-m). 5. But apparently the sheet number was still not considered prominent enough, because the next move was to increase its size and consistently to locate it at the top of the index diagram (LSS 136, copy Cu-m). 6. Later, before January 1920, a repeat sheet number was added (occasionally to type 4) in the top right hand corner. 7. Prices were increased in January 1920, to 2/- (paper), 3/- (cloth), 4/- (dissected). It is in this form that the design is most commonly found, mostly as end cards, but occasionally pasted onto the white hinged cards in use up to about 1915. All LSS sheets except 112, 146, all the Scottish sheets, all Irish Third Edition sheets except *Killarney* are recorded. 8. Later there were occasional detail changes in the style of the price statement or the sheet name, which may be found in upper and lower case lettering. The earliest and a late state of the design are illustrated on figure 10. See also appendix 6 where this information is set out in tabular form. I am grateful to David Archer and Graham Cornell in particular for adding substantially to my own records of these matters.

and the need to add newly recorded copies were telling arguments against continuing to include it, and anyway it was impractical to revisit all the collections that Guy examined in order to confirm the current accuracy of his listing. Thus a new order of priorities has been adopted, based on the premise that any student eager to inspect as many different states of these maps as possible will at some point be drawn towards Cambridge. Copies in copyright collections are noted first, followed by those in Guy's personal collection of some 950 coloured third edition maps (not just LSS), now housed in the Map Department of the University Library, Cambridge. This library has in addition its copyright collection to offer, as well as another near complete run of all 152 LSS sheets, the gift of another collector. Additional states located in other public collections are recorded next;[174] where no other source has been located, privately owned copies are noted (PC): the authors and the Charles Close Society would be pleased to learn of publicly held copies of any of these states.

One point of distinction between states of the LSS overlooked by Guy was the relettering of the marginalia. It can of course be difficult to confirm whether two copies of apparently the same state do in fact have different lettering unless those two copies are available side by side for detailed comparison. For those interested in exploring this matter further, there are three areas on the map worth examining: the wording *(Large Sheet Series)* in the top right hand corner, which could be removed altogether, and if present is not always in the same position relative to the sheet number; secondly the detail centre bottom, especially those featuring the "CCR 3/-" price statement (Crown Copyright Reserved against a "folded in sections" price of 3/-) which may be relettered, and thirdly the imprint bottom right. In many instances another hand,[175] in a less sloping italic, replaced the original, and minor correction and railway revision notices were usually placed together above or below the rights of way statement. Sometimes only the rights of way statement itself was relettered, especially when the words "Track or Footpath" were restored to it. Sometimes the evidence suggests that this relettering occurred at the same time (probably in 1916)[176] as the increase in price to 3/-, but many instances have now been discovered where the increase in price preceded the relettering of the price statement. A further clue is that the later hand usually preferred the lower case "folded in sections" to the conventional "folded in Sections".[177] Thus a quick and effective test is to look for the alternative form of the word "sections" against known CCR 3/- states. Since this remains a matter worthy of investigation, entailing the examination of perhaps many additional copies in order to identify further instances, the difference between the two is noted in the list below: those recorded with CCR priced at 3/- with "Sections" are marked "C:", those with "sections" are "C.". Other variants noted are described in footnotes.

Unless otherwise noted, every map state listed in this volume has been seen by the compiler, or the details confirmed with its owner. The compilation process began by attempting to examine every state that Guy listed, in order to confirm the accuracy of the details he recorded. However, users of Guy's cartobibliographies will notice the presence of some states there which have been omitted here. A check of the sources he quoted suggests that in some cases they were included in error. Furthermore he was himself unable to confirm other doubtful states, and where renewed investigation has proved no more successful in locating a copy, it has mostly been decided to omit these as well. Information about new sources which will confirm any of Guy's listings currently omitted would of course be welcomed. Finally Guy would have felt vindicated to learn that four LSS states which he was unsuccessful in finding but which he felt certain did exist, have emerged during the course of this investigation. These are, using his own codes, 108.1u, 111.1u, 118.0u, 128.0u. There are further similar discoveries of the Scottish map.

Further references to Guy Messenger's published work are given in the form "KGM".

Roger Hellyer

---

[174] The abbreviations given in column 12 of the lists below are explained on page viii.
[175] Examine, for instance, copies of sheets 21, 22, 124, 125, 145. There are several more instances. We have taken as an example sheet 125, illustrated on figure 17.
[176] The actual date of the price increase remains uncertain: see page 84 for further information.
[177] See the examples from sheet 85 at the top of figure 16.

Layout of the cartobibliography

This is a cartobibliography of the one-inch third edition maps in colour. By default the reader may assume a map to be black, with hachures in brown, contours in red or orange, main roads in sienna (burnt sienna from about August 1904), water in blue and woods in green. Exceptions to this norm are detailed in footnotes, or by cross reference to Richard Oliver's essay. References to outline maps are given in footnotes, and they are listed in appendix 1. A list of sheets with enhanced colour schemes, issued between 1913 and 1922, is given in appendix 4.

The entry for each sheet in the cartobibliography comprises a heading, and a list of printings.

The heading contains three elements:

1. Sheet number and name, or, in the case of district maps, sheet title, together with any sheet numbers quoted. Where the name is altered during the life of the map, the alternative forms are noted, with cross reference letters to column 2. Sheet names were often omitted or deleted during part of 1911 and 1912, and in some instances never restored. The first confirmed instance was the 2.11 printing of LSS 85, the last was the 3.12 printing of LSS 64, by which time LSS 73 had already been issued in its 2.12 printing with a sheet name. The sheet names offered for those which never had them are taken from Ellis Martin covers.

2. Date of revision, as printed on the map. Where the date varies during the life of the map, the alternative forms are noted, with cross reference letters to column 2.

3. Dimensions of the mapped area: width by height (in inches) or area covered (in miles). Where the two-inch divisions appear in the border, they are taken as the unit of measurement. Where part divisions are involved, the measurement may be approximate, some consideration having been given to the question of paper distortion.

The list contains thirteen columns:

1. Date of publication, or printing. Dates of printing are quoted where present. This may be when the imprint, often including a publication date, is transferred from an engraved original, as is typical of Scottish series sheets, or a publication date is lacking, as with some military maps. District maps generally have publication dates. On Irish maps the original Southampton imprint in the bottom right hand corner was usually left in place until about 1945, with alterations to dates and reprint notes as necessary. About that time the imprint wording was altered to "Compiled and Printed by the Ordnance Survey Department and Published by the Director at the Ordnance Survey Office, Phoenix Park, Dublin", together with a publication date. "Phoenix Park" was initially omitted. This notice was transferred to bottom centre in about 1948. The first part of the imprint was soon deleted, and "Published by the Director at the Ordnance Survey Office, Phoenix Park, Dublin" became standard.

2. Headings: "Ordnance Survey of England" (ose), "Ordnance Survey of England and Scotland" (oses), "Ordnance Survey of England and Wales" (osew), "Ordnance Survey of Ireland" (osi), "Ordnance Survey of Scotland" (oss). Together with cross reference letter, where necessary, for variations in sheet name or revision date: "x" indicates no name. The "o" symbol refers to LSS series sheets where "(Large Sheet Series)" is deleted from the top right hand corner.

3.   Print code – the "+" symbols accumulate those of previous editions. The punctuation of print codes is ignored (some have "-" or even "/" as separators, and full stops), and a conventional system is adopted here. Print codes are given in the form "3.05" (month.year) until 1922, the latest recorded being 6.22 on Scotland sheets 85 and 94. There was a gap in production of revised reprints during the first world war between 12.14 (LSS 135) and 11.19 in Ireland (sheet 36) and 1.20 in Scotland (sheets 8, 30, 57.57A). This was succeeded by a print code offering the number of copies printed and the year, in the form "1000/25". So far as the maps which are the subject of this book are concerned, such print codes were in use between 1922 and 1932.

4.   Date of minor corrections (England and Wales, Scotland) / road classification (Ireland), shown in the form "3.05" (month.year).

5.   Date of railways revised or inserted, shown in the form "3.05r" or "3.05i" (month.year), respectively. A supplementary letter "s" denotes sheets, mostly from 1910, that carry in both legend and map the new station symbol drawn as an open circle or rectangle (though in the case of several Scottish sheets there are no railways present); with the symbol on the map but omitted from the legend "+"; sheets reprinted with the symbol in the legend but not the map "*"; railway stations with red infill "S". See also appendix 5.

6.   Date of magnetic variation. Those with † are inferred; it is unfortunate that many maps issued in covers had their margins trimmed to the extent that this information is often missing.

7.   Copyright statements: "All rights of reproduction reserved" (A), which might be altered from 1912 to "Crown Copyright Reserved" (C). The earliest known incidence of this is on the 5.12 reprint of LSS 77. "Copyright Reserved" (c) appears on some OSI maps published in Dublin after 1922. This was often achieved by blanking out the word "Crown", so the remaining legend appears off centre. For the use of "C:" and "C." see page 82.

8.   Sheet prices. Initially there was one (1/- for small sheets, 1/6 for large), sometimes specified as for the paper flat form. Two prices were listed (1/-,1/6 for small sheets, 1/6,2/- for large) from about August 1905, the first for the map flat or folded unmounted into a cover, the second for the version mounted on cloth. A third price (2/- for small sheet maps, 2/6 for large), introduced in 1906 (the earliest recorded in July), was for the dissected on cloth ("folded in sections") form.[178] Prices are listed here in this order. The word "net" was added from the end of 1906.[179] The cost of the dissected form map rose to 3/- (2/6 for Ireland SSS), at a date which still lacks confirmation, apparently sometime in 1916. The OS catalogue to 1 April 1915 gives 2/6 as the price of the dissected map; the next known, to 1 January 1917, gives 3/-.[180] Very few small-scale maps were issued between these two dates, owing to the security ban on publishing topographical maps which might benefit the enemy. Of the small-scale maps in current use, there are virtually no dated reprints between 1915 and 1919. The Ireland half-inch map alone continued in production, though no issues were announced in the publication reports between June 1914 and 1918. The probability is that copies were printed, then stockpiled. This series thus becomes the best, if tenuous, guide to the pattern of sheet prices in general. The one Irish half-inch map first printed in 1915 still has the 2/6 dissected price. Significantly, so does one of the twelve first printed in 1916; the remainder have 3/-. Furthermore an experimental one-inch map, printed in 1916 on Popular Edition sheet lines, also has a 2/6 dissected price.[181] The next

---

[178] Though the meaning of "dissected" as a specific form of map packaging is today widely understood, it was not a word at the time in use by the Ordnance Survey, which preferred "folded in sections" on maps, "mounted in sections" (if anything) on map covers, and "cut into sections and mounted to fold in covers" in its catalogues.
[179] The earliest instances so far recorded are on half-inch maps published in December 1906.
[180] *Catalogue of the 6-inch and 25-inch county maps and town plans of England and Wales and the Isle of Man, and of the one-inch and smaller scale maps, and other publications of the Ordnance Survey of the United Kingdom. To 1st April, 1915.* London: HMSO, 1915; ......*To 1st January, 1917.* London: HMSO, 1917.
[181] Sheet 120: see appendix 4.

price rise was part of the general increase in sheet prices at the start of 1920, to 2/-,3/-,4/-.[182] With these increases prices were removed altogether from the map face, shown here as "np" (no price), though earlier price ranges occasionally survive. Prices may be restored to the few Scottish sheets reprinted after 1926. Variations in these prices usually reflect irregular circumstances, such as enlarged sheets covering coastal areas, or, conversely, standard size coastal sheets covering tiny land areas.

In Dublin the price of large sheets was increased to 2/-,3/-,4/- by 1929,[183] and this price is still recorded on maps printed in 1944 – even 1946 on half-inch maps. By 1946 the price was limited on the one-inch to a single figure of 2/-, sometimes specifically noted as for the paper flat version. The price statement seems to have been deleted altogether by 1949. These dates should be treated with a degree of caution. Any price rises that may have occurred in Belfast after 1922 were altered by hand, or stamped on individual one-inch sheets, though half-inch maps published in the late 1930s reflected a similar rise to 2/-,3/-,4/-.

9.   Borders and alpha-numeric representation.
        w: alpha-numeric border in two-inch blocks, approximately half-inch wide
        n: alpha-numeric border in two-inch blocks, approximately quarter-inch wide
        g: alpha-numeric border depicting in some way a measurement of the graticule
        s: simple border – unmeasured line or lines
Preceded where relevant by "AN" for two-inch alpha-numeric squaring system across the map face.

10.   Date of appearance in the Ordnance Survey *Supplement to catalogue of* [eg] *England & Wales. Publications issued from* [eg] *1st to 31st July, 1909* (conventionally abbreviated "OSPR" in accordance with its continuation as the *Ordnance Survey Publication Report*). References in the form "3/05" are to monthly supplements, in the form "1918/2" to quarterly or periodic supplements.

11.   KGM's state and substate codes, in the form "82.1x" or "SAL.0u" (England and Wales LSS, and Scotland third editions only) or, for maps not covered in his cartobibliographies, cross reference to the relevant section in Hellyer (1999),[184] in the form "7.1.2". KGM's codes apply only to the states of the maps that he recorded and is intended to serve as a cross reference to his listing: it was thus decided not to invent additional codes for newly recorded states.

12.   Location of copy, in accordance with the list of priorities discussed on page 82. The abbreviations used are explained on page viii. References to "book" imply inclusion of that map in a book: further details may be found in the footnotes below the entry. Specimen extracts found in Ordnance Survey catalogues and the like are usually omitted.

13.   Footnote reference.

Note. The sheet numbers of **combined sheets** are fully expressed in the cartobibliography. Elsewhere this procedure was usually felt to be pedantic, and they may be expressed in the forms "16.17" or "16 / 17", or "16 / 17pt" where a part sheet is involved, depending on the space available. Sheet numbers, such as those of the Shetland Isles sheets which correctly contain more than two sheet numbers, may be condensed still further, in the form "123+".

---

[182] As shown in the *Revised price list (1920)*, print code OSO 5000 26.1.20. This list is most frequently to be found as an insert in *A description of the Ordnance Survey small scale maps with specimens & indexes*. Southampton: Ordnance Survey, [1919].

[183] In point of fact the price rise was almost certainly that of January 1920. There is only an element of doubt because, as in Great Britain, prices were removed from Irish map reprints in 1920, and after 1922 no maps relevant to this book have been recorded that were reprinted in Dublin until 1929.

[184] Roger Hellyer, *Ordnance Survey small-scale maps : indexes 1801-1998*. Kerry: David Archer, 1999.

Cartobibliography

1. One-inch Third Edition Map of England and Wales : small sheet series

Sheets typically have "(Third Edition)" after the Ordnance Survey heading, top left, and the sheet number top right. Sheet names appear top centre. Standard sheet coverage is 18 by 12 miles.

Sheets 1 to 17 were not published in colour.

Sheet 18 *Brampton*   Revised 1903   18 by 12
1906   ose   -   -   -   1906   A 1/-,1/6,2/-   n   11/06   7.1.2   Cpt

Sheet 19 *Hexham*   Revised 1902-3   18 by 12
1906   ose   -   -   -   1906   A 1/-,1/6,2/-   n   11/06   7.1.2   Cpt

Sheets 20 to 24 were not published in colour.

Sheet 25 *Alston*   Revised 1903   18 by 12
1905   ose   -   -   -   1905   A 1/-,1/6   n   11/05   7.1.2   Cpt

Sheet 26 *Wolsingham*   Revised 1903   18 by 12
1906   ose   -   -   -   1906   A 1/-,1/6,2/-   n   9/06   7.1.2   Cpt

Sheets 27 to 29 were not published in colour.

Sheet 30 *Appleby*   Revised 1903   18 by 12
1906   ose   -   -   -   1905   A 1/-,1/6   n   3/06   7.1.2   Cpt

Sheets 31 to 35, 37 to 41, 36.45.46.56.57 (Isle of Man) *were not published in colour.*

Sheet 42 *Northallerton*   Revised 1904   18 by 12
1907   ose   -   -   -   1907   A 1/-,1/6,2/-   n   3/07   7.1.2   Cpt

Sheets 43, 44, 47 to 55, 58 to 62 were not published in colour.

Sheet 63 *York*   Revised 1904-5   18 by 12
1906   ose   -   -   -   1906   A 1/-,1/6,2/-   n   12/06   7.1.2   Cpt

Sheets 64 to 91 were not published in colour.

Sheets 92. 93. *Holyhead*   Revised 1903   20 by 12
1906   osew   -   -   -   1906   A 1/-,1/6   n   3/06   7.1.2   Cpt
With an extrusion for Middle Mouse.

Sheets 94. 106. *Bangor*   Revised 1903   18 by 20
1906   osew   -   -   -   1906   A 1/6,2/-   n   3/06   7.1.2   Cpt-m

Sheets 95. 107. *Denbigh*   Revised 1904   18 by 20
1906   osew   -   -   -   1906   A 1/6,2/-,2/6   n   11/06   7.1.2   Cpt

Sheet 96 *Liverpool*   Revised 1904   18 by 12
1906   osew   -   -   -   1906   A 1/-,1/6,2/-   n   10/06   7.1.2   Cpt

1	2	3	4	5	6	7	8	9	10	11	12	13

Sheets 97 to 104 were not published in colour.

Sheet 105. Part of sheet 118. *Carnarvon*   Revised 1903   18 by 18

1	2	3	4	5	6	7	8	9	10	11	12	13
1906	osew	-	-	-	1906	A	1/6,2/-,2/6	n	11/06	7.1.2	Cpt-m	

Sheet 106 see sheet 94.106, sheet 107 see sheet 95.107.

Sheet 108 *Flint*   Revised 1904   18 by 12

1	2	3	4	5	6	7	8	9	10	11	12	13
1907	osew	-	-	-	1907	A	1/-,1/6,2/-	n	3/07	7.1.2	Cpt	

Sheets 109 to 116 were not published in colour.

Sheets 117. 133. 134. Part of sheet 118. *Pwllheli*   Revised 1903   26 by 18

1	2	3	4	5	6	7	8	9	10	11	12	13
1907	osew	-	-	-	1907	A	1/6,2/-,2/6	n	3/07	7.1.2	Cpt-m	
1907	osew	-	-	-	1907	A	1/6,2/-,2/6	n		49.Ou	Og	1

1. Copies, presumably of the original issue, overprinted with "(Large Sheet Series) sheet 49" positioned left of the SSS sheet number (see figure 14). See also LSS sheet 49.

Sheet 118 see sheets 105.118 and 117.133.134.118.

Sheet 119 *Snowdon*   Revised 1903   18 by 12

1	2	3	4	5	6	7	8	9	10	11	12	13
1906	osew	-	-	-	1906	A	1/-,1/6	n	3/06	7.1.2	Cpt-m	

Sheet 120 *Corwen*   Revised 1903-4   18 by 12

1	2	3	4	5	6	7	8	9	10	11	12	13
1906	osew	-	-	-	1906	A	1/-,1/6	n	3/06	7.1.2	Cpt	

This was one of the last sheets to be offered for sale in red covers, in March 1906.

Sheets 121 to 132 were not published in colour.

Sheets 133 and 134 see sheet 117.133.134.118.

Sheet 135 *Harlech*   Revised 1903   18 by 12

1	2	3	4	5	6	7	8	9	10	11	12	13
1906	osew	-	-	-	1906	A	1/-,1/6	n	3/06	7.1.2	Cpt-m	

Sheet 136 *Bala*   Revised 1903-4   18 by 12

1	2	3	4	5	6	7	8	9	10	11	12	13
1906	osew	-	-	-	1905	A	1/-,1/6	n	3/06	7.1.2	Cpt	

Sheet 137 *Oswestry*   Revised 1904   18 by 12

1	2	3	4	5	6	7	8	9	10	11	12	13
1907	osew	-	-	-	1907	A	1/-,1/6,2/-	n	3/07	7.1.2	Cpt-m	

Sheet 138 *Wem*   Revised 1904   18 by 12

1	2	3	4	5	6	7	8	9	10	11	12	13
1907	osew	-	-	-	1907	A	1/-,1/6,2/-	n	8/07	7.1.2	Cpt	

Sheets 139 to 148 were not published in colour.

Sheet 149 *Barmouth*   Revised 1903   18 by 12

1	2	3	4	5	6	7	8	9	10	11	12	13
1906	osew	-	-	-	1906	A	1/-,1/6	n	3/06	7.1.2	Cpt	

Sheet 150 *Dinas-Mawddwy*   Revised 1903-4   18 by 12

1	2	3	4	5	6	7	8	9	10	11	12	13
1907	osew	-	-	-	1907	A	1/-,1/6,2/-	n	3/07	7.1.2	Cpt	

Sheet 151 was not published in colour.

Sheet 152 *Shrewsbury*   Revised 1904   18 by 12

1	2	3	4	5	6	7	8	9	10	11	12	13
1907	ose	-	-	-	1907	A	1/-,1/6,2/-	n	7/07	7.1.2	Cpt	

Sheets 153 to 184 were not published in colour.

Sheet 185 *Northampton* .... Revised 1904-5 ...... 18 by 12
1906 ose - - - 1906 A 1/-,1/6,2/- n 10/06 7.1.2 Cpt

Sheets 186 to 201 were not published in colour.

Sheet 202 *Towcester* .... Revised 1904 ...... 18 by 12
1906 ose - - - 1906 A 1/-,1/6,2/- n 12/06 7.1.2 Cpt

Sheet 203 *Bedford* .... Revised 1904 ...... 18 by 12
1906 ose - - - 1906 A 1/-,1/6,2/- n 11/06 7.1.2 Cpt

Sheet 204 *Biggleswade* .... Revised 1904 ...... 18 by 12
1906 ose - - - 1906 A 1/-,1/6,2/- n 11/06 7.1.2 Cpt

Sheet 205 *Saffron Walden* .... Revised 1905 ...... 18 by 12
1907 ose - - - 1907 A 1/-,1/6,2/- n 7.1.2 Lu
Not in OSPR. This sheet, probably the last SSS to be made, was not sent to the copyright libraries. It was certainly put on sale, but superseded in May 1908 when the LSS replacements were published.

Sheets 206 to 215 were not published in colour.

Sheet 216 *Tewkesbury* .... Revised 1903-4 ...... 18 by 12
1906 ose - - - 1906 A 1/-,1/6 n 6/06 7.1.2 Cpt-m

Sheet 217 *Moreton in Marsh* .... Revised 1903 ...... 18 by 12
1906 ose - - - 1906 A 1/-,1/6 n 3/06 7.1.2 Cpt

Sheet 218 *Chipping Norton* .... Revised 1902 ...... 18 by 12
1905 ose - - - 1905 A 1/- n 9/05 7.1.2 Cpt-m

Sheet 219 *Buckingham* .... Revised 1902 ...... 18 by 12
1905 ose - - - 1905 A 1/-,1/6 n 10/05 7.1.2 Cpt
1905 ose 2.07 - 1.07r 1905 A 1/-,1/6,2/- n 7.1.2 Lu

Sheet 220 *Leighton Buzzard* .... Revised 1902 ...... 18 by 12
1906 ose - - 3.06i 1906 A 1/-,1/6,2/- n 7/06 7.1.2 Cpt

Sheet 221 *Hitchin* .... Revised 1902-3 ...... 18 by 12
1905 ose - - - 1905 A 1/-,1/6 n 10/05 7.1.2 Cpt
1905 ose 3.07 - 2.07r 1905 A 1/-,1/6,2/- n 7.1.2 Lu

Sheet 222 *Great Dunmow* .... Revised 1902 ...... 18 by 12
1906 ose - - - 1906 A 1/-,1/6,2/- n 9/06 7.1.2 Cpt

Sheet 223 *Braintree* .... Revised 1904 ...... 18 by 12
1906 ose - - - 1906 A 1/-,1/6,2/- n 7/06 7.1.2 Cpt

Sheet 224. Part of sheet 242. *Colchester* .... Revised 1904 ...... 18 by 17
1906 ose - - - 1906 A 1/6,2/-,2/6 n 11/06 7.1.2 Cpt
Overlap: 6 by 5 miles with sheet 241.242.

Sheets 225 to 231 were not published in colour.

1	2	3	4	5	6	7	8	9	10	11	12	13

Sheet 232 *Abergavenny* — Revised 1904 — 18 by 12

| 1907 | osew | - | - | - | none | A | 1/-,1/6,2/- | n | | 7.1.2 | Cpt | |

OSPR reference not found.

Sheet 233 *Monmouth* — Revised 1904 — 18 by 12

| 1906 | ose | - | - | - | 1906 | A | 1/-,1/6,2/- | n | 11/06 | 7.1.2 | Cpt | |

Sheet 234 *Gloucester* — Revised 1903-4 — 18 by 12

| 1906 | ose | - | - | - | 1906 | A | 1/-,1/6 | n | 2/06 | 7.1.2 | Cpt-m | |

Sheet 235 *Cirencester* — Revised 1903 — 18 by 12

| 1905 | ose | - | - | - | 1905 | A | 1/-,1/6 | n | 11/05 | 7.1.2 | Cpt-m | |

Sheet 236 *Oxford* — Revised 1902 — 18 by 12

| 1905 | ose | - | - | - | 1905 | A | 1/- | n | 3/05 | 7.1.2 | Cpt | |

Sheet 237 *Thame* — Revised 1902 — 18 by 12

| 1905 | ose | - | - | - | 1905 | A | 1/-,1/6 | n | 10/05 | 7.1.2 | Cpt | |

Sheet 238 *Aylesbury* — Revised 1902 — 18 by 12

| 1905 | ose | - | - | - | 1905 | A | 1/- | n | 3/05 | 7.1.2 | Cpt | |
| 1905 | ose | 1.06 | - | - | 1905 | A | 1/-,1/6 | n | | 7.1.2 | Og | |

Sheet 239 *Hertford* — Revised 1902 — 18 by 12

| 1905 | ose | - | - | - | 1905 | A | 1/- | n | 3/05 | 7.1.2 | Cpt | |
| 1905 | ose | 3.06 | - | 8.05r | 1905 | A | 1/-,1/6 | n | | 7.1.2 | Eg | |

Sheet 240 *Epping* — Revised 1902-3 — 18 by 12

| 1905 | ose | - | - | - | 1905 | A | 1/-,1/6 | n | 10/05 | 7.1.2 | Cpt | |
| 1905 | ose | 1.07 | - | - | 1905 | A | 1/-,1/6,2/- | n | | 7.1.2 | Cu-m | |

Sheet 241. Part of sheet 242. *Chelmsford* — Revised 1904 — 24 by 12

| 1906 | ose | - | - | - | 1906 | A | 1/6,2/-,2/6 | n | 9/06 | 7.1.2 | Cpt | |

Overlap: 6 by 5 miles with sheet 224.242.

Sheet 242 see sheets 224.242 and 241.242.

Sheets 243 to 248 were not published in colour.

Sheets 249. 263. *Cardiff and Newport* — Revised 1904 — 18 by 24

| 1906 | osew | - | - | - | 1906 | A | 1/6,2/-,2/6 | n | 1/07 | 7.1.2 | Cpt | |

Sheet 250 *Chepstow* — Revised 1904 — 18 by 12

| 1906 | osew | - | - | - | 1906 | A | 1/-,1/6 | n | 6/06 | 7.1.2 | Cpt | |

Sheet 251 *Malmesbury* — Revised 1904 — 18 by 12

| 1905 | ose | - | - | - | 1905 | A | 1/-,1/6 | n | 12/05 | 7.1.2 | Cpt | |

Sheet 252 *Swindon* — Revised 1903 — 18 by 12

| 1905 | ose | - | - | - | 1905 | A | 1/-,1/6 | n | 10/05 | 7.1.2 | Cpt-m | |

Sheet 253 *Abingdon* — Revised 1902 — 18 by 12

| 1904 | ose | - | - | - | 1904 | A | 1/- | w | | 7.1.1 | Cpt | |
| 1904 | ose | 11.05 | - | - | 1905 | A | 1/-,1/6 | n | | 7.1.2 | Og | |

OSPR reference not found.

1	2	3	4	5	6	7	8	9	10	11	12	13

Sheet 254 *Henley on Thames* — Revised 1902 — 18 by 12

1	2	3	4	5	6	7	8	9	10	11	12
1904	ose	-	-	-	1904	A	1/-	w	7/04	7.1.1	Cpt
1904	ose	11.05	-	-	1905	A	1/-,1/6	n		7.1.2	Og

Sheet 255 *Beaconsfield* — Revised 1902 — 18 by 12

1	2	3	4	5	6	7	8	9	10	11	12
1904	ose	-	-	-	1904	A	1/-	w	11/04	7.1.1	Cpt
1904	ose	11.05	-	-	1905	A	1/-,1/6	n		7.1.2	Og

Sheet 256 *North London* — Revised 1902 — 18 by 12

1	2	3	4	5	6	7	8	9	10	11	12
1905	ose	-	-	-	1905	A	1/-	n	3/05	7.1.2	Cpt
1905	ose	7.06	-	6.06r	1906	A	1/-,1/6,2/-	n		7.1.2	Og

Sheet 257 *Romford* — Revised 1903 — 18 by 12

1	2	3	4	5	6	7	8	9	10	11	12
1905	ose	-	-	-	1905	A	1/-	n	6/05	7.1.2	Cpt-m
1905	ose	6.06	-	10.05r	1905	A	1/-,1/6,2/-	n		7.1.2	Cu-m

Sheet 258. Part of sheet 259. *Shoeburyness* — Revised 1904 — 23 by 12

1	2	3	4	5	6	7	8	9	10	11	12
1906	ose	-	-	-	1906	A	1/6,2/-	n	5/06	7.1.2	Cpt-m

Sheets 260 to 262 were not published in colour.

Sheet 263 see sheet 249.263.

Sheet 264 was not published in colour.

Sheet 265 *Bath* — Revised 1903-4 — 18 by 12

1	2	3	4	5	6	7	8	9	10	11	12
1907	ose	-	-	-	1906	A	1/-,1/6,2/-	n	3/07	7.1.2	Cpt-m

Sheet 266 *Marlborough* — Revised 1902 — 18 by 12

1	2	3	4	5	6	7	8	9	10	11	12
1905	ose	-	-	-	1905	A	1/-,1/6	n	10/05	7.1.2	Cpt
1905	ose	3.06	-	6.05r	1905	A	1/-,1/6	n		7.1.2	Lu

Sheet 267 *Hungerford* — Revised 1901-2 — 18 by 12

1	2	3	4	5	6	7	8	9	10	11	12
1904	ose	-	-	-	1904	A	1/-	w	2/04	7.1.1	Cpt
1904	ose	6.05	-	-	1905	A	1/-,1/6	w		7.1.1	Og

Sheet 268 *Reading* — Revised 1901-2 — 18 by 12

1	2	3	4	5	6	7	8	9	10	11	12
1904	ose	-	-	-	1904	A	1/-	w	8/04	7.1.1	Cpt
1904	ose	8.05	-	-	1905	A	1/-,1/6	n		7.1.2	Lu

Sheet 269 *Windsor* — Revised 1901-2 — 18 by 12

1	2	3	4	5	6	7	8	9	10	11	12
1904	ose	-	-	-	1904	A	1/-	w	8/04	7.1.1	Cpt-m
1904	ose	8.05	-		1905	A	1/-,1/6	n		7.1.2	Rg
1904	ose	3.07+	-	3.07r	1905	A	1/-,1/6,2/-	n		7.1.2	Og

Sheet 270 *South London* — Revised 1901-2 — 18 by 12

1	2	3	4	5	6	7	8	9	10	11	12
1904	ose	-	-	-	1904	A	1/-	w	12/04	7.1.1	Cpt
1906	ose	2.06	-	1.06i	1904	A	1/-,1/6	w		7.1.1	Eg
1906	ose	5.06	-	1.06r	1906	A	1/-,1/6,2/-	n		7.1.2	PC

Sheet 271 *Dartford* — Revised 1903 — 18 by 12

1	2	3	4	5	6	7	8	9	10	11	12
1905	ose	-	-	-	1905	A	1/-,1/6	n	12/05	7.1.2	Cpt
1905	ose	4.07	-	3.07r	1907	A	1/-,1/6,2/-	n		7.1.2	Cu-m

1	2	3	4	5	6	7	8	9	10	11	12	13

Sheet 272 *Chatham* — Revised 1903-4 — 18 by 12

| 1905 | ose | - | | - | - | 1905 | A 1/-,1/6 | n | 12/05 | 7.1.2 | Cpt | |

Sheets 273. 274. Parts of sheets 289. 290. *East Kent (North)* — Revised 1903-4 — 28 by 20

| 1906 | ose | - | | - | - | 1906 | A 1/6,2/- | n | 6/06 | 118.Os | Cpt-m | |

Sheets 289 and 290 see also sheet 305.306.321.289.290. This sheet was reissued as sheet 118 in the Large Sheet Series, q.v. The East Kent north and south sheets are recorded dissected and mounted together with cover title *East Kent. Sheets 273, 274, 289, 290, 305, 306, 321*, priced five shillings net.

Sheets 275 to 280 were not published in colour.

Sheet 281 *Frome* — Revised 1903-4 — 18 by 12

| 1906 | ose | - | | - | - | 1906 | A 1/-,1/6,2/- | n | 12/06 | 7.1.2 | Cpt | |

A pre-publication extract appears as plate XVIII in Major C.F. Close, *Text book of topographical and geographical surveying.* London: HMSO, 1905, "showing the combination of contours and vertical hachures".

Sheet 282 *Devizes* — Revised 1902 — 18 by 12

| 1905 | ose | - | | - | - | 1905 | A 1/- | n | 7/05 | 7.1.2 | Cpt-m | |

Sheet 283 *Andover* — Revised 1901 — 18 by 12

| 1904 | ose | - | | - | - | 1904 | A 1/- | w | 9/04 | 7.1.1 | Cpt | |
| 1904 | ose | 9.05 | | - | - | 1905 | A 1/-,1/6 | n | | 7.1.2 | Og | |

Sheet 284 *Basingstoke* — Revised 1901 — 18 by 12

| 1904 | ose | - | | - | - | 1904 | A 1/- | w | 10/04 | 7.1.1 | Cpt | |
| 1904 | ose | 1.06 | | - | - | 1905 | A 1/-,1/6 | n | | 7.1.2 | Eg | |

Sheet 285 *Aldershot* — Revised 1901 — 18 by 12

1904	ose	-		-	-	1904	A 1/-	w	10/04	7.1.1	Cpt	
1904	ose	7.05		-	-	1904	A 1/-,1/6	w		7.1.1	Cu-m	
1904	ose	2.07+		-	2.07r	1907	A 1/-,1/6,2/-	n		7.1.2	Eg	

Sheet 286 *Reigate* — Revised 1901 — 18 by 12

1904	ose	-		-	4.04i	1904	A 1/-	w	8/04	7.1.1	Cpt	
1904	ose	10.05		-	-	1905	A 1/-,1/6	n		7.1.2	Og	1
1904	ose	6.09+		-	*	1909	A 1/-,1/6,2/-	n		7.1.2	Eg	2

1. Another issue is recorded, with uncoloured woods. 2. This 1909 reprint, nearly two years later than any other in the small sheet series, was presumably a short term expedient, with the four large sheets that replaced it all published by the end of the year. The railway symbol in the legend precedes any other recorded by more than a year.

Sheet 287 *Sevenoaks* — Revised 1903 — 18 by 12

| 1905 | ose | - | | - | - | 1905 | A 1/-,1/6 | n | 10/05 | 7.1.2 | Cpt-m | |
| 1905 | ose | 4.07 | | - | 2.07r | 1907 | A 1/-,1/6,2/- | n | | 7.1.2 | Og | |

Sheet 288 *Maidstone* — Revised 1903 — 18 by 12

| 1905 | ose | - | | - | 8.05i | 1905 | A 1/-,1/6 | n | 1/06 | 7.1.2 | Cpt-m | |

Sheets 289 and 290 see sheets 273.274.289.290 and 305.306.321.289.290.

Sheets 291 to 296 were not published in colour.

Sheet 297 *Wincanton* — Revised 1903 — 18 by 12

| 1907 | ose | - | | - | - | 1906 | A 1/-,1/6,2/- | n | 3/07 | 7.1.2 | Cpt-m | |

1	2	3	4	5	6	7	8	9	10	11	12	13

Sheet 298 *Salisbury* — Revised 1902-3 — 18 by 12

1	2	3	4	5	6	7	8	9	10	11	12
1905	ose	-	-	-	1905	A	1/-,1/6	n	9/05	7.1.2	Cpt

Sheet 299 *Winchester* — Revised 1901 — 18 by 12

1	2	3	4	5	6	7	8	9	10	11	12
1904	ose	-	-	-	1904	A	1/-	w	2/04	7.1.1	Cpt
1904	ose	8.05	-	-	1905	A	1/-,1/6	n		7.1.2	Og
1904	ose	7.07+	-	-	1907	A	1/-,1/6,2/-	n		7.1.2	Og

Sheet 300 *Alresford* — Revised 1901 — 18 by 12

1	2	3	4	5	6	7	8	9	10	11	12
1903	ose	-	-	-	1903	A	1/-	w	12/03	7.1.1	Cpt
1903	ose	8.04	-	-	1904	A	1/-	w		7.1.1	Eg
1903	ose	11.06+	-	3.06i	1906	A	1/-,1/6,2/-	n		7.1.2	Lu

Sheet 301 *Haslemere* — Revised 1901 — 18 by 12

1	2	3	4	5	6	7	8	9	10	11	12
1904	ose	-	-	-	1904	A	1/-	w	2/04	7.1.1	Cpt
1904	ose	9.05	-	-	1905	A	1/-,1/6	n		7.1.2	Eg

Sheet 302 *Horsham* — Revised 1901 — 18 by 12

1	2	3	4	5	6	7	8	9	10	11	12
1904	ose	-	-	-	1904	A	1/-	w	2/04	7.1.1	Cpt
1904	ose	6.05	-	-	1905	A	1/-,1/6	w		7.1.1	Cu-m

Sheet 303 *Tunbridge Wells* — Revised 1903 — 18 by 12

1	2	3	4	5	6	7	8	9	10	11	12
1905	ose	-	-	-	1905	A	1/-,1/6	n	8/05	7.1.2	Cpt
1905	ose	4.07	-	2.07r	1907	A	1/-,1/6,2/-	n		7.1.2	Eg

Sheet 304 *Tenterden* — Revised 1903 — 18 by 12

1	2	3	4	5	6	7	8	9	10	11	12
1905	ose	-	-	-	1905	A	1/-,1/6	n	12/05	7.1.2	Cpt

Sheets 305. 306. 321. Parts of sheets 289. 290. *East Kent (South)* — Revised 1904 — 28 by 18

1	2	3	4	5	6	7	8	9	10	11	12
1906	ose	-	-	-	1906	A	1/6,2/-	n	6/06	128.Os	Cpt-m

Sheets 289 and 290 see also sheet 273.274.289.290. This sheet was reissued as sheet 128 in the Large Sheet Series, q.v. The East Kent north and south sheets are recorded dissected and mounted together with cover title *East Kent. Sheets 273, 274, 289, 290, 305, 306, 321,* priced five shillings net.

Sheets 307 to 312 were not published in colour.

Sheet 313 *Shaftesbury* — Revised 1903 — 18 by 12

1	2	3	4	5	6	7	8	9	10	11	12
1906	ose	-	-	-	1906	A	1/-,1/6	n	3/06	7.1.2	Cpt

Sheet 314 *Ringwood* — Revised 1902-3 — 18 by 12

1	2	3	4	5	6	7	8	9	10	11	12
1905	ose	-	-	-	1905	A	1/-	n	6/05	7.1.2	Cpt
1905	ose	7.06	-	-	1905	A	1/-,1/6,2/-	n		7.1.2	Lu

Sheet 315 *Southampton* — Revised 1901 — 18 by 12

1	2	3	4	5	6	7	8	9	10	11	12
1904	ose	-	-	-	1904	A	1/-	w	4/04	7.1.1	Cpt
1904	ose	9.05	-	-	1905	A	1/-,1/6	n		7.1.2	Eg

Sheet 316. Part of sheet 331. *Portsmouth* — Revised 1901 — 18 by 18

1	2	3	4	5	6	7	8	9	10	11	12
1904	ose	-	-	-	1904	A	1/6	w		7.1.1	Cpt
1904	ose	4.05	-	-	1905	A	1/6	w		7.1.1	Eg

Overlap: c.9¼ by c.3½ miles with sheet 344.345.330.331. OSPR reference not found.

Sheets 317. 332. *Chichester and Bognor*   Revised 1901   18 by 20¾

1903	ose	-	-	-	1903	A	1/6	w	11/03	7.1.1	Cpt
1903	ose	2.05	-	-	1905	A	1/6	w		7.1.1	Eg
1903	ose	7.07+	-	7.07r	1907	A	1/6,2/-,2/6	n		7.1.2	Cu-m

The first sheet of the series to be published.

Sheets 318. 333. *Brighton and Worthing*   Revised 1901   18 by 15

1904	ose	-	-	-	1904	A	1/6	w	2/04	7.1.1	Cpt
1904	ose	2.05	-	-	1905	A	1/-	w		7.1.1	PC
1904	ose	1.06	-	-	1905	A	1/-,1/6	w		7.1.1	Cu-m

Sheets 319. 334. *Eastbourne and Lewes*   Revised 1903   18 by 19

| 1905 | ose | - | - | - | 1905 | A | 1/6,2/- | n | 9/05 | 7.1.2 | Cpt |
| 1905 | ose | 2.07 | - | 1.07r | 1905 | A | 1/6,2/-,2/6 | n | | 7.1.2 | Cu-m |

Sheet 320 *Hastings*   Revised 1903   18 by 12

| 1905 | ose | - | - | - | 1905 | A | 1/-,1/6 | n | 12/05 | 7.1.2 | Cpt |

Sheet 321 see sheet 305.306.321.289.290.

Sheets 322 to 326 were not published in colour.

Sheets 327. 341. *Bridport*   Revised 1905   18 by 18

| 1906 | ose | - | - | - | 1906 | A | 1/-,1/6,2/- | n | 12/06 | 7.1.2 | Cpt |

Sheets 328. 342. *Dorchester and Weymouth*   Revised 1903   18 by 24

| 1906 | ose | - | - | 10.05r | 1906 | A | 1/6,2/- | n | 3/06 | 7.1.2 | Cpt |

Sheets 329. 343. *Bournemouth and Swanage*   Revised 1903   18 by 20

| 1904 | ose | - | - | - | 1904 | A | 1/6 | w | 12/04 | 7.1.1 | Cpt |
| 1904 | ose | 11.05 | - | - | 1904 | A | 1/6,2/- | w | | 7.1.1 | Cu-m |

Sheet 330 *Lymington*   Revised 1901   18 by 12

| 1904 | ose | - | - | - | 1904 | A | 1/- | w | 8/04 | 7.1.1 | Cpt |
| 1904 | ose | 5.06 | - | - | 1906 | A | 1/-,1/6,2/- | n | | 7.1.2 | Eg |

See also sheet 344.345.330.331. Overlap with this sheet: c.14½ by c.9½ miles.

Sheet 331 see sheets 316.331 and 344.345.330.331.

Sheet 332 see sheet 317.332, sheet 333 see sheet 318.333, sheet 334 see sheet 319.334.

Sheets 335 to 340 were not published in colour.

Sheet 341 see sheet 327.341, sheet 342 see sheet 328.342, sheet 343 see sheet 329.343.

Sheets 344. 345. Parts of sheets 330. 331. *Isle of Wight*   Revised 1901   24 by 18

| 1904 | ose | - | - | - | 1904 | A | 1/6 | w | | 7.1.1 | Cpt |
| 1904 | ose | 4.06 | - | 1.05r | 1904 | A | 1/6,2/- | w | | 7.1.1 | Cu-m |

Overlaps: c.9¼ by c.3½ miles with sheet 316.331, c.14½ by c.9½ with 330. OSPR reference not found.

Sheets 346 to 360 were not published in colour.

District maps

The ideal sequence of maps in this section is not obvious. Separating out those sheets intended for civilian use would have divorced them from the military maps to which they naturally relate. Furthermore, to have attempted to subdivide military training areas from manoeuvre maps would have misplaced the three "manoeuvre maps" which cover Aldershot district (ie the Command), which are not manoeuvre maps at all in the conventional sense of being made for specific manoeuvres on a single occasion. They seem better to fit the category of long-term training area maps. This conclusion is supported by the map imprints: the long-term training areas (including the *Aldershot District Manoeuvre* maps) have "Published by the Director General at the Ordnance Survey Office, Southampton", whereas manoeuvre maps (including *Wareham*) are just "Printed at the Ordnance Survey Office, Southampton". In the end it was easiest to list all maps in a single sequence. Certain maps (eg *Wareham*) seemed out of place in an alphabetical listing. Thus, for better or worse, this list is ordered chronologically.

Aldershot District Manœuvre Map

Parts of sheets 268. 269. 284. 285. 300. 301.							Revised 1901-2			18 by 26
1904	ose	-	-	-	1904	A 2/-	w	10/04	ALD.O	Cpt
		1.05					w		ALD.1	
		1912		1912r			n		ALD.2	

The 1904 printing is without overprint, and is the successor to similar maps covering the identical area also without overprint, based on the first revision. The earlier map was published in 1896, and was in effect the first published Ordnance Survey one-inch map in colour. Roads, hachures, contours and water were coloured, but not woodland. It was republished with new hachures in 1899, and last reprinted in May 1904. This 1904 second revision map has in addition a green woodland plate. KGM listed reprints of this map without citing his sources. He apparently saw the 1.05 reprint (which he noted as in the standard tall red cover of the time), but perhaps not the 1912 which could have been reported to him. They have not been recorded by this writer and thus cannot be verified.

Aldershot District Manœuvre Map. (North)

Parts of sheets 268. 269. 284. 285.							Revised 1901-2			27 by 18½		
1905	ose	-	-	-	1905	A 1/6,2/-	n	10/05	ALN.O	Cpt	1,3
1905	ose	5.06	-	-	1905†	A 1/6,2/-	n		ALN.1	Cu-m	2,3
1905	ose	2.07+	-	1.07r	1905†	A 1/6,2/-,2/6	n		ALN.2	PC	3
1905	ose	6.09++	-	4.09r	1909	A 1/6,2/-,2/6	n		ALN.3	Cu-m	
1905	ose	7.11+++	-	7.11r	1911	A 1/6,2/-,2/6	n		ALN.4	PC	4
1905	ose	7.11+++	-	7.11r	1911	A 1/6,2/-,2/6	n		-	PC	5
1905	ose	7.11+++	-	7.11r	1911	A 1/6,2/-,2/6	n		-	Og	6

Aldershot (South) adjoins this sheet, without overlap, with a continuous alpha-numeric system covering the two sheets. There is no green woodland plate. 1. The boundary of the Aldershot Command area is in orange. Government lands are shaded red and leasehold ground on which troops are permitted to manoeuvre, green. 2. The colour of the Command boundary is altered to red. 3. These three printings each have the same magnetic variation value (16°20'30"), but the date is unfortunately trimmed from the recorded copies of the 5.06 and 2.07 printings. 4. The component sheets are no longer listed. County names appear in the border. 5. Government and leasehold grounds are bordered red and blue, but unshaded. 6. Conservancy areas and danger zones are added, marked in red.

Aldershot District Manœuvre Map. (South)

Parts of sheets 284. 285. 300. 301. 316. 317.   Revised 1901   27 by 18½

1	2	3	4	5	6	7 8	9	10	11	12	13
1905	ose	-	-	-	1905	A 1/6,2/-	n	10/05	ALS.O	Cpt	1
1905	ose	5.06	-	1.06r	1905	A 1/6,2/-	n		ALS.1	Cu-m	2,3
1905	ose	10.07+	-	9.07r	1907†	A 1/6,2/-,2/6	n		ALS.2	PC	3
1905	ose	10.09++	-	10.09r	1909†	A 1/6,2/-,2/6	n		ALS.3	PC	3
1905	ose	8.12+++	-	8.12r	1912	A 1/6,2/-,2/6	n		-	PC	4
1905	ose	8.12+++	-	8.12r	1912	A 1/6,2/-,2/6	n		-	PC	5
1905	ose	8.12+++	-	8.12r	1912	A 1/6,2/-,2/6	n		ALS.4	Cu-m	6
1905	ose	8.12+++	-	8.12r	1912	A 1/6,2/-,2/6	n		-	PC	7

Aldershot (North) adjoins this sheet, without overlap, with a continuous alpha-numeric system covering the two sheets. There is no green woodland plate. 1. The boundary of the Aldershot Command area is in orange. Government lands are shaded red and leasehold ground on which troops are permitted to manoeuvre, green. 2. The colour of the Command boundary is altered to red. 3. The 5.06 printing has the same magnetic variation value as the contemporary north sheet (16°20'30"). Unfortunately the dates of the 10.07 and 10.09 reprints are uncertain, being trimmed from the recorded copies, but with altered values they are likely to have been updated. 4. The component sheets are no longer listed. County names appear in the border. With the Butser Hill area added to the Command. 5. The Butser Hill area is not overprinted. 6. The Woolmer Instructional Military Railway is named in small red letters. 7. The Woolmer Instructional Military Railway is named in large italic red letters.

Aldershot : Public School Provisional Brigade

No revision date   10 by 7

1	2	3	4	5	6	7 8	9	11	12
nd	-	-	-	-	-	A np	s	-	PC

Without road or wood infills. This is an extract map derived from the 1905 or 1906 printing of *Aldershot District Manœuvre Map (North)*.

Salisbury Plain

Sheet 282. Parts of sheets 281. 283. 297. 298. 299.   Revised a. 1903 b. 1901-4   26¼ by 20½

1	2	3	4	5	6	7 8	9	10	11	12	13
1906	ose.a	-	-	-	1905	A 1/6,2/-	n	6/06	SAL.O	Cpt	1
1906	ose.a	-	-	-	1905	A 1/6,2/-	n		-	PC	2
1909	ose.a	-	-	-	1909	A 1/6,2/-,2/6	n		SAL.1	Cu-m	3
1909	ose.b	10.09	-	-	1909	A 1/6,2/-,2/6	n		-	PC	3
1909	ose.b	10.12+	-	8.12r	1912	C 1/6,2/-,2/6	n		-	BL	4
1909	ose.b	10.12+	-	8.12r	1912	C 1/6,2/-,2/6	n		SAL.2	BL	5

War Department Land on Salisbury Plain

1	2	3	4	5	6	7 8	9	11	12	13
1909	ose.b	2150/27++	-	8.12r	1927	C 1/6,2/-,2/6	n	-	PC	6

1. Without overprint. 2. Another edition, with the boundary of the War Department lands overprinted in red. 3. With War Department Property revised to 1908. Cultivated areas along the Avon valley are shown in screened red, with crossings marked to pass from one side of these areas to the other. An additional overprint in black marks the perimeters of camps on the plain. 4. The component sheets are no longer listed. With War Department Property revised ostensibly to 1908, but additional lands are absorbed in the Tilshead area, and since 1911 appears as a superseded date on the next, this is the more probable revision date here. 5. With War Department Property revised to 1911. Further revisions by War Department 1914. The 1909 publication date is unclear and may be read as 1908. See figure 19. 6. Classified *For Official use only*. Corrected and reprinted 2150/27. Further Revisions by War Department 1926. Recorded in a H.7 buff cover, without index diagram, with George V coat of arms.

Military Manœuvre Map, 1906 : Wareham and Surrounding Country

Parts of sheets 328. 329. 342. 343.   No revision date   24 by 18

1	2	3	4	5	6	7 8	9	10	11	12
1906	ose	-	-	-	1906	A 1/6,2/-,2/6	n	9/06	WAR.O	Cpt

Wareham and Surrounding Country. Parts of sheets 328. 329. 342. 343.

1	2	3	4	5	6	7 8	9	11	12	13
1906	ose	9.07	-	-	1907	A 1/6,2/-,2/6	n	WAR.1	BL	1

Neither version carries an overprint. 1. Though obviously repackaged for sale to the public, the imprint is unaltered, and continues to refer to the map as "Printed at the Ordnance Survey Office, Southampton, in 1906", not "published". See figure 17.

Strensall Manoeuvre Map, 1906

Not found. Listed without details in Nicholson (1988), but he also apparently had not seen the map. It was probably based on the second national revision, but there is no certainty that the map was coloured. Outline third edition sheets north and east of sheet 63, which covers the Strensall area, were published in 1906, but only SSS 63 itself appeared in colour, and that not before December.

Windsor and Neighbourhood. Sheet 269. Parts of sheets 255. 285.　　No revision date　18 by 25½
1907　ose　-　　-　-　-　　A np　　s　　　7.3.3　PC

Prepared specially for Eton College Rifle Volunteer Corps. The map was "printed", not "published". See figure 19.

Aldershot Command. Manœuvres, 1907
Sheets 219. 237. Parts of sheets 220. 238.　　　No revision date　27 by 21½
1907　ose　-　　-　-　-　　A np　　s　　-　book

There is no green woodland plate, and the contours are uncoloured. The manoeuvre area is overprinted in red. In *Aldershot Command staff tour and manoeuvres, September 1907* (copy PRO WO 279/517). Also made was a black outline edition, with the manoeuvre area overprint (copy PC). The map was "prepared and printed at the Ordnance Survey".

Southern & Eastern Command Manœuvre Map, 1907
Parts of sheets 282. 298. 314.　　　　No revision date　15 by 27¼
1907　ose　-　　-　-　-　　A np　　s　　-　Ob

A black outline map, with sienna roads and brown hachures. Water, woods and contours are all on the black plate. With an overprint of restricted and out of bounds areas in screened red, training gallops in solid red, and the manoeuvre area boundary in blue. A peculiar feature of the map is a fictitious coastline following the River Avon from Rushall to Fordingbridge, with an inlet at Salisbury south of the railway to Wilton Park. The "sea" is screened blue, and has a five fathom line in black, and two named features, Figheldean Bay and Wilton Bay. With direction arrows along the top margin, apparently unrelated to roads, "to" Marlborough, Swindon, Avebury, Devizes and Calne, and, in a group in the north-west corner, "from" Chippenham, Melksham, Box and Bath. The copy recorded, once the property of the Staff College Museum, is in the Bodleian Library, Oxford, at C17:61(65).

Aldershot Command. Manœuvres 1908
Sheets 300. 316. Parts of sheets 299. 315.　　　No revision date　30¾ by 24
1908　ose　-　　-　-　-　-　-　　s　　-　PC

A fully coloured map, with training area boundary overprinted in red, prohibited areas shaded in red. Most marginal matter is unusually set within the neat line. Copies issued in covers may have a leaflet describing *Water arrangements during field operations* pasted inside the front cover.

Eastern Command Manoeuvre Map, 1908

Not found. Listed in Nicholson (1988), but he also apparently had not seen the map, which he noted as covering the New Forest area. There is no certainty that the map was coloured.

Admission to the Staff College. Parts of sheets 235. 236. 252. 253.　No revision date　c.23½ by 24
1908　ose　-　　-　-　-　　A np　　s　　-　book

Made for the August 1908 examination paper. Most of the standard marginalia is in place. In *Report on the examination for admission to the Staff College, Camberley, held in August, 1908, with copies of the examination papers.* London: HMSO, 1909.

2. One-inch Third Edition Map of England and Wales (Large Sheet Series)

Sheets typically have "(Third Edition)" after the Ordnance Survey heading, top left, and "(Large Sheet Series)" before the sheet number, top right. Sheet names appear top centre. Standard sheet coverage is 27 by 18 miles.

Sheet 1 a. *Norham* b. *River Tweed*   Revised 1901   18 by 27

1907	ose.a	-	-	-	1907	A	1/6,2/-,2/6	n	12/07	1.Ou	Cpt-m	1
1917	oses.b	-	-	s	1917	C.	1/6,2/-,3/-	n		1.Ry	Cg	2
1917	oses.b	11.20	-	s	1917	C	np	n		1.Rp	Cu-m	2

Black Outline Edition One-inch Map, CCR 1/-, based on 1.Ry (1.Ro, OSPR 1918/3). 1. The Scottish area is blank. 2. The Scottish area is filled.

Sheet 2 *Holy Island*   Revised 1901   18 by 27

| 1907 | ose | - | - | - | 1907 | A | 1/6,2/-,2/6 | n | 12/07 | 2.Ou | Cpt-m | |
| 1907 | ose | - | - | - | 1907 | A | 1/6,2/-,3/- | n | | 2.Ov | BL-r | |

Black Outline Edition One-inch Map, ARRR 1/-, based on 2.Ov (2.Oo, OSPR 1918/3).

Sheet 3 a. *Otterburn* b. *The Cheviots*   Revised 1901-2   27 by 18

1907	ose.a	-	-	-	1907	A	1/6,2/-,2/6	n	12/07	3.Ou	Cpt-m	1
1917	oses.b	-	-	s	1917	C.	1/6,2/-,3/-	n		3.Ry	Cu-m	2
1917	oses.b	11.20	-	s	1917	C	np	n		3.Rp	Rg	2

Black Outline Edition One-inch Map, CCR 1/-, based on 3.Ry (3.Ro, OSPR 1918/3). 1. The Scottish area is blank. 2. The Scottish area is filled.

Sheet 4 *Rothbury*   Revised 1902   27 by 18

1907	ose	-	-	-	1907	A	1/6,2/-,2/6	n	12/07	4.Ou	Cpt-m	
1907	ose	-	-	-	1907	A	1/6,2/-,3/-	n		4.Ov	Lu	1
1907	ose	-	-	-	1907	C.	1/6,2/-,3/-	n		4.Oy	Cu-m	1
1907	ose	5.22	-	-	1907	C	np	n		4.Op	BL-r	

Black Outline Edition One-inch Map, ARRR 1/-, based on 4.Ov (4.Oo, OSPR 1918/3). 1. Sheets 4, 65, 95, 111 are the only confirmed cases of a change of copyright statement combined with the 1/6,2/-,3/- price state; see also sheets 66 and 97.

Sheet 5 a. *Longtown.* Revised 1902-3 b. *Gretna.* Revised 1901-3   27 by 18

| 1907 | ose.a | - | - | - | 1907 | A | 1/6,2/-,2/6 | n | 12/07 | 5.Ou | Cpt-m | 1 |
| 1917 | oses.b | 12.21 | - | - | 1917 | C | np | n | | 5.Rp | Cu-m | 2 |

KGM 5.Ry omitted (see page 82). A 1917 printing of this sheet has not been recorded. The publication and magnetic variation dates of the 12.21 printing suggest that, as with sheets 1 and 3, a new edition of the map was prepared in 1917 with mapping of Scotland added, but it may be that in the case of sheet 5 it was not printed until stocks of the original printing had sufficiently run down. Perhaps this did not occur before 1921. There are at least two variants to the Ellis Martin cover intended for this sheet. The earliest known, with sheet name *Longtown and District,* is demonstrably for the 1907 printing since the artist went to the trouble of drawing the index diagram with the Scottish area still blank. It is improbable that Martin began drawing cover designs before taking up full time employment by the Survey in May 1919, and anyway, as figure 10 reveals, this version of the cover was still in use after January 1920 when the price of the map "folded in sections" was increased to 4/-. All of this lends support to the notion that the replacement issue was delayed. The Scottish area on the index diagram appearing on the later *Gretna and District* cover is filled. 1. The Scottish area is blank. 2. The Scottish area is filled. The two-inch blocks in the side margins are displaced half an inch north, requiring a half-inch "K" block at the bottom. It is an anomaly that the railway station symbol, applied to the 1917 printings of sheets 1 and 3, was not applied to sheet 5 as well.

Sheet 6 a. *Haltwhistle* b. *Hexham* — Revised 1902-3 — 27 by 18

1	2	3	4	5	6	7	8	9	10	11	12	13
1907	ose.a	-	-	-	1907	A	1/6,2/-,2/6	n	12/07	6.Ou	Cpt-m	
1907	ose.x	5.11	-	5.11r	1911	A	1/6,2/-,2/6	n		6.1u	Cu-m	
1907	ose.b	5.11	-	5.11r	1911	C.	1/6,2/-,3/-	n		6.1y	Cu-m	
1907	ose.b	10.20	-	5.11r	1911	C	np	n		6.1p	Cu-m	

The Scottish area is blank. *Black Outline Edition One-inch Map*, ARRR 1/-, based on 6.1u (6.1o, OSPR 1918/3).

Sheet 7 *Newcastle upon Tyne* — Revised 1902-3 — 27 by 18

1	2	3	4	5	6	7	8	9	10	11	12	13
1907	ose	-	-	-	1907	A	1/6,2/-,2/6	n	12/07	7.Ou	Cpt-m	
1907	ose.x	2.12	1.12	1.12r	1912	A	1/6,2/-,2/6	n		7.1u	Cu-m	
1907	ose	2.12	1.12	1.12r	1912	C.	1/6,2/-,3/-	n		7.1y	Cu-m	
1907	ose	12.20	1.12	1.12r	1912	C	np	n		7.1p	BL-r	
1907	ose	2.22	1.12	1.12r	1912	-	np	n		-	Ag	1

KGM 7.1z omitted (see page 82). 1. Copyright and rights of way statements are both deleted.

Sheet 8 a. *Silloth* b. *Silloth and Cockermouth* — Revised 1903 — 27 by 18

1	2	3	4	5	6	7	8	9	10	11	12	13
1907	ose.a	-	-	-	1907	A	1/6,2/-,2/6	n	12/07	8.Ou	Cpt-m	
1907	ose.b	11.14	-	10.14r	1914	C	1/6,2/-,2/6	n		8.1x	Cu-m	

The Scottish area is blank. Overlap: 6 by 18 miles with sheet 9. *Black Outline Edition One-inch Map*, CCR 1/-, based on 8.1x (8.1o, OSPR 1918/4).

Sheet 9 *Carlisle and Penrith* — Revised 1903 — 27 by 18

1	2	3	4	5	6	7	8	9	10	11	12	13
1907	ose	-	-	-	1907	A	1/6,2/-,2/6	n	12/07	9.Ou	Cpt-m	
1907	ose	8.14	-	6.14r	1914	C	1/6,2/-,2/6	n		9.1x	Cu-m	
1907	ose	-	-	6.14r*	1914	C.	1/6,2/-,3/-	n		9.1y	PC	
1907	ose	1.21	-	6.14r*	1914	C	np	n		9.1p	BL-r	

Overlap: 6 by 18 miles with sheet 8. KGM 9.1x.2 omitted (see page 82). In the south-east corner the county area of Westmorland is erroneously named Durham.

Sheet 10 a. *Stanhope* b. *Wear Dale* — Revised 1902-3 — 27 by 18

1	2	3	4	5	6	7	8	9	10	11	12	13
1907	ose.a	-	-	-	1907	A	1/6,2/-,2/6	n	2/08	10.Ou	Cpt-m	
1907	ose.b	11.14	-	10.14r	1914	C	1/6,2/-,2/6	n		10.1x	Cu-m	
1907	ose.b	11.14	-	10.14r	1914	C	np	n		-	Rg	
1907	ose.b	-	-	10.14r	1914	C	np	n		10.1z	Cu-m	

Sheet 11 a. *Durham* b. *Sunderland, Durham and Hartlepool* — Revised 1902-3 — 27 by 18

1	2	3	4	5	6	7	8	9	10	11	12	13
1907	ose.a	-	-	-	1907	A	1/6,2/-,2/6	n	2/08	11.Ou	Cpt	
1907	ose.b	11.14	-	-	1914	C	1/6,2/-,2/6	n		11.1x	Cu-m	
1907	ose.b	11.14	-	-	1914	C:	1/6,2/-,3/-	n		11.1y	Cu-m	

Sheet 12 *Whitehaven and Keswick* — Revised 1903 — 27 by 18

1	2	3	4	5	6	7	8	9	10	11	12	13
1907	ose	-	-	-	1907	A	1/6,2/-,2/6	n	6/07	12.Ou	Cpt-m	1
1907	ose	4.14	4.14	4.14r	1914	C	1/6,2/-,2/6	n		12.1x	Cu-m	2
1907	ose	4.14	4.14	4.14r	1914	C.	1/6,2/-,3/-	n		12.1y	Cu-m	
1907	ose	4.14	4.14	4.14r	1914	C	np	n		12.1z	Cu-m	

Overlap: 6 by 18 miles with sheet 13. 1. Printed with only thirteen divisions along the north and south margins, the thirteenth being three inches wide. 2. A fourteenth division one inch wide was added.

Sheet 13 *Ullswater and Ambleside* — Revised 1903 — 27 by 18

1	2	3	4	5	6	7	8	9	10	11	12	13
1907	ose	-	-	-	1907	A	1/6,2/-,2/6	n	9/07	13.Ou	Cpt-m	
1907	ose	-	-	-	1907	C.	1/6,2/-,3/-	n		13.Oy	BL-r	
1907	ose	4.20	-	-	1907	C	np	n		13.Op	Cu-m	

Overlap: 6 by 18 miles with sheet 12. *Black Outline Edition One-inch Map*, ARRR 1/-, based on 13.Ou (13.Oo, OSPR 1918/3). KGM 13.Ox omitted (see page 82).

Sheet 14 a. *Barnard Castle* b. *Barnard Castle and Kirkby Stephen*   Revised 1904   27 by 18

| 1907 | ose.a | - | - | - | 1907 | A | 1/6,2/-,2/6 | n | 6/07 | 14.0u | Cpt-m | |
| 1907 | ose.b | 12.13 | - | 12.13r | 1913 | C | 1/6,2/-,2/6 | n | | 14.1x | Cu-m | |

Black Outline Edition One-inch Map, CCR 1/-, based on 14.1x (14.1o, OSPR 1918/3).

Sheet 15 a. *Darlington* b. *Darlington and Middlesbrough*   Revised 1904   27 by 18

1907	ose.a	-	-	-	1907	A	1/6,2/-,2/6	n	6/07	15.0u	Cpt-m	
1907	ose.b	4.14	3.14	3.14r	1914	C	1/6,2/-,2/6	n		15.1x	Cu-m	
1907	ose.b	4.14	3.14	3.14r	1914	C:	1/6,2/-,3/-	n		-	LDg	1
1907	ose.b	4.14	3.14	3.14r	1914	C.	1/6,2/-,3/-	n		15.1y	Cu-m	2
1907	ose.b	4.14	3.14	3.14r	1914	C	np	n		15.1z	BL-r	

Black Outline Edition One-inch Map, CCR 1/-, based on 15.1y (15.1o, OSPR 1918/3). 1. "........folded in Sections". 2. "........folded in sections" (see page 82).

Sheet 16 a. *Whitby* b. *Whitby and Saltburn*   Revised 1904   28 by 18

1907	ose.a	-	-	-	1907	A	1/6,2/-,2/6	n	8/07	16.0u	Cpt-m	
1907	ose.b	9.14	-	9.14r	1914	C	1/6,2/-,2/6	n		16.1x	Cu-m	1
1907	ose.b	9.14	-	-	1914	C	1/6,2/-,2/6	n		-	Lu	1
1907	ose.b	9.14	-	-	1914	C.	1/6,2/-,3/-	n		16.1y	Cu-m	
1907	ose.b	11.20	-	-	1914	C	np	n		16.1p	Cu-m	

Black Outline Edition One-inch Map, CCR 1/-, based on 16.1y (16.1o, OSPR 1918/3). 1. The Admiralty survey date is carelessly erased.

Sheet 17 *Isle of Man*   Revised 1905   21 by 26¼

1906	ose	-	-	-	1906	A	1/6,2/-,2/6	n	12/06	17.0u	Cpt-m	
1906	ose	7.10	-	-	1910	A	1/6,2/-,2/6	n		17.1u	Cu-m	
1906	ose	7.10	-	-	1910	C.	1/6,2/-,3/-	n		17.1y	Cu-m	
1906	ose	4.20	-	-	1910	C	np	n		17.1p	Cu-m	

No contours are printed on this sheet. With extrusions to cover the Calf of Man and Maughold Head. This was the first sheet of this series to be issued, and the first OS one-inch map of the island in colour. The earliest covers lack an index, which was otherwise almost universally applied for this series, on the back card. *Black Outline Edition One-inch Map*, ARRR 1/-, based on 17.1u (17.1o, OSPR 1918/4).

Sheet 18 a. *Barrow in Furness* b. *Barrow in Furness and Coniston*   Revised 1903-4   18 by 26

1907	ose.a	-	-	-	1907	A	1/6,2/-,2/6	n	8/07	18.0u	Cpt-m	
1907	ose.b	3.14	3.14	3.14r	1914	C	1/6,2/-,2/6	n		18.1x	Cu-m	
1907	ose.bo	12.20	3.14	3.14r	1914	C	np	n		18.1p	BL-r	

Overlaps: 3 by 18 miles with sheet 19, 3 by 8 with 24. *Black Outline Edition One-inch Map*, CCR 1/-, based on 18.1x (18.1o, OSPR 1918/3).

Sheet 19 *Kendal*   Revised 1903-4   27 by 18

1907	ose	-	-	-	1907	A	1/6,2/-,2/6	n	9/07	19.0u	Cpt	
1907	ose.x	5.11	5.11	5.11r*	1911	A	1/6,2/-,2/6	n		19.1u	Cu-m	
1907	ose	5.11	5.11	5.11r*	1911	C:	1/6,2/-,3/-	n		19.1y	Cu-m	
1907	ose	9.20	5.11	5.11r*	1911	C	np	n		19.1p	Cu-m	

Overlap: 3 by 18 miles with sheet 18. *Black Outline Edition One-inch Map*, ARRR 1/-, based on 19.1u (19.1o, OSPR 1918/3).

Sheet 20 a. *Hawes* b. *Hawes and Leyburn*   Revised 1904   27 by 18

1907	ose.a	-	-	-	1907	A	1/6,2/-,2/6	n	8/07	20.0u	Cpt-m	
1907	ose.b	1.14	1.14	1.14r	1914	C	1/6,2/-,2/6	n		20.1x	Cu-m	
1907	ose.b	1.14	1.14	1.14r	1914	C:	1/6,2/-,3/-	n		20.1y	Cu-m	
1907	ose.b	2.21	1.14	1.14r	1914	C	np	n		20.1p	Cu-m	

Black Outline Edition One-inch Map, CCR 1/-, based on 20.1y (20.1o, OSPR 1918/3).

Sheet 21 a. *Thirsk* b. *Northallerton and Ripon* Revised 1904 27 by 18

1	2	3	4	5	6	7	8	9	10	11	12	13
1907	ose.a	-	-	-	1907	A	1/6,2/-,2/6	n	6/07	21.Ou	Cpt-m	
1907	ose.b	1.14	1.14	1.14r	1914	C	1/6,2/-,2/6	n		21.1x	Cu-m	
1907	ose.b	1.14	1.14	1.14r	1914	C:	1/6,2/-,3/-	n		21.1y	Cu-m	1
1907	ose.b	1.14	1.14	1.14r	1914	C.	1/6,2/-,3/-	n		-	Lu	2

Black Outline Edition One-inch Map, CCR 1/-, based on 21.1y (21.1o, OSPR 1918/4). KGM 21.1z omitted (see page 82). 1. "........folded in Sections". 2. "........folded in sections" (see page 82).

Sheet 22 *Pickering* Revised 1904-5 27 by 18

1	2	3	4	5	6	7	8	9	10	11	12	13
1907	ose	-	-	-	1907	A	1/6,2/-,2/6	n	9/07	22.Ou	Cpt-m	
1907	ose	6.12	5.12	5.12r	1912	C	1/6,2/-,2/6	n		22.1x	Cu-m	
1907	ose	10.14+	10.14	10.14r	1914	C	1/6,2/-,2/6	n		22.2x	Cu-m	
1907	ose	10.14+	10.14	10.14r	1914	C.	1/6,2/-,3/-	n		22.2y	Cu-m	

Overlap: 9 by 18 miles with sheet 23. *Black Outline Edition One-inch Map,* CCR 1/-, based on 22.2y (22.2o, OSPR 1918/4).

Sheet 23 a. *Scarborough* b. *Scarborough and Flamborough Head* Revised 1904-5 27 by 18

1	2	3	4	5	6	7	8	9	10	11	12	13
1907	ose.a	-	-	-	1907	A	1/6,2/-,2/6	n	8/07	23.Ou	Cpt-m	
1907	ose.b	3.14	-	1.14r	1914	C	1/6,2/-,2/6	n		23.1x	Cu-m	
1907	ose.b	3.14	-	1.14r	1914	C:	1/6,2/-,3/-	n		-	Cu	1
1907	ose.b	3.14	-	1.14r	1914	C.	1/6,2/-,3/-	n		23.1y	Cu-m	2
1907	ose.b	1.21	-	1.14r	1914	C	np	n		23.1p	Cu-m	

Overlap: 9 by 18 miles with sheet 22. An outline printing, with roads and contours in red, is recorded, based on 23.1y (copy PC). 1. "........folded in Sections". 2. "........folded in sections" (see page 82).

Sheet 24 *Lancaster and Fleetwood* Revised 1903-12 27 by 18

1	2	3	4	5	6	7	8	9	10	11	12	13
1913	ose	-	-	s	1913	C	1/6,2/-,2/6	n	11/13	24.Ox	Cpt-m	
1913	ose.o	-	-	s	1913	C	np	n		24.Oz	Cu-m	

Overlap: 3 by 8 miles with sheet 18.

Sheet 25 *Skipton* Revised 1910-11 27 by 18

1	2	3	4	5	6	7	8	9	10	11	12	13
1913	ose	-	-	s	1913	C	1/6,2/-,2/6	n	11/13	25.Ox	Cpt-m	
1913	ose.o	8.20	-	s	1913	C	np	n		25.Op	Cu-m	

Sheet 26 *Harrogate* Revised 1910-11 27 by 18

1	2	3	4	5	6	7	8	9	10	11	12	13
1913	ose	-	-	s	1913	C	1/6,2/-,2/6	n	7/13	26.Ox	Cpt-m	
1913	ose	-	-	s	1913	C:	1/6,2/-,3/-	n		26.Oy	Cu-m	1
1913	ose	-	-	s	1913	C.	1/6,2/-,3/-	n		-	Cu-m	2
1913	ose	12.20	-	s	1913	C	np	n		26.Op	Cu-m	

1. "........folded in Sections". 2. "........folded in sections" (see page 82).

Sheet 27 *York* Revised 1904-5 27 by 18

1	2	3	4	5	6	7	8	9	10	11	12	13
1908	ose	-	-	-	1908	A	1/6,2/-,2/6	n	3/08	27.Ou	Cpt-m	
1908	ose	8.12	7.11	8.12r	1912	C	1/6,2/-,2/6	n		27.1x	Cu-m	
1908	ose	8.12	7.11	8.12r	1912	C.	1/6,2/-,3/-	n		27.1y	BL-r	
1908	ose	10.20	7.11	8.12r	1912	C	np	n		27.1p	Cu-m	

Overlap: 9 by 18 miles with sheet 28. *Black Outline Edition One-inch Map,* CCR 1/-, based on 27.1y (27.1o, OSPR 1918/4).

Sheet 28 a. *Great Driffield* b. *Great Driffield and Bridlington* Revised 1904-5   27 by 18

1	2	3	4	5	6	7	8	9	10	11	12	13
1908	ose.a	-	-	-	1908	A	1/6,2/-,2/6	n	3/08	28.Ou	Cpt-m	
1908	ose.b	7.12	6.12	6.12r	1912	A	1/6,2/-,2/6	n		28.1u	Cu-m	
1908	ose.b	7.12	6.12	6.12r	1912	A	1/6,2/-,3/-	n		28.1v	Cu-m	
1908	ose.bo	1.21	6.12	6.12r	1912	C	np	n		28.1p	Wc	

Overlap: 9 by 18 miles with sheet 27. *Black Outline Edition One-inch Map,* ARRR 1/-, based on 28.1v (28.1o, OSPR 1918/4). KGM 28.1y omitted (see page 82).

Sheet 29 *Preston, Southport and Blackpool*   Revised 1911-2   27 by 18

1	2	3	4	5	6	7	8	9	10	11	12	13
1913	ose	-	-	s	1913	C	1/6,2/-,2/6	n	12/13	29.Ox	Cpt-m	
1913	ose	-	-	s	1913	C:	1/6,2/-,3/-	n		29.Oy	Cu-m	
1913	ose	-	-	+	1913	C	np	n		29.Oz	BL-r	1
1913	ose	1000/23	-	+	1913	C	np	n		29.Op	Cu-m	1

Overlap: 22 by c.3¼ miles with sheet 34. 1. The original legend is replaced, presumably in error, by one appropriate to the small sheet coloured map of Ireland. This has a trigonometrical point and level (25 feet) in place of the traditional contour symbol, an Irish style lightship, and no windpump symbol (see figure 15). This particular legend used also lacks station symbols, and thus fails to reflect their continuing presence on the map.

Sheet 30 *Accrington, Burnley and Halifax*   Revised 1908-12   27 by 18

1	2	3	4	5	6	7	8	9	10	11	12	13
1913	ose	-	-	s	1913	C	1/6,2/-,2/6	n	12/13	30.Ox	Cpt-m	
1913	ose	-	-	s	1913	C:	1/6,2/-,3/-	n		30.Oy	Rg	
1913	ose	4.20	-	s	1913	C	np	n		30.Op.1	Cu-m	
1913	ose	1000/23	-	s	1913	C	np	n		30.Op.2	Cu-m	

KGM 30.Oz omitted (see page 82). An outline printing, with water in blue and contours in red, is recorded, based on 30.Oy (copy PC). Also recorded is a special printing from the black plate only (therefore no water, hachures or contours), based on 30.Oy, with the price deleted. It has a heading overprinted in red *Old Large Sheet Series 1-inch. Fully coloured outline made up from small sheets by transfer from copper (engraved)* (copies LDg, Sg). Similar one-inch Popular Edition and quarter-inch Third Edition printings are also recorded, presumably for some common purpose.

Sheet 31 *Bradford, Leeds and Wakefield*   Revised 1908-10   27 by 18

1	2	3	4	5	6	7	8	9	10	11	12	13
1913	ose	-	-	s	1913	C	1/6,2/-,2/6	n	9/13	31.Ox	Cpt-m	
1913	ose	-	-	s	1913	C:	1/6,2/-,3/-	n		31.Oy	Cu-m	
1913	ose	-	-	s	1913	C	np	n		31.Oz	BL-r	

An outline printing, with water in blue and contours in red, is recorded, based on 31.Ox (copy PC).

Sheet 32 *Goole*   Revised 1905   27 by 18

1	2	3	4	5	6	7	8	9	10	11	12	13
1908	ose	-	-	-	1908	A	1/6,2/-,2/6	n	3/08	32.Ou	Cpt-m	
1908	ose	7.12	3.10	7.12r	1912	C	1/6,2/-,2/6	n		32.1x	Cu-m	
1908	ose	7.12	3.10	7.12r	1912	C:	1/6,2/-,3/-	n		32.1y	Cu-m	

Sheet 33 *Hull*   Revised 1905   27 by 18

1	2	3	4	5	6	7	8	9	10	11	12	13
1908	ose	-	-	-	1908	A	1/6,2/-,2/6	n	3/08	33.Ou	Cpt	
1908	ose	10.12	9.11	8.12r	1912	C	1/6,2/-,2/6	n		33.1x	Mg	
1908	ose	11.14+	9.11	10.14r	1914	C	1/6,2/-,2/6	n		33.2x	Cu-m	
1908	ose	11.14+	9.11	-	1914	C	1/6,2/-,2/6	n		-	Cu	

With an extrusion to cover Kilnsea Warren.

1	2	3	4	5	6	7	8	9	10	11	12	13

Sheet 34 *Liverpool, Southport and Chester*   Revised 1904-12   26 by c.33¼

1913	osew	-	-	s	1913	C	1/6,2/-,2/6	n	12/13	34.Ox	Cpt-m	
1913	osew	-	-	s	1913	C.	1/6,2/-,3/-	n		34.Oy	Cu-m	
1913	osew	-	-	s	1913	C	np	n		34.Oz	Cu-m	

Index diagrams of the Large Sheet Series typically show this sheet in portrait style with dimensions 18 by 27 miles; in the event a much larger sheet was published, extended north to cover Southport. Overlaps: 22 by c.3¼ miles with sheet 29, 13 by 18 with 35, 13 by 12 with 43, 13 by 12 with 44.

Sheet 35 *Bolton, Warrington and St. Helens*   Revised 1904-11   27 by 18

1913	ose	-	-	s	1913	C	1/6,2/-,2/6	n	12/13	35.Ox	Cpt-m	
1913	ose	-	-	s	1913	C:	1/6,2/-,3/-	n		35.Oy	Cu-m	
1913	ose	-	-	s	1913	C	np	n		35.Oz	Cu-m	

Overlap: 13 by 18 miles with sheet 34.

Sheet 36 *Manchester, Stockport and Oldham*   Revised 1905-11   27 by 18

1913	ose	-	-	s	1913	C	1/6,2/-,2/6	n	12/13	36.Ox	Cpt-m	
1913	ose	-	-	s	1913	C:	1/6,2/-,3/-	n		-	Cu	1
1913	ose	-	-	s	1913	C.	1/6,2/-,3/-	n		36.Oy	Cu-m	2
1913	ose	8.21	-	s	1913	C	np	n		36.Op	Cu-m	

Black Outline Edition One-inch Map, CCR 1/-, based on 36.Oy (36.Oo, OSPR 1918/2). 1. "…..folded in Sections". 2. "……..folded in sections" (see page 82).

Sheet 37 a. *Sheffield and Doncaster* b. *Sheffield, Barnsley and Doncaster*

     Revised 1905-8   27 by 18

1910	ose.a	-	-	-	1910	A	1/6,2/-,2/6	n	12/10	37.Ou	Cpt-m	
1910	ose.b	8.12	-	7.12r	1912	A	1/6,2/-,2/6	n		37.1u	Cu-m	
1910	ose.b	8.12	-	7.12r	1912	C:	1/6,2/-,3/-	n		37.1y	Rg	

Black Outline Edition One-inch Map, ARRR 1/-, based on 37.1u (37.1o, OSPR 1918/4).

Sheet 38 *Gainsborough*   Revised 1905-6   27 by 18

1908	ose	-	-	-	1908	A	1/6,2/-,2/6	n	12/08	38.Ou	Cpt-m	
1908	ose	11.12	4.11	8.12r	1912	C	1/6,2/-,2/6	n		38.1x	Cu-m	
1908	ose	11.12	4.11	8.12r	1912	C:	1/6,2/-,3/-	n		38.1y	Cu-m	

[*Black Outline Edition One-inch Map*], CCR 1/6,2/-,3/-, based on 38.1y (38.1o, not in OSPR, copy Og). The heading, price adjustment and edition note are lacking, but is otherwise consistent with others in the Og Black Outline set, acquired on 12 February 1920, presented by the Director General, Ordnance Survey. It is possible that the entire Black Outline Edition programme was abandoned part way through the conversion process of this sheet.

Sheet 39 *Grimsby and Louth*   Revised 1905-6   27 by 18

1908	ose	-	-	-	1908	A	1/6,2/-,2/6	n	10/08	39.Ou	Cpt-m	
1908	ose	1.10	-	1.10r	1910	A	1/6,2/-,2/6	n		39.1u	Cu-m	
1908	ose	7.12+	4.11	7.12r	1912	C	1/6,2/-,2/6	n		39.2x	Cu-m	
1908	ose	7.12+	4.11	7.12r	1912	C:	1/6,2/-,3/-	n		39.2y	Cu-m	

Sheet 40 *Anglesey*   Revised 1903   27 by c.17½

1910	osew	-	-	-	1910	A	1/6,2/-,2/6	n	9/10	40.Ou	Cpt-m	
1910	osew	-	-	-	1910	C.	1/6,2/-,3/-	n		40.Oy	Cu-m	
1910	osew	11.20	-	-	1910	C	np	n		40.Op	Cu-m	

With an extrusion to cover Middle Mouse. Overlaps: 19 by 2½ miles with sheet 41, 5½ by 11½ with 42.

Sheet 41 a. *Carnarvon* b. *Snowdon* — Revised 1903 — 27 by 18

1	2	3	4	5	6	7 8	9	10	11	12	13
1910	osew.a	-	-	-	1910	A 1/6,2/-,2/6	n	8/10	41.0u	Cpt-m	
1910	osew.b	3.14	3.14	3.14r	1914	C 1/6,2/-,2/6	n		41.1x	Cu-m	
1910	osew.b	3.14	3.14	3.14r	1914	C: 1/6,2/-,3/-	n		-	Cu	1
1910	osew.b	3.14	3.14	3.14r	1914	C. 1/6,2/-,3/-	n		41.1y	Cu-m	2
1910	osew.b	8.21	3.14	3.14r	1914	C np	n		41.1p	BL-r	

Overlaps: 19 by 2½ miles with sheet 40, 13½ by 9 with 42, 13½ by 3 with 49, 13½ by 9 with 50. 1. "........folded in Sections". 2. "........folded in sections" (see page 82).

Sheet 42 a. *Llandudno* b. *Bangor, Llandudno and Colwyn Bay* — Revised 1903-4 — 27 by 18

1	2	3	4	5	6	7 8	9	10	11	12	13
1909	osew.a	-	-	-	1909	A 1/6,2/-,2/6	n	12/09	42.0u	Cpt-m	
1909	osew.x	1.12	-	1.12r	1912	A 1/6,2/-,2/6	n		42.1u	Cu-m	
1909	osew.b	7.14+	7.14	7.14r	1914	C 1/6,2/-,2/6	n		42.2x	Cu-m	
1909	osew.b	7.14+	-	-	1914	C: 1/6,2/-,3/-	n		42.2y	Cu-m	1
1909	osew.b	7.14+	-	-	1914	C. 1/6,2/-,3/-	n		-	Cu-m	2
1909	osew.b	4.20	-	-	1914	C np	n		42.2p	Cu-m	

Overlaps: 5½ by 11½ miles with sheet 40, 13½ by 9 with 41. *Black Outline Edition One-inch Map*, CCR 1/-, based on 42.2y (42.2o, OSPR 1918/4). Copies of the coloured map have been recorded in H.4 covers named *Colwyn Bay District* (1.12) and *Penmaenmawr District*. 1. "........folded in Sections". 2. "........folded in sections" (see page 82).

Sheet 43 *Flint* — Revised 1904 — 27 by 18

1	2	3	4	5	6	7 8	9	10	11	12	13
1908	osew	-	-	-	1908	A 1/6,2/-,2/6	n	8/08	43.0u	Cpt	
1908	osew	7.09	-	7.09r*	1909	A 1/6,2/-,2/6	n		43.1u	Cu-m	
1908	osew	7.09	-	7.09r*	1909	C. 1/6,2/-,3/-	n		43.1y	Cu-m	
1908	osew	-	-	7.09r*	1909	C np	n		43.1z	Cu-m	1
1908	osew	4.20	-	7.09r*	1909	C np	n		43.1p	Cu-m	

Overlap: 13 by 12 miles with sheet 34. With an extrusion to cover the Point of Air. *Black Outline Edition One-inch Map*, ARRR 1/-, based on 43.1u (43.1o, OSPR 1918/4). 1. Copies of this printing were supplied for use in Armstrong College, Newcastle-upon-Tyne.

Sheet 44 a. *Northwich* b. *Chester and Northwich* — Revised 1904-5 — 27 by 18

1	2	3	4	5	6	7 8	9	10	11	12	13
1908	ose.a	-	-	-	1908	A 1/6,2/-,2/6	n	12/08	44.0u	Cpt-m	
1908	ose.x	10.11	10.11	9.11r	1911	A 1/6,2/-,2/6	n		44.1u	Cu-m	
1908	ose.b	1.14+	10.11	1.14r	1914	C 1/6,2/-,2/6	n		44.2x	Cu-m	1
1908	ose.b	1.14+	10.11	1.14r	1914	C. 1/6,2/-,3/-	n		44.2y	Cu-m	
1908	ose.b	1.14+	10.11	1.14r	1914	C np	n		44.2z	Cu-m	

Overlap: 13 by 12 miles with sheet 34. *Black Outline Edition One-inch Map*, CCR 1/-, based on 44.2y (44.2o, OSPR 1918/2). 1. Some copies were supplied for use in Glasgow Provincial Training College.

Sheet 45 a. *Buxton* b. *Macclesfield, Buxton, and Leek* — Revised 1905-6 — 27 by 18

1	2	3	4	5	6	7 8	9	10	11	12	13
1909	ose.a	-	-	-	1909	A 1/6,2/-,2/6	n	9/09	45.0u	Cpt-m	
1909	ose.a	10.10	-	9.10i	1910	A 1/6,2/-,2/6	n		45.1u	Cu-m	
1909	ose.b	5.13+	5.13	5.13i	1913	C 1/6,2/-,2/6	n		45.2x	Cu-m	
1909	ose.b	5.13+	5.13	5.13i	1913	C: 1/6,2/-,3/-	n		45.2y	Cu-m	1
1909	ose.b	5.13+	5.13	5.13i	1913	C: 1/6,2/-,3/-	n		-	Cu-m	1
1909	ose.b	5.13+	5.13	5.13i	1913	C np	n		45.2z	Cu-m	
1909	ose.b	8.21	5.13	5.13i	1913	C np	n		45.2p	Cu-m	

Black Outline Edition One-inch Map, CCR 1/-, based on 45.2y (45.2o, OSPR 1918/4). 1. Both these printings have "folded in Sections" – one has "3/-, net", the other "3/- net". The 3/- is also relettered.

Sheet 46 a. *Chesterfield* b. *Matlock, Chesterfield and Worksop*   Revised 1906-7   27 by 18

1910	ose.a	-		-	1910	A	1/6,2/-,2/6	n	2/10	46.0u	Cpt-m	
1910	ose.b	8.12	-	8.12r	1912	C	1/6,2/-,2/6	n		46.1x	Cu-m	
1910	ose.b	8.12	-	8.12r	1912	C:	1/6,2/-,3/-	n		46.1y	Cu-m	
1910	ose.bo	8.12	-	8.12r	1912	C	np	n		46.1z	Cu-m	

Black Outline Edition One-inch Map, CCR 1/-, based on 46.1y (46.1o, OSPR 1918/4).

Sheet 47 *Lincoln*   Revised 1906   27 by 18

1909	ose	-		-	-	1909	A	1/6,2/-,2/6	n	9/09	47.0u	Cpt
1909	ose	6.12	-	1.12r	1912	A	1/6,2/-,2/6	n		47.1u	Cu-m
1909	ose	6.12	-	1.12r	1912	A	1/6,2/-,3/-	n		47.1v	Cu
1909	ose	4.20	-	1.12r	1912	C	np	n		47.1p	BL-r

Sheet 48 a. *Spilsby* b. *Horncastle and Skegness*   Revised 1906   29 by 18

1909	ose.a	-		-	-	1909	A	1/6,2/-,2/6	n	3/09	48.0u	Cpt-m
1909	ose.a	2.11	2.11	2.11r	1911	A	1/6,2/-,2/6	n		48.1u	BL-c
1909	ose.b	6.12+	2.11	6.12r	1912	C	1/6,2/-,2/6	n		48.2x	Cu-m
1909	ose.bo	6.12+	2.11	6.12r	1912	C	np	n		48.2z	BL-r

With an extrusion to cover Outer Knock. *Black Outline Edition One-inch Map,* CCR 1/-, based on 48.2x (48.2o, not in OSPR, copy BL-r).

Small **sheets 117. 133. 134. Part of sheet 118.** *Pwllheli*   Revised 1903   26 by 18

1907	osew	-		-	-	1907	A	1/6,2/-,2/6	n	3/07	7.1.2	Cpt-m

Renumbered large **sheet 49** *Pwllheli*

1907	osew	-		-	-	1907	A	1/6,2/-,2/6	n		49.0u	Og	1
1907	osew	-		-	-	1913	C	1/6,2/-,2/6	n	6/13	49.1x	Cpt-m	2

Overlap: 13½ by 3 miles with sheet 41. 1. Some copies, presumably of the original printing, of the combined SSS sheet 117.133.134.118 are overprinted with "(Large Sheet Series) Sheet 49" positioned to the left of the original sheet number (see figure 14). It is not known when this occurred, or how many copies were affected. But, significantly, only four are recorded, and only one of those in covers. 2. OSPR 6/13 provides this information: *Note. The combined Map of Pwllheli, comprising Sheets 117, 133, 134 and parts of Sheet 118, published on 7th March, 1907, is identical with Sheet 49 of the Large Sheet Series and will in future be issued as such.*

Sheet 50 *Ffestiniog*   Revised 1903-4   27 by 18

1909	osew	-		-	-	1909	A	1/6,2/-,2/6	n	11/09	50.0u	Cpt-m
1909	osew	3.12	-	1.12r	1912	A	1/6,2/-,2/6	n		50.1u	Cu-m
1909	osew	3.12	-	1.12r	1912	A	1/6,2/-,3/-	n		50.1v	Cu-m
1909	osew	11.20	-	1.12r	1912	C	np	n		50.1p	Cu-m

Overlap: 13½ by 9 miles with sheet 41.

Sheet 51 a. *Llangollen* b. *Llangollen, Oswestry, and Wrexham*   Revised 1903-4   27 by 18

1908	osew.a	-		-	-	1908	A	1/6,2/-,2/6	n	7/08	51.0u	Cpt
1908	osew.b	6.12	6.12	6.12r	1912	A	1/6,2/-,2/6	n		51.1u	Cu-m
1908	osew.b	6.12	6.12	6.12r	1912	A	1/6,2/-,3/-	n		51.1v	Cu-m
1908	osew.b	12.20	6.12	6.12r	1912	C	np	n		51.1p	Cu-m

Sheet 52 a. *Crewe* b. *Crewe, Market Drayton and Whitchurch*   Revised 1904-5   27 by 18

1908	osew.a	-		-	-	1908	A	1/6,2/-,2/6	n	8/08	52.0u	Cpt
1908	osew.b	8.13	-	8.13r*	1913	C	1/6,2/-,2/6	n		52.1x	Cu-m
1908	osew.b	8.13	-	8.13r*	1913	C:	1/6,2/-,3/-	n		52.1y	PC	1
1908	osew.b	8.13	-	8.13r*	1913	C.	1/6,2/-,3/-	n		-	BL-r	2

Black Outline Edition One-inch Map, CCR 1/-, based on 52.1y (52.1o, OSPR 2/19). KGM 52.1u omitted (see page 82). 1. "........folded in Sections". 2. "........folded in sections" (see page 82).

Sheet 53 a. *Longton* b. *Stoke upon Trent and Uttoxeter*   Revised 1905   27 by 18

1	2	3	4	5	6	7	8	9	10	11	12	13
1908	ose.a	-		-	-	1908	A	1/6,2/-,2/6	n	12/08	53.Ou	Cpt-m	
1908	ose.x	2.12	-	1.12r	1912	A	1/6,2/-,2/6	n		53.1u	Cu-m	
1908	ose.b	11.14+	-	11.14r	1914	C	1/6,2/-,2/6	n		53.2x	Cu	
1908	ose.b	11.14+	-	-	1914	C.	1/6,2/-,3/-	n		53.2y	Cu-m	
1908	ose.b	11.14+	-	-	1914	C	np	n		53.2z	Cu-m	

Black Outline Edition One-inch Map, CCR 1/-, based on 53.2y (53.2o, OSPR 2/19).

Sheet 54 *Nottingham and Derby*   Revised 1905-6   27 by 18

1	2	3	4	5	6	7	8	9	10	11	12	13
1909	ose	-		-	-	1909	A	1/6,2/-,2/6	n	9/09	54.Ou	Cpt	
1909	ose	5.12	-	5.12r	1912	A	1/6,2/-,2/6	n		54.1u	Cu-m	
1909	ose	5.12	-	5.12r	1912	A	1/6,2/-,3/-	n		54.1v	Mg	
1909	ose	5.12	-	5.12r	1912	A	np	n		54.1w	Cu-m	

KGM 54.1u.1 omitted (see page 82): no copies have been found, and the practice of omitting the sheet name otherwise ended two months earlier.

Sheet 55 *Grantham*   Revised 1906-7   27 by 18

1	2	3	4	5	6	7	8	9	10	11	12	13
1909	ose	-		-	-	1909	A	1/6,2/-,2/6	n	6/09	55.Ou	Cpt	
1909	ose	4.12	-	4.12r	1912	A	1/6,2/-,2/6	n		55.1u	Cu-m	
1909	ose	4.12	-	4.12r	1912	A	1/6,2/-,3/-	n		55.1v	Cu-m	
1909	ose	4.12	-	1912r	1912	C	np	n		55.1z	Rg	

Sheet 56 *Boston*   Revised 1906-7   27 by 18

1	2	3	4	5	6	7	8	9	10	11	12	13
1910	ose	-		-	-	1910	A	1/6,2/-,2/6	n	5/10	56.Ou	Cpt-m	
1910	ose	4.12	-	1.12r	1912	A	1/6,2/-,2/6	n		56.1u	Cu	
1910	ose	4.12	-	1.12r	1912	A	1/6,2/-,3/-	n		56.1v	BL-r	
1910	ose	4.12	-	1.12r	1912	A	np	n		56.1w	Cu-m	

Sheet 57 a. *Hunstanton* b. *Hunstanton and Fakenham*   Revised 1907-8   27 by 18

1	2	3	4	5	6	7	8	9	10	11	12	13
1910	ose.a	-		-	-	1910	A	1/6,2/-,2/6	n	8/10	57.Ou	Cpt-m	
1910	ose.b	5.12	-	4.12r	1912	A	1/6,2/-,2/6	n		57.1u	Cu-m	
1910	ose.b	5.12	-	4.12r	1912	A	1/6,2/-,3/-	n		57.1v	Cu-m	

Sheet 58 *Cromer*   Revised 1908   27 by 18

1	2	3	4	5	6	7	8	9	10	11	12	13
1910	ose	-		-	s	1910	A	1/6,2/-,2/6	n	12/10	58.Ou	Cpt-m	
1910	ose	4.12	4.12	4.12rs	1912	A	1/6,2/-,2/6	n		58.1u	Cu-m	1
1910	ose	4.12	4.12	4.12rs	1912	A	1/6,2/-,3/-	n		58.1v	Cu-m	1

Overlap: 9 by 3 miles with sheet 68. 1. *Railways rvised to April 1912* [sic].

Sheet 59 *Barmouth*   Revised 1903-4   27 by 18

1	2	3	4	5	6	7	8	9	10	11	12	13
1910	osew	-		-	-	1910	A	1/6,2/-,2/6	n	3/10	59.Ou	Cpt-m	
1910	osew	-		-	-	1910	C.	1/6,2/-,3/-	n		59.Oy	Cu-m	
1910	osew	11.20	-	-	1910	C	np	n		59.Op	Cu-m	
1910	osew	-		-	-	1910	-	np	n		-	book	1

Black Outline Edition One-inch Map, CCR 1/-, based on 59.Oy (59.Oo, OSPR 3/19). 1. Recorded with the heading *Training for war* in *Report on the examination for admission to the Staff Colleges at Camberley and Quetta, held in February-March 1922. With copies of the examination papers and remarks of the examiners thereon.* London: HMSO, 1922.

Sheet 60 *Welshpool*   Revised 1903-4   27 by 18

1	2	3	4	5	6	7	8	9	10	11	12	13
1908	osew	-		-	-	1908	A	1/6,2/-,2/6	n	8/08	60.Ou	Cpt-m	
1908	osew	-		-	-	1908	A	1/6,2/-,3/-	n		60.Ov	Cu-m	

1	2	3	4	5	6	7	8	9	10	11	12	13

Sheet 61 *Shrewsbury*   Revised 1904-5   27 by 18

1908	ose	-	-	-	1908	A	1/6,2/-,2/6	n	7/08	61.Ou	Cpt-m	
1908	ose	7.13	-	5.13r	1913	C	1/6,2/-,2/6	n		61.1x	Cu-m	1
1908	ose	1.21	-	5.13r	1913	C	np	n		61.1p	Cu-m	
1908	ose	1.21	-	5.13r	1913	C	np	n		-	book	2

1. Some copies were supplied for use in the Officers' Training Corps, Shrewsbury School contingent. 2. Recorded with the heading *Training for war* in *Report on the examination for admission to the Staff Colleges at Camberley and Quetta, held in February-March 1922. With copies of the examination papers and remarks of the examiners thereon.* London: HMSO, 1922. The print code, probably 1.21, has been poorly erased.

Sheet 62 a. *Lichfield* b. *Cannock Chase*   Revised 1905   27 by 18

1908	ose.a	-	-	-	1908	A	1/6,2/-,2/6	n	7/08	62.Ou	Cpt-m	
1908	ose.x	11.11	-	9.11r	1911	A	1/6,2/-,2/6	n		62.1u	Cu-m	
1908	ose.b	7.14+	-	6.14r	1914	C	1/6,2/-,2/6	n		62.2x	Cu-m	
1908	ose.b	7.14+	-	6.14r	1914	C:	1/6,2/-,3/-	n		62.2y	Cu-m	

Sheet 63 *Leicester*   Revised 1905-6   27 by 18

1909	ose	-	-	-	1909	A	1/6,2/-,2/6	n	3/09	63.Ou	Cpt-m	
1909	ose	6.12	-	5.12r	1912	C	1/6,2/-,2/6	n		63.1x	Cu-m	
1909	ose	6.12	-	5.12r	1912	C:	1/6,2/-,3/-	n		63.1y	Cu	
1909	ose	6.12	-	5.12r	1912	C	np	n		63.1z	Cu-m	

Sheet 64 a. *Oakham* b. *Melton Mowbray, Oakham and Stamford*   Revised 1906   27 by 18

1909	ose.a	-	-	-	1909	A	1/6,2/-,2/6	n	3/09	64.Ou	Cpt-m	
1909	ose.x	3.12	-	2.12r	1912	A	1/6,2/-,2/6	n		64.1u.1	Cu-m	
1909	ose.b	3.12	-	2.12r	1912	A	1/6,2/-,2/6	n		64.1u.2	Cu-m	
1909	ose.b	3.12	-	2.12r	1912	C:	1/6,2/-,3/-	n		64.1y	Cu-m	
1909	ose.b	3.12	-	2.12r	1912	C	np	n		64.1z	Cu-m	

Sheet 65 *Peterborough and Wisbech*   Revised 1906-7   27 by 18

1910	ose	-	-	-	1910	A	1/6,2/-,2/6	n	5/10	65.Ou	Cpt-m	
1910	ose	3.12	-	1.12r	1912	A	1/6,2/-,2/6	n		65.1u	Cu-m	
1910	ose	3.12	-	1.12r	1912	A	1/6,2/-,3/-	n		65.1v	Cu	1
1910	ose	3.12	-	1.12r	1912	C.	1/6,2/-,3/-	n		65.1y	Cu-m	1
1910	ose	3.12	-	1.12r	1912	C	np	n		65.1z	BL-r	

1. Sheets 4, 65, 95, 111 are the only confirmed cases of a change of copyright statement combined with the 1/6,2/-,3/- price state; see also sheets 66 and 97.

Sheet 66 a. *Swaffham* b. *King's Lynn and Swaffham*   Revised 1907-8   27 by 18

1910	ose.a	-	-	s	1910	A	1/6,2/-,2/6	n	12/10	66.Ou	Cpt-m	
1910	ose.b	4.12	-	4.12rs	1912	A	1/6,2/-,2/6	n		66.1u	Cu-m	
1910	ose.b	4.12	-	4.12rs	1912	A	1/6,2/-,3/-	n		66.1v	Cu-m	
1910	ose.b	4.12	-	4.12rs	1912	C	1/6,2/-,3/-	n		66.1y		

Black Outline Edition One-inch Map, CCR 1/-, based on 66.1y (66.1o, OSPR 3/19). KGM 66.1y has not been recorded (the copies he cited being 66.1v), and thus cannot be verified. But the fact that the outline printing has a CCR copyright statement suggests that it may indeed exist, or at least have been prepared. There are few confirmed cases of a change of copyright statement combined with the 1/6,2/-, 3/- price state; see sheets 4, 65, 95, 111, also 97.

Sheet 67 *Norwich*   Revised 1908   27 by 18

1910	ose	-	-	s	1910	A	1/6,2/-,2/6	n	12/10	67.Ou	Cpt	
1910	ose	4.12	-	4.12rs	1912	A	1/6,2/-,2/6	n		67.1u	Cu-m	
1910	ose	4.12	-	4.12rs	1912	A	1/6,2/-,3/-	n		67.1v	Cu-m	

Overlap: 9 by 18 miles with sheet 68.

1	2	3	4	5	6	7	8	9	10	11	12	13

Sheet 68 a. *Great Yarmouth* b. *Great Yarmouth and Lowestoft*   Revised 1907-8   18 by 27

1910	ose.a	-	-	s	1910	A	1/6,2/-,2/6	n	12/10	68.Ou	Cpt-m	
1910	ose.b	4.12	-	4.12rs	1912	A	1/6,2/-,2/6	n		68.1u	PC	
1910	ose.b	4.12	-	4.12rs	1912	A	1/6,2/-,3/-	n		68.1v	Cu-m	1
1910	ose.b	4.12	-	4.12rs	1912	A	1/6,2/-,3/-	n		-	Cu-m	1
1910	ose.b	4.12	-	4.12rs	1912	A	1/6,2/-,3/-	n		-	Cu-m	1

Overlaps: 9 by 3 miles with sheet 58, 9 by 18 with 67, 9 by 6 with 77. *Black Outline Edition One-inch Map,* ARRR 1/-, based on 68.1v (68.1o, OSPR 1918/2). KGM 68.1y omitted (see page 82). 1. The 3/- price statement on these three versions is differently lettered – the first has "3/-, net", the other two have "3/- net", one with a faint flattened "3", the other with a bold and rounded "3".

Sheet 69 *Aberystwyth*   Revised 1908-9   27 by 18

1912	osew	-	-	s	1912	A	1/6,2/-,2/6	n	8/12	69.Ou	Cpt-m	
1912	osew	-	-	s	1913	C	1/6,2/-,2/6	n		69.Ox	Cu-m	1
1912	osew	12.20	-	s	1913	C	np	n		69.Op	Cu-m	

1. The change in date and value of the magnetic variation (17°45'W to 17°36'W) is unusual in a state without a reprint code but with an altered copyright statement.

Sheet 70 unnamed [*Newtown*]   Revised 1908   27 by 18

| 1912 | osew.x | - | - | s | 1912 | A | 1/6,2/-,2/6 | n | 3/12 | 70.Ou | Cpt-m | |
| 1912 | osew.x | - | - | s | 1912 | A | 1/6,2/-,3/- | n | | 70.Ov | BL-r | |

Ellis Martin covers with names *Newtown and District* and *Knighton and District* (copy NLW) were issued for this sheet.

Sheet 71 a. *Ludlow* b. *Bridgnorth and Ludlow*   Revised 1906-7   27 by 18

1910	ose.a	-	-	-	1910	A	1/6,2/-,2/6	n	6/10	71.Ou	Cpt-m	
1910	ose.b	3.14	-	1.14r	1914	C	1/6,2/-,2/6	n		71.1x	Cu-m	
1910	ose.b	3.14	-	1.14r	1914	C:	1/6,2/-,3/-	n		71.1y	Cu-m	1

1. A copy printed without hachures is recorded, in Ellis Martin covers (copy PC).

Sheet 72 *Birmingham*   Revised 1906-7   27 by 18

1910	ose	-	-	-	1910	A	1/6,2/-,2/6	n	3/10	72.Ou	Cpt	
1910	ose	4.12	-	4.12r	1912	A	1/6,2/-,2/6	n		72.1u	Cu-m	
1910	ose	4.12	-	4.12r	1912	A	1/6,2/-,3/-	n		72.1v	Cu-m	

Sheet 73 *Coventry and Rugby*   Revised 1904-7   27 by 18

1909	ose	-	-	-	1909	A	1/6,2/-,2/6	n	3/09	73.Ou	Cpt-m	
1909	ose	2.12	-	1.12r	1912	A	1/6,2/-,2/6	n		73.1u	Cu-m	
1909	ose	2.12	-	1.12r	1912	C.	1/6,2/-,3/-	n		73.1y	Cu-m	

Black Outline Edition One-inch Map, ARRR 1/-, based on 73.1u (OSPR 1918/2, 73.1o). KGM 73.1x omitted (see page 82).

Sheet 74 *Kettering*   Revised 1904-5   27 by 18

1908	ose	-	-	-	1908	A	1/6,2/-,2/6	n	10/08	74.Ou	Cpt-m	
1908	ose	2.10	-	2.10r	1910	A	1/6,2/-,2/6	n		74.1u	Cu-m	
1908	ose	5.12+	-	4.12r	1912	A	1/6,2/-,2/6	n		74.2u	Cu-m	
1913	ose	7.13	-	7.13r	1913	C	1/6,2/-,2/6	n		74.Rx	Cu-m	1
1913	ose	7.13	-	7.13r	1913	C:	1/6,2/-,3/-	n		74.Ry	Cu-m	
1913	ose	7.13	-	7.13r	1913	C	np	n		74.Rz	Cu-m	

KGM 74.Ru omitted (see page 82). 1. Other than sheets 1, 3 and 5, which were given new publication dates when they were reissued with coverage of Scotland added, this is the only sheet in the series to be reissued with a significantly different publication date. There is no obvious reason why this occurred, though it has been suggested that a new stone had to be made, the original failing in some way.

Sheet 75 *Ramsey* — Revised 1905-7 — 27 by 18

1	2	3	4	5	6	7 8	9	10	11	12	13
1909	ose	-	-	-	1909	A 1/6,2/-,2/6	n	12/09	75.Ou	Cpt-m	
1909	ose.x	11.11	-	10.11r	1911	A 1/6,2/-,2/6	n		75.1u	Cu-m	
1909	ose.x	11.11	-	10.11r	1911	A 1/6,2/-,3/-	n		75.1v	Cu-m	

Ellis Martin covers have the sheet name *Huntingdon and District*.

Sheet 76 a. *Thetford* b. *Soham and Thetford* — Revised 1905-7 — 27 by 18

1	2	3	4	5	6	7 8	9	10	11	12	13
1909	ose.a	-	-	-	1909	A 1/6,2/-,2/6	n	12/09	76.Ou	Cpt-m	
1909	ose.b	6.12	-	4.12r	1912	A 1/6,2/-,2/6	n		76.1u	Cu-m	
1909	ose.b	6.12	-	4.12r	1912	A 1/6,2/-,3/-	n		76.1v	Cu-m	

Sheet 77 a. *Harleston* b. *Bungay, Harleston and Diss* — Revised 1905-7 — 27 by 18

1	2	3	4	5	6	7 8	9	10	11	12	13
1909	ose.a	-	-	-	1909	A 1/6,2/-,2/6	n	7/09	77.Ou	Cpt-m	
1909	ose.b	5.12	-	5.12r	1912	C 1/6,2/-,2/6	n		77.1x	Cu-m	1
1909	ose.b	5.12	-	5.12r	1912	C: 1/6,2/-,3/-	n		77.1y	Cu-m	

Overlaps: 9 by 6 miles with sheet 68, 9 by 12 with 88. 1. This is the earliest known printing to carry the new "Crown Copyright Reserved" copyright statement.

Sheet 78 unnamed [*Cardigan*] — Revised 1909 — 27 by 18

1	2	3	4	5	6	7 8	9	10	11	12	13
1911	osew.x	-	-	s	1911	A 1/6,2/-,2/6	n	1/12	78.Ou	Cpt-m	

Black Outline Edition One-inch Map, ARRR 1/-, based on 78.Ou (78.Oo, OSPR 1918/3). The adjoining sheet diagram erroneously shows an overlap on to sheet 89. Ellis Martin covers with name *Cardigan and District* were issued for this sheet.

Sheet 79 *Lampeter* — Revised 1908-9 — 27 by 18

1	2	3	4	5	6	7 8	9	10	11	12	13
1912	osew	-	-	s	1912	A 1/6,2/-,2/6	n	10/12	79.Ou	Cpt-m	

Black Outline Edition One-inch Map, ARRR 1/-, based on 79.Ou (79.Oo, OSPR 1918/2). See figure 3.

Sheet 80 unnamed [*New Radnor*] — Revised 1908 — 27 by 18

1	2	3	4	5	6	7 8	9	10	11	12	13
1911	osew.x	-	-	s	1911	A 1/6,2/-,2/6	n	1/12	80.Ou	Cpt-m	
1911	osew.x	-	-	s	1911	A 1/6,2/-,3/-	n		80.Ov	Cu-m	
1911	osew.x	-	-	s	1911	A np	n		80.Ow	BL-r	

Ellis Martin covers with name *New Radnor and District* were issued for this sheet.

Sheet 81 a. *Bromyard* b. *Leominster, Great Malvern, and Bromyard* Revised 1907 — 27 by 18

1	2	3	4	5	6	7 8	9	10	11	12	13
1910	ose.a	-	-	-	1910	A 1/6,2/-,2/6	n	7/10	81.Ou	Cpt-m	
1910	ose.b	6.12	-	6.12r	1912	C 1/6,2/-,2/6	n		81.1x	Cu-m	
1910	ose.b	6.12	-	6.12r	1912	C: 1/6,2/-,3/-	n		81.1y	Cu-m	

Sheet 82 *Stratford on Avon and Worcester* — Revised 1906-7 — 27 by 18

1	2	3	4	5	6	7 8	9	10	11	12	13
1910	ose	-	-	-	1910	A 1/6,2/-,2/6	n	3/10	82.Ou	Cpt-m	
1910	ose	6.12	-	5.12r	1912	C 1/6,2/-,2/6	n		82.1x	Cu-m	
1910	ose	6.12	-	5.12r	1912	C: 1/6,2/-,3/-	n		82.1y	Cu-m	

Sheet 83 *Warwick and Banbury* — Revised 1904-7 — 27 by 18

1	2	3	4	5	6	7 8	9	10	11	12	13
1909	ose	-	-	-	1909	A 1/6,2/-,2/6	n	7/09	83.Ou	Cpt-m	
1909	ose	1.14	-	12.13r	1914	C 1/6,2/-,2/6	n		83.1x	Cu-m	
1909	ose	1.14	-	12.13r	1914	C: 1/6,2/-,3/-	n		83.1y	Cu-m	

Sheet 84 *Northampton and Bedford* — Revised 1904-5 — 27 by 18

1	2	3	4	5	6	7 8	9	10	11	12	13
1908	ose	-	-	-	1908	A 1/6,2/-,2/6	n	7/08	84.Ou	Cpt-m	
1908	ose	4.12	-	1.12r	1912	A 1/6,2/-,2/6	n		84.1u	Cu-m	
1908	ose	4.12	-	1.12r	1912	A 1/6,2/-,3/-	n		84.1v	Cu-m	

1	2	3	4	5	6	7	8	9	10	11	12	13

Sheet 85 a. *Cambridge* b. *Cambridge and Royston* — Revised 1904-5 — 27 by 18

1	2	3	4	5	6	7 8	9	10	11	12	13
1908	ose.a	-	-	-	1908	A 1/6,2/-,2/6	n	5/08	85.0u	Cpt-m	
1908	ose.x	2.11	-	2.11r*	1911	A 1/6,2/-,2/6	n		85.1u	BL-c	1
1908	ose.b	10.12+	-	9.12r	1912	C 1/6,2/-,2/6	n		85.2x	Cu-m	
1908	ose.b	9.14++	-	9.14r	1914	C 1/6,2/-,2/6	n		85.3x.2	PC	2
1908	ose.x	9.14++	-	-	1914	C 1/6,2/-,2/6	n		85.3x.1	Cu	2,3
1908	ose.x	9.14++	-	-	1914	C 1/6,2/-,3/6	n		85.3y.1	Cu-m	4
1908	ose.x	9.14++	-	-	1914	C: 1/6,2/-,3/-	n		85.3y.2	PC	5
1908	ose.x	9.14++	-	-	1914	C. 1/6,2/-,3/-	n		85.3y.3	BL-r	5

1. Railway stations were added to the legend of this printing, only to disappear again on the next. 2. KGM listed these two states the other way round in the April 1989 supplement to his monograph, but since the later states all have no railway revision date or sheet name, the sequence offered here would seem the more probable. 3. This is only known instance of the removal of a sheet name after 1912. 4. The 3/6 price would have been the result of poor revision to the plate when the price increase from 2/6 to 3/- occurred. 5. The price is now clearly 3/-: the marginalia centre bottom is differently lettered on these two versions: the first has "…...folded in Sections" and "(362)" as the indication of the level of the sea, the second "……folded in sections" and "(326)". See figure 16.

Sheet 86 a. *Bury St. Edmunds* b. *Newmarket Sudbury and Bury St. Edmunds* — Revised 1905-6 — 27 by 18

1	2	3	4	5	6	7 8	9	10	11	12	13
1908	ose.a	-	-	-	1908	A 1/6,2/-,2/6	n	5/08	86.0u	Cpt	
1908	ose.b	7.12	-	5.12r	1912	A 1/6,2/-,2/6	n		86.1u	BL-c	
1908	ose.b	9.14+	-	9.14r	1914	C 1/6,2/-,2/6	n		86.2x	Cu-m	1
1908	ose.b	9.14+	-	9.14r	1914	C 1/6,2/-,3/6	n		-	PC	2
1908	ose.b	9.14+	-	9.14r	1914	C: 1/6,2/-,3/-	n		86.2y	Cu-m	3
1908	ose.b	9.14+	-	9.14r	1914	C. 1/6,2/-,3/-	n		-	Cu-m	4

Black Outline Edition One-inch Map, CCR 1/-, based on 86.2y (86.2o, OSPR 1918/3). 1. A copy is recorded with *Cambridge University School of Instruction : Pembroke College : No.34.* stamped on the integral cover (copy PC). There is no sign of change on the map itself. 2. The 3/6 price would have been the result of poor revision to the plate when the price increase from 2/6 to 3/- occurred. 3. "…….folded in Sections". 4. "……..folded in sections" (see page 82).

Sheet 87 *Ipswich* — Revised 1905-6 — 27 by 18

1	2	3	4	5	6	7 8	9	10	11	12	13
1908	ose	-	-	-	1908	A 1/6,2/-,2/6	n	3/08	87.0u	Cpt-m	
1908	ose	10.10	-	9.10r	1910	A 1/6,2/-,2/6	n		87.1u	Cu-m	
1908	ose	6.12+	-	4.12r	1912	A 1/6,2/-,2/6	n		87.2u	Cu-m	
1908	ose	6.12+	-	4.12r	1912	A 1/6,2/-,3/-	n		87.2v	Cu-m	
1908	ose	6.12+	-	4.12r	1912	A np	n		87.2w	Cu-m	

Overlap: 9 by 15 miles with sheet 88.

Sheet 88 *Saxmundham* — Revised 1905-7 — 18 by 27

1	2	3	4	5	6	7 8	9	10	11	12	13
1908	ose	-	-	-	1908	A 1/6,2/-,2/6	n	12/08	88.0u	Cpt-m	
1908	ose	8.09	-	7.09r	1909	A 1/6,2/-,2/6	n		88.1u	Cu-m	
1908	ose	9.14+	-	8.14r	1914	C 1/6,2/-,2/6	n		88.2x	Cu-m	
1908	ose	9.14+	-	-	1914	C: 1/6,2/-,3/-	n		88.2y	Cu-m	

Overlaps: 9 by 12 miles with sheet 77, 9 by 15 with 87.

Sheet 89 *Fishguard and St. David's* — Revised 1909 — 27 by 18

1	2	3	4	5	6	7 8	9	10	11	12	13
1912	osew	-	-	s	1912	A 1/6,2/-,2/6	n	10/12	89.0u	Cpt-m	
1912	osew	9.14	-	9.14rs	1914	C 1/6,2/-,2/6	n		89.1x	Cu-m	

Sheet 90 *Carmarthen*   Revised 1909   27 by 18

1	2	3	4	5	6	7	8	9	10	11	12	13
1911	osew.x	-		s	1911	A	1/6,2/-,2/6	n	1/12	90.Ou	Cpt-m	
1911	osew	9.14	-	10.14rs	1914	C	1/6,2/-,2/6	n		90.1x	Cu-m	1

Overlap: 13½ by 3 miles with sheet 100. 1. It is peculiar that the print code should be in advance of the railway revision date.

Sheet 91 *Valley of Towy*   Revised 1907-9   27 by 18

1	2	3	4	5	6	7	8	9	10	11	12	13
1912	osew	-		s	1912	A	1/6,2/-,2/6	n	10/12	91.Ou	Cpt-m	
1912	osew	10.14	-	10.14rs	1914	C	1/6,2/-,2/6	n		91.1x	Cu	

Sheet 92 *Brecon and Abergavenny*   Revised 1904-9   27 by 18

1	2	3	4	5	6	7	8	9	10	11	12	13
1912	osew.x	-		s	1912	A	1/6,2/-,2/6	n	3/12	92.Ou	Cpt-m	
1912	osew	8.13	-	8.13rs	1913	C	1/6,2/-,2/6	n		92.1x	Cu-m	
1912	osew	8.13	-	8.13rs	1913	C:	1/6,2/-,3/-	n		92.1y	BL-r	

Sheet 93 *Ross*   Revised 1903-8   27 by 18

1	2	3	4	5	6	7	8	9	10	11	12	13
1910	ose	-	-	-	1910	A	1/6,2/-,2/6	n	3/10	93.Ou	Cpt-m	

Black Outline Edition One-inch Map, ARRR 1/-, based on 93.Ou (93.Oo, OSPR 1918/3).

Sheet 94 a. *Cheltenham* b. *Gloucester and Cheltenham*   Revised 1903-4   27 by 18

1	2	3	4	5	6	7	8	9	10	11	12	13
1907	ose.a	-	-	-	1907	A	1/6,2/-,2/6	n	12/07	94.Ou	Cpt-m	
1907	ose.x	7.11	-	6.11r	1911	A	1/6,2/-,2/6	n		94.1u	Cu-m	
1907	ose.b	6.12+	-	6.12r	1912	A	1/6,2/-,2/6	n		94.2u	Cu-m	1
1907	ose.b	9.14++	-	8.14r	1914	A	1/6,2/-,2/6	n		-	Cu-m	
1907	ose.b	9.14++	-		1914	A	1/6,2/-,2/6	n		94.3u	Cu-m	

Black Outline Edition Map One-inch Map, ARRR 1/-, based on 9.14 with railway revision to 8.14 (94.3o, OSPR 1918/2). 1. Some copies were supplied for use in Cheltenham Training College.

Sheet 95 a. *Chipping Norton and Bicester* b. *Chipping Norton, Woodstock and Bicester*

                                                             Revised 1902   27 by 18

1	2	3	4	5	6	7	8	9	10	11	12	13
1907	ose.a	-	-	-	1907	A	1/6,2/-,2/6	n	10/07	95.Ou	Cpt-m	
1907	ose.b	5.12	-	4.12r	1912	A	1/6,2/-,2/6	n		95.1u	Cu-m	
1907	ose.b	8.14+	-	8.14r	1914	A	1/6,2/-,2/6	n		95.2u	Bc	
1907	ose.b	8.14+	-	8.14r	1914	A	1/6,2/-,3/-	n		95.2v	Cu-m	1
1907	ose.b	8.14+	-	8.14r	1914	C:	1/6,2/-,3/-	n		95.2y	BL-r	1

Black Outline Edition One-inch Map, ARRR 1/-, based on 95.2v (95.2o, OSPR 1918/3). See figure 18. 1. Sheets 4, 65, 95, 111 are the only confirmed cases of a change of copyright statement combined with the 1/6,2/-,3/- price state; see also sheets 66 and 97.

Sheet 96 a. *Leighton Buzzard* b. *Buckingham, Leighton Buzzard and Luton*

                                                             Revised 1902   27 by 18

1	2	3	4	5	6	7	8	9	10	11	12	13
1907	ose.a	-	-	-	1907	A	1/6,2/-,2/6	n	10/07	96.Ou	Cpt-m	
1907	ose.x	1.12	-	11.11r	1912	A	1/6,2/-,2/6	n		96.1u	Cu-m	
1907	ose.b	1.14+	-	1.14r	1914	C	1/6,2/-,2/6	n		96.2x	Cu-m	

Black Outline Edition One-inch Map, CCR 1/-, based on 96.2x (96.2o, OSPR 1918/2).

Sheet 97 *Hertford*   Revised 1902-3   27 by 18

1	2	3	4	5	6	7	8	9	10	11	12	13
1907	ose	-	-	-	1907	A	1/6,2/-,2/6	n	9/07	97.Ou	Cpt-m	
1907	ose	-	-	-	1907	A	1/6,2/-,3/-	n		97.Ov	Cu-m	
1907	ose	-	-	-	1907	C	1/6,2/-,3/-	n		97.Oy		

An outline printing, with water in blue and contours in red, is recorded, probably based on 97.Ou with the price deleted (copy PC). The copy recorded by KGM at LSE as 97.Oy (his working notes confirm that he meant CCR 3/-, not 2/6 as given in his book) is currently lost, possibly destroyed. No other copy has yet been located, thus it cannot be verified. There are few confirmed cases of a change of copyright statement combined with the 1/6,2/-,3/- price state; see sheets 4, 65, 95, 111, also 66.

Sheet 98 *Braintree*   Revised 1902-4   27 by 18

1907	ose	-	-	-	1907	A	1/6,2/-,2/6	n	10/07	98.Ou	Cpt-m	
1907	ose	1.14	12.13	12.13r	1914	C	1/6,2/-,2/6	n		98.1x	Cu-m	
1907	ose	1.14	12.13	12.13r	1914	C.	1/6,2/-,3/-	n		98.1y	Cu-m	

Overlap: 5 by 18 miles with sheet 99. *Black Outline Edition One-inch Map,* CCR 1/-, based on 98.1y (98.1o, OSPR 1918/2).

Sheet 99 *Colchester and Harwich*   Revised 1904   27 by 18

1907	ose	-	-	-	1907	A	1/6,2/-,2/6	n	10/07	99.Ou	Cpt-m	
1907	ose	6.12	-	5.12r	1912	C	1/6,2/-,2/6	n		-	Mg	1
1907	ose	6.14+	-	5.14r	1914	C	1/6,2/-,2/6	n		99.2x	Cu-m	
1907	ose	6.14+	-	5.14r	1914	C:	1/6,2/-,3/-	n		99.2y	Cu-m	2
1907	ose	6.14+	-	5.14r	1914	C:	1/6,2/-,3/-	n		-	Cu-m	2

Overlap: 5 by 18 miles with sheet 98. *Black Outline Edition One-inch Map,* CCR 1/-, based on 99.2y (99.2o, OSPR 1918/4). See also figure 10. 1. This is the only copy of this state recorded: it is a copy folded in covers held in the department's reserve collection. 2. Two printings of this state are recorded: the first listed has distinctly darker hachures, and "(Large Sheet Series)" set above the line of the sheet number, "Price" under "are given" and the sections price "3/- net"; the other has "Price" under "....n in Feet" and "3/-, net".

Sheet 100 unnamed [*Pembroke*]   Revised 1909   31½ by 18

| 1912 | osew.x | - | - | s | 1912 | A | 1/6,2/-,2/6 | n | 3/12 | 100.Ou | Cpt-m | |

Overlap: 13½ by 3 miles with sheet 90. Some indexes show Grassholm Island and The Smalls as present in this sheet, but (barring unrecorded printings), they are not covered in the Large Sheet Series. Ellis Martin covers with name *Pembroke and District* were issued for this sheet.

Sheet 101 unnamed [*Llanelly*]   Revised 1904-9   27 by 18

| 1911 | osew.x | - | - | s | 1911 | A | 1/6,2/-,2/6 | n | 6/11 | 101.Ou | Cpt-m | |
| 1911 | osew.x | - | - | s | 1911 | A | 1/6,2/-,3/- | n | | 101.Ov | Cu-m | |

Ellis Martin covers with name *Llanelly and District* were issued for this sheet.

Sheet 102 *Swansea and Merthyr Tydfil*   Revised 1904-8   27 by 18

| 1911 | osew | - | - | - | 1911 | A | 1/6,2/-,2/6 | n | 3/11 | 102.Ou | Cpt-m | 1 |
| 1911 | osew | - | - | - | 1911 | A | 1/6,2/-,3/- | n | | 102.Ov | Cu | |

Overlap: 21 by 6 miles with sheet 110. 1. Some copies were supplied for use in Cyfarthfa Castle municipal secondary school, Merthyr Tydfil.

Sheet 103 a. *Newport and Pontypool* b. *Newport, Blaenavon and Pontypool*

                Revised 1904   27 by 18

1908	osew.a	-	-	-	1908	A	1/6,2/-,2/6	n	10/08	103.Ou	Cpt-m	
1908	osew.b	7.12	5.12	5.12r	1912	C	1/6,2/-,2/6	n		103.1x	NLW	1
1908	osew.b	9.14+	5.12	9.14r	1914	C	1/6,2/-,2/6	n		103.2x	EXg	
1908	osew.b	9.14+	5.12	9.14r	1914	C:	1/6,2/-,3/-	n		103.2y	Cu-m	

Overlap: 6 by 6 miles with sheet 110. *Black Outline Edition One-inch Map,* CCR 1/-, based on 103.2y (103.2o, OSPR 1918/3). 1. The only copy so far recorded was supplied for use in the Lewis' School, Pengam. It thus remains open to question whether copies of this printing were also made for sale to the public, but for a revised reprint to have been designated solely for educational use would for this series be unusual.

Sheet 104 *Dursley*   Revised 1903-4   27 by 18

| 1907 | ose | - | - | - | 1907 | A | 1/6,2/-,2/6 | n | 10/07 | 104.Ou | Cpt-m | |
| 1907 | ose | - | - | - | 1907 | C. | 1/6,2/-,3/- | n | | 104.Oy | Cu-m | |

Black Outline Edition One-inch Map, ARRR 1/-, based on 104.Ou (104.Oo, OSPR 1918/2).

Sheet 105 *Swindon and Cirencester*   Revised 1902-3   27 by 18

1	2	3	4	5	6	7 8	9	10	11	12	13
1908	ose	-	-	-	1908	A 1/6,2/-,2/6	n	12/08	105.Ou	Cpt-m	
1908	ose	7.10	-	6.10r	1910	A 1/6,2/-,2/6	n		105.1u	Cu-m	
1908	ose	9.12+	4.12	6.12r	1912	A 1/6,2/-,2/6	n		105.2u	Cu-m	1

Black Outline Edition One-inch Map, ARRR 1/-, based on 105.2u (105.2o, OSPR 1918/4). 1. A copy is recorded printed without the blue water plate (copy PC).

Sheet 106 a. *Abingdon* b. *Oxford and Henley on Thames*   Revised 1902   27 by 18

1	2	3	4	5	6	7 8	9	10	11	12	13
1908	ose.a	-	-	-	1908	A 1/6,2/-,2/6	n	3/08	106.Ou	Cpt-m	
1908	ose.a	8.10	5.10	5.10i	1910	A 1/6,2/-,2/6	n		106.1u	Cu-m	
1908	ose.b	5.12+	4.12	4.12i	1912	A 1/6,2/-,2/6	n		106.2u	Cu-m	
1908	ose.b	10.14++	10.14	10.14r	1914	C 1/6,2/-,2/6	n		106.3x	Cu-m	
1908	ose.b	10.14++	10.14	10.14r	1914	C: 1/6,2/-,3/-	n		106.3y	Cu-m	

Black Outline Edition One-inch Map, CCR 1/-, based on 106.3y (106.3o, OSPR 1918/3).

Sheet 107 a. *Rickmansworth* b. *Watford and High Wycombe*   Revised 1902   27 by 18

1	2	3	4	5	6	7 8	9	10	11	12	13
1908	ose.a	-	-	-	1908	A 1/6,2/-,2/6	n	12/08	107.Ou	Cpt-m	
1908	ose.a	7.10	2.10	6.10r	1910	A 1/6,2/-,2/6	n		107.1u	Cu-m	
1908	ose.b	6.12+	2.10	5.12r	1912	A 1/6,2/-,2/6	n		107.2u	Cu-m	1
1908	ose.b	6.12+	2.10	5.12r	1912	C. 1/6,2/-,3/-	n		107.2y	Cu-m	
1908	ose.bo	6.12+	2.10	5.12r	1912	C. 1/6,2/-,3/-	n		-	Rg	
1908	ose.b	6.12+	2.10	5.12r	1912	C np	n		107.2z	Cu-m	

Black Outline Edition One-inch Map, ARRR 1/-, based on 107.2u (107.2o, OSPR 1918/2). 1. Also recorded overprinted with a 10,000-yard and quartered 2000-yard grid in a deep red, presumably for artillery training purposes. The principal squares are lettered A to O, the 2000 yard subdivisions 1 to 25, quartered a to d using pecked lines. The origin is in the north-west corner, with grid lines parallel to the sheet lines of the map (copy PC). See figure 6, and appendix 2.

Sheet 108 a. *Romford* b. *N.E. London and Epping Forest*   Revised 1902-3   27 by 18

1	2	3	4	5	6	7 8	9	10	11	12	13
1908	ose.a	-	-	-	1908	A 1/6,2/-,2/6	n	12/08	108.Ou	Cpt-m	
1908	ose.a	4.09	-	4.09r	1909	A 1/6,2/-,2/6	n		108.1u	PC	1
1908	ose.b	9.12+	3.10	8.12r	1912	A 1/6,2/-,2/6	n		108.2u	BL-c	
1908	ose.b	7.14++	6.14	6.14r	1914	C 1/6,2/-,2/6	n		108.3x	Cu-m	
1908	ose.b	7.14++	-	-	1914	C 1/6,2/-,2/6	n		-	Cu-m	
1908	ose.b	7.14++	-	-	1914	C: 1/6,2/-,3/-	n		108.3y	Cu-m	
1908	ose.bo	7.14++	-	-	1914	C: 1/6,2/-,3/-	n		-	Cu-m	2

Overlap: 3 by 18 miles with sheet 109. *Black Outline Edition One-inch Map,* CCR 1/-, see note 2 (108.3o, OSPR 1918/2). 1. See figure 5. 2. Apparently using the black plate prepared for the Black Outline Edition; it has "Price 1/- net" printed above the copyright statement and the usual price statement repositioned below; the price 1/- may be deleted by means of a ruled black line (see also sheet 115).

Sheet 109 *Shoeburyness*   Revised 1902-4   27 by 18

1	2	3	4	5	6	7 8	9	10	11	12	13
1908	ose	-	-	-	1908	A 1/6,2/-,2/6	n	11/08	109.Ou	Cpt	
1908	ose	6.09	-	4.09r	1909	A 1/6,2/-,2/6	n		109.1u	Cu-m	
1908	ose	6.09	-	4.09r	1909	A 1/6,2/-,3/-	n		109.1v	Cu-m	

Overlap: 3 by 18 miles with sheet 108.

Sheet 110 *Bridgend*   Revised 1904   27 by 18

1	2	3	4	5	6	7 8	9	10	11	12	13
1909	osew	-	-	-	1909	A 1/6,2/-,2/6	n	9/09	110.Ou	Cpt-m	
1909	osew.x	8.11	8.11	8.11r	1911	A 1/6,2/-,2/6	n		110.1u	PC	
1909	osew.x	8.11	8.11	8.11r	1911	A 1/6,2/-,3/-	n		110.1v	Cu-m	

Overlaps: 21 by 6 miles with sheet 102, 6 by 6 with 103, 6 by 12 with 111.

Sheet 111 *Cardiff and Weston super Mare*   Revised 1904-5   27 by 18

1908	osew	-	-	-	1907	A	1/6,2/-,2/6	n	2/08	111.Ou	Cpt-m	
1908	osew	4.09	-	3.09r	1909	A	1/6,2/-,2/6	n		111.1u	PC	
1908	osew	4.09	-	3.09r	1909	A	1/6,2/-,3/-	n		111.1v	Sg	1
1908	osew	4.09	-	3.09r	1909	C.	1/6,2/-,3/-	n		111.1y	BL-r	1

Overlap: 6 by 12 miles with sheet 110. *Black Outline Edition One-inch Map,* ARRR 1/-, based on 111.1v (111.1o, OSPR 1918/3). 1. Sheets 4, 65, 95, 111 are the only confirmed cases of a change of copyright statement combined with the 1/6,2/-,3/- price state; see also sheets 66 and 97.

Sheet 112 a. *Bath* b. *Bristol and Bath*   Revised 1903-5   27 by 18

1907	ose.a	-	-	-	1907	A	1/6,2/-,2/6	n	11/07	112.Ou	Cpt-m	
1907	ose.x	9.11	8.11	8.11r	1911	A	1/6,2/-,2/6	n		112.1u	Cu-m	
1907	ose.b	3.14+	1.14	1.14r	1914	C	1/6,2/-,2/6	n		112.2x	Cu-m	1
1907	ose.b	3.14+	1.14	1.14r	1914	C.	1/6,2/-,3/-	n		112.2y	Cu-m	

Black Outline Edition One-inch Map, CCR 1/-, based on 112.2y (112.2o, OSPR 1918/2). 1. Some copies were supplied for use by Bath Education Committee.

Sheet 113 *Marlborough*   Revised 1901-2   27 by 18

1908	ose	-	-	-	1908	A	1/6,2/-,2/6	n	12/08	113.Ou	Cpt-m	
1908	ose	1.11	-	12.10r	1911	A	1/6,2/-,2/6	n		113.1u	Cu-m	
1908	ose	6.12+	-	4.12r	1912	A	1/6,2/-,2/6	n		113.2u	Cu-m	
1908	ose	6.12+	-	4.12r	1912	A	1/6,2/-,3/-	n		113.2v	Cu-m	

KGM 113.Oo (*recte* 113.2o) omitted (see page 82).

Sheet 114 a. *Reading* b. *Reading and Newbury*   Revised 1901-2   27 by 18

1909	ose.a	-	-	-	1909	A	1/6,2/-,2/6	n	9/09	114.Ou	Cpt-m	
1909	ose.b	5.12	4.12	4.12r	1912	A	1/6,2/-,2/6	n		114.1u	Cu-m	
1909	ose.b	5.12	4.12	4.12r	1912	C.	1/6,2/-,3/-	n		114.1y	Cu-m	

Black Outline Edition One-inch Map, ARRR 1/-, based on 114.1u (114.1o, OSPR 1918/3). KGM 114.1x omitted (see p.82).

Sheet 115 a. *Weybridge* b. *Windsor and Richmond*   Revised 1901-2   27 by 18

1909	ose.a	-	-	-	1909	A	1/6,2/-,2/6	n	10/09	115.Ou	Cpt-m	
1909	ose.x	8.11	8.11	8.11r	1911	A	1/6,2/-,2/6	n		115.1u	Cu-m	1,2
1909	ose.x	8.11	8.11	8.11r	1911	A	1/6,2/-,3/-	n		115.1v.1	Cu-m	3
1909	ose.bo	8.11	8.11	8.11r	1911	A	1/-	n		-	PC	4,6
1909	ose.bo	8.11	8.11	8.11r	1911	A	1/6,2/-,3/-	n		115.1v.2	Cu-m	5,6
1909	ose.b	8.11	8.11	8.11r	1911	C.	1/6,2/-,3/-	n		115.1y	Cu-m	

Black Outline Edition One-inch Map, ARRR 1/- (115.1o, OSPR 1918/2). See also note 4. 1. Also recorded overprinted with a 12,000-yard and quartered 2000-yard grid in red, presumably for artillery training purposes. The principal squares are lettered A to L, the 2000 yard subdivisions 1 to 36, quartered a to d using thin lines. The origin is in the north-west corner, with grid lines parallel to the sheet lines of the map (copy PC). The squaring is apparently the same as appears on sheet 124 (qv). 2. Also recorded overprinted with a six-mile and quartered one-mile grid in red, presumably for artillery training purposes. The principal squares are lettered A to O, the one-mile subdivisions 1 to 36, quartered a to d using thin lines. The origin is in the north-west corner, with grid lines parallel to the sheet lines of the map. The red line at the outer limits of the six-mile squares around the edge of the sheet is present (copy PC). 3. Another printing as in note 2, with the overlay fitting slightly differently, perhaps because of the stretch of the paper. There is no red line representing the outer limit of the six-mile squares around the edge of the sheet (copy PC). See appendix 2. 4. This state was apparently prepared for the Black Outline Edition; it has "Price 1/- net" printed above the copyright statement. 5. In addition to the 1/- price as described in note 4, the usual price statement was repositioned below the copyright statement; the price 1/- may be deleted by means of a ruled black line (see also sheet 108). See figure 16. 6. The LSS heading is deleted. See figure 14.

Sheet 116 a. *Croydon and Sevenoaks* b. *Croydon, Gravesend, and Sevenoaks*

								Revised 1901-3		27 by 18	
1909	ose.a	-	-	-	1909	A	1/6,2/-,2/6	n	11/09	116.Ou	Cpt-m
1909	ose.b	5.12	-	5.12r	1912	A	1/6,2/-,2/6	n		116.1u	Cu-m
1909	ose.b	5.12	-	5.12r	1912	A	1/6,2/-,3/-	n		116.1v	Cu-m
1909	ose.bo	5.12	-	5.12r	1912	C.	1/6,2/-,3/-	n		116.1y	Cu-m
1909	ose.bo	5.12	-	5.12r	1912	C	np	n		116.1z	Mg

Black Outline Edition One-inch Map, ARRR 1/-, based on 116.1v (116.1o, OSPR 1918/2).

Sheet 117 *Chatham and Sheerness*

								Revised 1903-4		27 by 18	
1909	ose	-	-	-	1909	A	1/6,2/-,2/6	n	12/09	117.Ou	Cpt-m
1909	ose.x	8.11	-	5.11r	1911	A	1/6,2/-,2/6	n		117.1u	Cu-m
1909	ose.x	8.11	-	5.11r	1911	A	1/6,2/-,3/-	n		117.1v	Cu-m

Overlap: 9 by 16 miles with sheet 118. Ellis Martin covers have the sheet name *Maidstone and District.*

Small **sheets 273. 274. Parts of sheets 289. 290.** a. *East Kent (North)* Revised 1903-4 28 by 20

1906	ose.a	-	-	-	1906	A	1/6,2/-	n	6/06	118.Os	Cpt-m

Renumbered large **sheet 118** b. *Canterbury* c. *Canterbury and Margate*

1909	ose.b	-	-	-	1909	A	1/6,2/-,2/6	n		118.Ou	Cu-m
1909	ose.b	11.10	-	11.10r	1910	A	1/6,2/-,2/6	n	3/11	118.1u	Cpt-m
1909	ose.c	3.14+	-	12.13r	1914	C	1/6,2/-,2/6	n		118.2x	Cu-m
1909	ose.c	3.14+	-	12.13r	1914	C:	1/6,2/-,3/-	n		118.2y	Cu-m

Overlaps: 9 by 16 miles with sheet 117, 9 by 4 with 127. Imprint, sheet number, name and other marginal detail such as price and magnetic variation were altered when this combined small sheet was remodelled as a member of the large sheet series.

Sheet 119 *Barnstaple*

								Revised 1906-8		18 by 27	
1910	ose	-	-	-	1910	A	1/6,2/-,2/6	n	6/10	119.Ou	Cpt-m
1911	ose.x	8.11	-	8.11r	1911	A	1/6,2/-,2/6	n		119.1u	Cu-m

With an inset of Lundy Island. Overlap: 3 by 13 miles with sheet 129.

Sheet 120 *Exmoor*

								Revised 1906		27 by 18	
1909	ose	-	-	-	1909	A	1/6,2/-,2/6	n	11/09	120.Ou	Cpt-m
1909	ose	9.12	6.12	8.12r	1912	A	1/6,2/-,2/6	n		120.1u	Cu-m
1909	ose	9.12	6.12	8.12r	1912	A	1/6,2/-,3/-	n		120.1v	Cu-m

Sheet 121 *Bridgwater*

								Revised 1905		27 by 18	
1908	ose	-	-	-	1908	A	1/6,2/-,2/6	n	2/08	121.Ou	Cpt-m
1908	ose.x	6.11	-	6.11r*	1911	A	1/6,2/-,2/6	n		121.1u	Cu-m
1908	ose.x	6.11	-	6.11r*	1911	A	1/6,2/-,3/-	n		121.1v	Mg

Sheet 122 *Frome and Wincanton*

								Revised 1903-5		27 by 18	
1907	ose	-	-	-	1907	A	1/6,2/-,2/6	n	12/07	122.Ou	Cpt-m
1907	ose	10.10	-	10.10r	1910	A	1/6,2/-,2/6	n		122.1u	Cu-m
1907	ose	10.10	-	10.10r	1910	A	1/6,2/-,3/-	n		122.1v	Cu-m

KGM 122.1w omitted (see page 82).

Sheet 123 *Salisbury and Stonehenge*

								Revised 1901-3		27 by 18	
1908	ose	-	-	-	1908	A	1/6,2/-,2/6	n	3/08	123.Ou	Cpt-m
1908	ose	10.10	-	9.10r	1910	A	1/6,2/-,2/6	n		123.1u	Cu-m
1908	ose	6.12+	-	4.12r	1912	A	1/6,2/-,2/6	n		123.2u	Cu-m

Sheet 124 *Winchester and Alton*   Revised 1901   27 by 18

1	2	3	4	5	6	7	8	9	10	11	12	13
1909	ose	-	-	-	1909	A	1/6,2/-,2/6	n	11/09	124.Ou	Cpt-m	
1909	ose	6.12	-	5.12r	1912	A	1/6,2/-,2/6	n		124.1u	Cu-m	1,2
1909	ose	6.12	nd	5.12r	1912	C.	1/6,2/-,3/-	n		124.1y	Cu-m	

Black Outline Edition One-inch Map, ARRR 1/-, based on 124.1u (124.1o, OSPR 1918/3). 1. An outline printing, with water in blue and contours in red, is recorded, based on 124.1u with the price deleted. It was used at least twice for Officers' Training Corps examinations, in November 1919 and March 1920. The 1920 printing appears in *Report on the Examinations for Certificate "A" held in March, 1920, for cadets of the junior and senior divisions, Officers Training Corps. With copies of the examination papers.* London: HMSO, 1920. The print code is deleted, or has faded, from this issue. 2. Also recorded overprinted with a 12,000-yard and quartered 2000-yard grid in red, presumably for artillery training purposes. The principal squares are lettered A to L, the 2000 yard subdivisions 1 to 36, quartered a to d using thin lines. The origin is in the north-west corner, with grid lines parallel to the sheet lines of the map (copy PC). The squaring is apparently the same as appears on the first of the two sheet 115 examples (qv). See appendix 2.

Sheet 125 *Guildford and Horsham*   Revised 1901   27 by 18

1	2	3	4	5	6	7	8	9	10	11	12	13
1909	ose	-	-	-	1909	A	1/6,2/-,2/6	n	12/09	125.Ou	Cpt-m	
1909	ose.x	5.11	-	5.11r	1911	A	1/6,2/-,2/6	n		125.1u	Cu-m	
1909	ose	5.14+	5.14	5.14r	1914	C	1/6,2/-,2/6	n		125.2x	Cu-m	
1909	ose	5.14+	5.14	5.14r	1914	C:	1/6,2/-,3/-	n		125.2y	Cu-m	1
1909	ose.o	5.14+	5.14	5.14r	1914	C.	1/6,2/-,3/-	n		-	Cu-m	2

Black Outline Edition One-inch Map, CCR 1/-, based on 125.2y (125.2o, OSPR 1918/3). KGM made reference in a letter dated 10 January 1986 to his purchase of a coloured state with sheet price 1/- (see also sheets 108, 115), but nothing further is known of this. 1. "…..folded in Sections". 2. "…..folded in sections" (see page 82 and figure 17).

Sheet 126 a. *Tunbridge Wells and East Grinstead*   b. *Tunbridge Wells and Redhill*

                                          Revised 1901-3   27 by 18

1	2	3	4	5	6	7	8	9	10	11	12	13
1909	ose.a	-	-	-	1909	A	1/6,2/-,2/6	n	11/09	126.Ou	Cpt-m	
1909	ose.x	6.11	-	5.11r	1911	A	1/6,2/-,2/6	n		126.1u	Cu-m	
1909	ose.b	6.11,7.14	-	6.14r	1914	C	1/6,2/-,2/6	n		-	Og	1
1909	ose.b	6.11,8.14	-	6.14r	1914	C	1/6,2/-,2/6	n		126.2x	Cu-m	
1909	ose.b	6.11,8.14	-	6.14r	1914	C:	1/6,2/-,3/-	n		126.2y.1	Cu-m	2
1909	ose.bo	-	-	6.14r	1914	C.	1/6,2/-,3/-	n		126.2y.2	Cu-m	3
1909	ose.bo	4.20	-	1914i	1914	C	np	n		126.2p	Cu-m	

Black Outline Edition One-inch Map, CCR 1/-, based on 126.2y.1 (126.2o, OSPR 1918/2). KGM 126.2z omitted (see page 82). 1. A copy (PC) of the July 1914 printing is attached to the only known example of what appears to be an Ordnance Survey experimental standard series cover (H.9. See figure 9, and, for further discussion, page 37). It is in bookfold format with a *Diagram of sheets of the map* from 78 to 152 (on cloth, usually found as the adhesive back card attached to dissected maps before the first world war) pasted inside the front. Space is reserved in the lower half for sheet name and number, which are here overprinted in red. No retail price is given. There seems to be no reason to avoid the obvious date implications. The printing of the map is markedly different to that of August 1914. In spite of the issue date and identical railway revision date, the south-west side of the Groombridge triangle still appears as a single line "Disused Ry" rather than the double track in use on the 8.14. Furthermore the changes listed by KGM to post and telegraph facilities in the 8.14 printing (which he read as 6.14) have yet to be made. However the new sheet name and magnetic variation data are in place. 2. "…..folded in Sections". 3. "…..folded in sections" (see page 82).

Sheet 127 a. *Tenterden* b. *Ashford and Tenterden*   Revised 1903-4   27 by 18

1	2	3	4	5	6	7	8	9	10	11	12	13
1909	ose.a	-	-	-	1909	A	1/6,2/-,2/6	n	12/09	127.Ou	Cpt-m	
1909	ose.b	5.12	-	5.12r	1912	A	1/6,2/-,2/6	n		127.1u	Cu-m	
1909	ose.b	5.12	-	5.12r	1912	A	1/6,2/-,3/-	n		127.1v	Cu-m	

Overlaps: 9 by 4 miles with sheet 118, 9 by 14 with 128, 27 by 6 with 138.

Small sheets 305. 306. 321. Parts of sheets 289. 290. a. *East Kent (South)*   Revised 1904   28 by 18

| 1906 | ose.a | - | | - | - | 1906 | A | 1/6,2/- | n | 6/06 | 128.Os | Cpt-m |

Renumbered large **sheet 128** b. *Folkestone and Ashford* c. *Dover, Folkestone and Ashford*

1909	ose.b	-		-	-	1909	A	1/6,2/-,2/6	n		128.Ou	PC
1909	ose.c	7.12		-	7.12r	1912	A	1/6,2/-,2/6	n	11/12	128.1u	Cpt-m
1909	ose.c	7.12		-	7.12r	1912	A	1/6,2/-,3/-	n		128.1v	Cu-m
1909	ose.c	7.12		-	7.12r	1912	A	np	n		128.1w	Cu-m

Overlaps: 9 by 14 miles with sheet 127, 9 by 10 with 138. Imprint, sheet number, name and other marginal detail such as price and magnetic variation were altered when this combined small sheet was remodelled as a member of the large sheet series.

Sheet 129 a. *Bude* b. *Clovelly and Bude*   Revised 1906-8   18 by 27

| 1910 | ose.a | - | | - | - | 1910 | A | 1/6,2/-,2/6 | n | 7/10 | 129.Ou | Cpt-m |
| 1910 | ose.b | 10.12 | | - | 9.12r | 1912 | C | 1/6,2/-,2/6 | n | | 129.1x | Cu-m | 1 |

Overlaps: 3 by 13 miles with sheet 119, 3 by 14 with 130, 6 by 5 with 139, 12 by 5 with 140. 1. This is a very late printing still to have the words "Crown Copyright Reserved" in large lettering.

Sheet 130 unnamed [*Okehampton*]   Revised 1907-8   27 by 18

| 1911 | ose.x | - | | - | - | 1911 | A | 1/6,2/-,2/6 | n | 6/11 | 130.Ou | Cpt-m |

Overlaps: 3 by 14 miles with sheet 129, 9 by 9 with 131, 18 by 9 with 140, 9 by 9 with 141. Ellis Martin covers with name *Okehampton and District* were issued for this sheet.

Sheet 131 *Tiverton*   Revised 1906-7   27 by 18

| 1910 | ose | - | | - | - | 1910 | A | 1/6,2/-,2/6 | n | 5/10 | 131.Ou | Cpt-m |
| 1910 | ose | 7.14 | | - | - | 1914 | C | 1/6,2/-,2/6 | n | | 131.1x | Cu-m |

Overlap: 9 by 9 miles with sheet 130.

Sheet 132 *Chard*   Revised 1904-7   27 by 18

| 1910 | ose | - | | - | - | 1910 | A | 1/6,2/-,2/6 | n | 3/10 | 132.Ou | Cpt-m |

Overlap: 27 by 6 miles with sheet 142.

Sheet 133 *Yeovil and Blandford*   Revised 1903-5   27 by 18

1908	ose	-		-	-	1908	A	1/6,2/-,2/6	n	3/08	133.Ou	Cpt-m
1908	ose	7.10		-	6.10r	1910	A	1/6,2/-,2/6	n		133.1u	Cu-m
1908	ose	3.14+		12.13	12.13r	1914	C	1/6,2/-,2/6	n		133.2x	Cu-m

Overlap: 9 by 5 miles with sheet 144.

Sheet 134 a. *Ringwood* b. *Romsey and Ringwood*   Revised 1901-3   27 by 18

1909	ose.a	-		-	-	1909	A	1/6,2/-,2/6	n	8/09	134.Ou	Cpt
1909	ose.a	10.10		-	10.10r	1910	A	1/6,2/-,2/6	n		134.1u	Cu-m
1909	ose.b	4.14+		12.13	12.13r	1914	C	1/6,2/-,2/6	n		134.2x	Cu-m
1909	ose.b	4.14+		12.13	12.13r	1914	C:	1/6,2/-,3/-	n		134.2y	Cu-m

Overlaps: 18 by 5 miles with sheet 144, 9 by 5 with 145.

Sheet 135 a. *Fareham* b. *Southampton and Portsmouth*   Revised 1901   27 by 18

1908	ose.a	-		-	-	1908	A	1/6,2/-,2/6	n	10/08	135.Ou	Cpt-m
1908	ose.a	4.10		-	3.10r	1910	A	1/6,2/-,2/6	n		135.1u	Cu-m
1908	ose.b	5.12+		-	4.12r	1912	A	1/6,2/-,2/6	n		135.2u	Cu-m	1
1908	ose.b	12.14++		-	-	1914	C	1/6,2/-,2/6	n		135.3x	Cu-m
1908	ose.b	12.14++		-	-	1914	C:	1/6,2/-,3/-	n		135.3y	Cu-m

Overlap: 18 by 5 miles with sheet 145. 1. Also recorded overprinted in red with a 2000-yard alpha-numeric squaring system, with 400-yard subdivisions numbered 1 to 25. Part of the overprint cancels the two-inch blocks in the border of the map. The system may not be unique to this sheet, since part of square 9A is in the north-west corner. The system is parallel to the sheet lines of the map. The purpose of the map has not been discovered (copy PC). See figure 2 and appendix 2.

Sheet 136 a. *Arundel* b. *Worthing, Chichester and Littlehampton*   Revised 1901   27 by 18

1909	ose.a	-	-	-	1909	A	1/6,2/-,2/6	n	12/09	136.0u	Cpt-m	
1909	ose.b	6.12	5.12	5.12r	1912	A	1/6,2/-,2/6	n		136.1u	Cu-m	
1909	ose.b	6.12	5.12	5.12r	1912	A	1/6,2/-,3/6	n		136.1v	Cu-m	1
1909	ose.b	6.12	5.12	5.12r	1912	A	np	n		136.1w	Cu-m	

With an extrusion to cover Selsey Bill. 1. The 3/6 price would have been the result of poor revision to the plate when the price increase from 2/6 to 3/- occurred.

Sheet 137 a. *Lewes* b. *Brighton, Eastbourne and Lewes*   Revised 1901-3   27 by 18

1909	ose.a	-	-	-	1909	A	1/6,2/-,2/6	n	12/09	137.0u	Cpt-m
1909	ose.b	7.12	5.12	5.12r	1912	A	1/6,2/-,2/6	n		137.1u	Cu-m
1909	ose.b	7.12	5.12	5.12r	1912	A	1/6,2/-,3/-	n		137.1v	Cu

Sheet 138 a. *Hastings* b. *Hastings, Winchelsea and Rye*   Revised 1903-4   27 by 18

1910	ose.a	-	-	-	1910	A	1/6,2/-,2/6	n	2/10	138.0u	Cpt-m
1910	ose.b	7.12	-	7.12r	1912	C	1/6,2/-,2/6	n		138.1x	Cu-m
1910	ose.b	7.12	-	7.12r	1912	C:	1/6,2/-,3/-	n		138.1y	Cu-m
1910	ose.b	nc	-	7.12r	1912	C	np	n		138.1z	BL-r

Overlaps: 27 by 6 miles with sheet 127, 9 by 10 with 128. KGM 138.1u omitted (see page 82).

Sheet 139 *Boscastle and Padstow*   Revised 1905-8   27 by 18

| 1910 | ose | - | - | - | 1910 | A | 1/6,2/-,2/6 | n | 2/10 | 139.0u | Cpt-m |

Overlap: 6 by 5 miles with sheet 129.

Sheet 140 unnamed [*Launceston*]   Revised 1907-8   27 by 18

| 1911 | ose.x | - | - | s | 1911 | A | 1/6,2/-,2/6 | n | 10/11 | 140.0u | Cpt-m |

Overlaps: 12 by 5 miles with sheet 129, 18 by 9 with 130, 27 by c.3¼ with 148, 4½ by 6 with 149. Ellis Martin covers with name *Launceston and District* were issued for this sheet.

Sheet 141 *Exeter and Teignmouth*   Revised 1907-8   27 by 18

| 1911 | ose | - | - | s | 1911 | A | 1/6,2/-,2/6 | n | 3/11 | 141.0u | Cpt-m |
| 1911 | ose | - | - | s | 1911 | A | 1/6,2/-,3/- | n | | 141.0v | Cu-m |

Overlaps: 9 by 9 miles with sheet 130, 22½ by 6 with 149. See figure 18.

Sheet 142 *Lyme Regis*   Revised 1905-8   27 by 18

| 1910 | ose | - | - | - | 1910 | A | 1/6,2/-,2/6 | n | 3/10 | 142.0u | Cpt-m |
| 1910 | ose.x | - | - | 6.11r | 1911 | A | 1/6,2/-,2/6 | n | | 142.1u | Cu-m |

Overlap: 27 by 6 miles with sheet 132. Ellis Martin covers with name *Axminster and District* were issued for this sheet.

Sheet 143 *Weymouth*   Revised 1903-5   27 by 18

| 1908 | ose | - | - | - | 1907 | A | 1/6,2/-,2/6 | n | 2/08 | 143.0u | Cpt-m |
| 1908 | ose | - | - | - | 1907 | A | 1/6,2/-,3/- | n | | 143.0v | Cu-m |

Overlap: 9 by 13 miles with sheet 144.

Sheet 144 a. *Poole Harbour* b. *Bournemouth and Swanage*   Revised 1903   27 by 18

1909	ose.a	-	-	-	1908	A	1/6,2/-,2/6	n	3/09	144.0u	Cpt-m
1908	ose.a	10.10	10.10	10.10r	1910	A	1/6,2/-,2/6	n		144.1u	Cu-m
1908	ose.b	9.12+	3.10	8.12r	1912	A	1/6,2/-,2/6	n		144.2u	Cu-m
1908	ose.b	9.12+	3.10	8.12r	1912	C:	1/6,2/-,3/-	n		144.2y	Cu-m

Overlaps: 9 by 5 miles with sheet 133, 18 by 5 with 134, 9 by 13 with 143.

1	2	3	4	5	6	7	8	9	10	11	12	13

Sheet 145 *Isle of Wight* — Revised 1901 — 27 by 18

1909	ose	-	-	-	1909	A	1/6,2/-,2/6	n	12/09	145.Ou	Cpt-m	
1909	ose	-	-	-	1909	A	1/6,2/-,2/6	n	-		book	1
1909	ose	6.12	-	5.12r	1912	A	1/6,2/-,2/6	n		145.1u	Cu-m	
1909	ose	6.12	-	5.12r	1912	C:	1/6,2/-,3/-	n		145.1y	Cu-m	

Overlaps: 9 by 5 miles with sheet 134, 18 by 5 with 135. KGM 145.1x omitted (see page 82). 1. Another edition, overprinted for use in *The Land Defence of the United Kingdom : Isle of Wight.* London: War Office A.1458, 1911 (copy PRO WO 33/522).

Sheet 146 *Truro* — Revised 1905 — 27 by 18

| 1909 | ose | - | - | - | 1909 | A | 1/6,2/-,2/6 | n | 6/09 | 146.Ou | Cpt-m | |
| 1909 | ose.x | 8.11 | - | 8.11r | 1911 | A | 1/6,2/-,2/6 | n | | 146.1u | Cu | |

Overlap: 4 by 18 miles with sheet 147.

Sheet 147 unnamed [*Bodmin*] — Revised 1905-8 — 27 by 18

| 1911 | ose.x | - | - | - | 1911 | A | 1/6,2/-,2/6 | n | 7/11 | 147.Ou | Cpt-m | |

Overlaps: 4 by 18 miles with sheet 146, 9 by c.14¾ with 148. Ellis Martin covers with name *Bodmin and District* were issued for this sheet.

Sheet 148 unnamed [*Plymouth*] — Revised 1908-9 — 27 by 18

| 1911 | ose.x | - | | s | 1911 | A | 1/6,2/-,2/6 | n | 7/11 | 148.Ou | Cpt-m | |
| 1911 | ose.x | - | | s | 1911 | A | 1/6,2/-,3/- | n | | 148.Ov | Cu-m | |

With an inset of Eddystone Rocks. Overlaps: 27 by c.3¼ miles with sheet 140, 9 by c.14¾ with 147, 4½ by c.15¼ with 149, 9 by 11 with 150. Ellis Martin covers with name *Plymouth and District* were issued for this sheet.

Sheet 149 *Torquay* — Revised 1908-9 — 27 by 18

| 1911 | ose | - | | s | 1911 | A | 1/6,2/-,2/6 | n | 3/11 | 149.Ou | Cpt-m | |
| 1911 | ose | - | | s | 1911 | A | 1/6,2/-,3/- | n | - | | PC | |

Overlaps: 4½ by 6 miles with sheet 140, 22½ by 6 with 141, 4½ by c.15¼ with 148, 22½ by c.8¼ with 150.

Sheet 150 *Kingsbridge* — Revised 1908-9 — 28½ by 18

| 1911 | ose | - | | s | 1911 | A | 1/6,2/-,2/6 | n | 3/11 | 150.Ou | Cpt-m | |

Overlaps: 9 by 11 miles with sheet 148, 22½ by c.8¼ with 149. *Black Outline Edition One-inch Map,* ARRR 1/-, based on 150.Ou (150.Oo, OSPR 1918/2).

Sheet 151 *Land's End* — Revised 1905 — 25 by 18

1908	ose	-	-	-	1908	A	1/6,2/-,2/6	n	12/08	151.Ou	Cpt-m	
1908	ose.x	5.11	-	4.11r	1911	A	1/6,2/-,2/6	n		151.1u	Cu-m	1
1908	ose.x	5.11	-	4.11r	1911	A	1/6,2/-,3/-	n		151.1v	Cu	

With an inset of the Isles of Scilly, the first one-inch map of the islands to be issued by the Ordnance Survey in colour. Ellis Martin covers with name *Penzance and District* were issued for this sheet. 1. Latitude and longitude values are added around the inset of the Isles of Scilly.

Sheet 152 *Falmouth and Lizard Point* — Revised 1905 — 27 by 18

1909	ose	-	-	-	1909	A	1/6,2/-,2/6	n	5/09	152.Ou	Cpt-m	
1909	ose.x	5.11	-	5.11r	1911	A	1/6,2/-,2/6	n		152.1u	Cu-m	
1909	ose.x	5.11	-	5.11r	1911	C:	1/6,2/-,3/-	n		152.1y	Cu-m	

District maps

In the top margin of maps published to 1911 were listed the component Large Sheet Series sheet numbers. From 1912 this information was usually deleted in reprints and not given in new maps.

Brighton & Worthing District   Revised 1901-3   30 by 20

1	2	3	4	5	6	7	8	9	10	11	12	13
1912	ose	-	-	-	1912	A	1/6,2/-,2/6	n	3/12	BRG.Ou	Cpt-m	
1912	ose	-	-	-	1912	C:	1/6,2/-,3/-	n		BRG.Oy	Cu-m	
1912	ose	-	-	-	1912	C	np	n		BRG.Oz	BL-r	

Cambridge District. Parts of sheets 85 & 86.   Revised 1904-5   27¼ by 18

1	2	3	4	5	6	7	8	9	10	11	12	13
1910	ose	-	-	-	1910	A	1/6,2/-,2/6	ANg	9/10	CAM.Ou	Cpt-m	1
1910	ose.o	12.12	-	11.12r	1912	C	1/6,2/-,2/6	ANg		CAM.1x	Cu-m	1,2
1910	ose.o	12.12	-	-	1912	C	np	ANg		CAM.1z	Cu-m	3

Degrees of latitude and longitude form a diced inside border next to the neat line. With an alpha-numeric squaring system. Magnetic variation diagrams are printed with different values on each side. 1. Copies were made available to Cambridge University Officers' Training Corps (overprinted on covers, not the maps). 2. The "(Large Sheet Series)" heading and component sheet numbers are deleted. 3. A copy is recorded with a price alteration label dated 1 September 1945.

Dorking and Leith Hill District   Revised 1901-2   28½ by 18½

1	2	3	4	5	6	7	8	9	10	11	12	13
1914	ose	-	-	s	1914	C	1/6,2/-,2/6	g	6/14	DOR.Ox	Cpt-m	1
1914	ose	-	-	s	1914	C	1/6,2/-,2/6	g		-	PC	1
1914	ose	-	-	s	1914	C:	1/6,2/-,3/-	g		DOR.Oy	Cu-m	2
1914	ose	-	-	s	1914	C	np	g		DOR.Oz	Cu-m	
1914	ose	2000/22	-	s	1914	C	np	g		DOR.Op.1	Cu-m	
1914	ose	4000/25+	-	s	1914	C	np	g		DOR.Op.2	Cu-m	

With an extrusion to cover Horsham. One of a group of maps issued between 1913 and 1922 with enhanced colour schemes (see page 18, appendix 4 and figure 7). 1. There are at least two variations in the strength of green used for woodland: in what is presumably the earlier woodland is a light grey-green, similar to, though stronger than, the lowest layer tint; in the second the woodland green contrasts strongly with the lowest layer which is unchanged. 2. The lowest layer tint is discernibly greener.

Felixstowe see *Ipswich and Felixstowe*

Folkestone and Dover District   Revised 1903-4   29¼ by 19¼

1	2	3	4	5	6	7	8	9	10	11	12	13
1913	ose	-	-	-	1913	C	1/6,2/-,2/6	n	3/13	FOL.Ox	Cpt-m	
1913	ose	-	-	-	1913	C	np	n		FOL.Oz	Cu-m	

With an extrusion to cover Faversham. With blue water tint in place of the usual water lining.

Hastings and Bexhill District   Revised 1903   30 by 20

1	2	3	4	5	6	7	8	9	10	11	12	13
1912	ose	-	-	-	1912	A	1/6,2/-,2/6	n	3/12	HAS.Ou	Cpt-m	
1912	ose	500/27	-	-	1912	A	1/6,2/-,3/-	n		-	PC	1

1. The copyright and price states are anachronistic, but the alteration in price could imply an intermediate, unrecorded, state.

Ilkley District   Revised 1904-11   20 by 27¼

1	2	3	4	5	6	7	8	9	10	11	12	13
1914	ose	-	-	s	1914	C	1/6,2/-,2/6	g	7/14	ILK.Ox	Cpt-m	
1914	ose	6.20	-	s	1914	C	np	g		ILK.Op	Cu-m	
1914	ose	6.20	-	S	1914	C	np	g		-	Cu-m	

With extrusions to cover Ripon, Harrogate and Leeds. One of a group of maps issued between 1913 and 1922 with enhanced colour schemes (see page 18 and appendix 4).

Ipswich and Felixstowe. Parts of sheets 87. 99.   Revised 1904-5   27 by 18

1911	ose.x	-	-	-	1911	A	1/6,2/-,2/6	n	5/11	IPS.Ou	Cpt	1
1911	ose.o	3.14	-	2.14r	1914	C	1/6,2/-,2/6	n		IPS.1x	PC	2
1911	ose.o	3.14	-	2.14r	1914	C:	1/6,2/-,3/-	n		IPS.1y	Cu-m	

KGM IPS.Ou.2 and IPS.1z omitted (see page 82). The map was listed in OSPR 5/11 as "Special Map of Felixstowe District, parts of Sheets 87, 99", and H.4 covers were printed entitled *Felixstowe District*. However, no printing with a *Felixstowe* title on the map face has yet been recorded. 1. The BL copy is in BL-c (not in Cook and McIntosh (1991)). See figure 14. 2. The "(Large Sheet Series)" heading and component sheet numbers are deleted.

Land's End and Lizard District   Revised 1905   30½ by 21½

1912	ose	-	-	-	1912	A	1/6,2/-,2/6	n	3/12	LEL.Ou	Cpt-m
1912	ose	6.13	-	6.13r	1913	C	1/6,2/-,2/6	n		LEL.1x	Cu-m

With extrusions to cover rocks off Falmouth, Lizard Head, Land's End and Cape Cornwall. KGM LEL.1z omitted (see page 82).

London (North)   Revised 1901-3   29 by 19

1912	ose	-	-	-	1912	A	1/6,2/-,2/6	ANn	10/12	LNN.Ou	Cpt-m
1912	ose	-	-	-	1912	A	1/6,2/-,3/-	ANn		LNN.Ov	Cu-m

With an alpha-numeric squaring system. *London (South)* adjoins this sheet, without overlap. See figure 18.

London (South)   Revised 1901-3   29 by 19

1912	ose	-	-	-	1912	A	1/6,2/-,2/6	ANn	10/12	LNS.Ou	Cpt-m
1912	ose	-	-	-	1912	A	1/6,2/-,3/-	ANn		LNS.Ov	Cu-m
1912	ose	2000/23	-	-	1912	A	np	ANn		-	Cu-m

With an alpha-numeric squaring system. *London (North)* adjoins this sheet, without overlap.

Maidenhead, Windsor and Henley District   Revised 1901-2   29⅞ by 20

1912	ose	-	-	-	1912	A	1/6,2/-,2/6	n	7/12	MAI.Ou	Cpt-m
1912	ose	2.13	-	2.13r	1913	C	1/6,2/-,2/6	n		MAI.1x	Cu-m
1912	ose	2.13	-	2.13r	1913	C:	1/6,2/-,3/-	n		MAI.1y	Cu-m

KGM MAI.1p omitted (see page 82).

Newquay District   Revised 1905-6   29½ by 20¼

1912	ose	-	-	-	1912	A	1/6,2/-,2/6	n	6/12	NEW.Ou	Cpt-m
1912	ose	-	-	-	1912	A	1/6,2/-,3/-	n		NEW.Ov	Cu-m

a. ***Oxford District.*** Parts of sheets 95. 96. 105. 106. b. ***Oxford and District*** Revised 1902 27 by 18

1911	ose.a	-	-	-	1911	A	1/6,2/-,2/6	ANg	3/11	OXF.Ou	Cpt	1
1911	ose.bo	6.12	5.12	5.12r	1912	A	1/6,2/-,2/6	ANg		OXF.1u	Cu-m	1,2
1911	ose.bo	6.12	5.12	5.12r	1912	A	1/6,2/-,3/-	ANg		OXF.1v	Cu-m	

Degrees of latitude and longitude form a diced inside border next to the neat line. With an alpha-numeric squaring system. Magnetic variation diagrams are printed with different values on each side (see figures 1 and 19). 1. Copies were made available to Oxford University Officers' Training Corps (overprinted on covers, not the maps). 2. The "(Large Sheet Series)" heading and component sheet numbers are deleted.

Pwllheli and Criccieth District   Revised 1903   29½ by 20¾

1913	ose	-	-	-	1913	C	1/6,2/-,2/6	n	6/13	PWL.Ox	Cpt-m
1913	ose	-	-	-	1913	C	1/6,2/-,3/-	n		PWL.Oy	

With an inset of the western end of the Lleyn Peninsula. With blue water tint in place of the usual water lining. The heading top left is, erroneously, "Ordnance Survey of England", not "England and Wales". The reprint is not verified; the one copy seen by KGM apparently belonged to a friend of his who had purchased it new some sixty years earlier.

1	2	3	4	5	6	7	8	9	10	11	12	13

Reading and District
Revised 1901-2 — 29 by 19

1	2	3	4	5	6	7	8	9	10	11	12	13
1912	ose	-	-	-	1912	A	1/6,2/-,2/6	n	8/12	REA.Ou	Cpt-m	
1912	ose	-	-	-	1912	A	1/6,2/-,3/-	n		REA.Ov	Cu-m	

With an extrusion to cover the outskirts of Newbury.

Rugby District
Revised 1904-7 — 29⅛ by 19¼

1	2	3	4	5	6	7	8	9	10	11	12	13
1912	ose	-	-	-	1912	A	1/6,2/-,2/6	n	8/12	RUG.Ou	Cpt-m	
1912	ose	4.20	-	-	1912	C	np	n		RUG.Op	Cu-m	

With an extrusion to cover Nuneaton.

Sidmouth, Budleigh Salterton & Exmouth District
Revised 1906-8 — 27⅝ by 17¾

1	2	3	4	5	6	7	8	9	10	11	12	13
1912	ose	-	-	-	1912	A	1/6,2/-,2/6	n	3/12	SID.Ou	Cpt-m	
1912	ose	12.13	-	12.13r	1913	C	1/6,2/-,2/6	n		SID.1x	Cu-m	
1912	ose	12.13	-	12.13r	1913	-	np	n		SID.1z	Cu-m	1
1912	ose	4.20+	-	12.13r	1913	C	np	n		SID.1p	Cu-m	

Copies of the map have been recorded in Ellis Martin (H.10.2) cover entitled *Exmouth District* (4.20). 1. Copyright and rights of way notes are omitted.

Staffordshire Potteries and District
Revised 1905-6 — 19⅜ by 27

1	2	3	4	5	6	7	8	9	10	11	12	13
1913	ose	-	-	-	1913	C	1/6,2/-,2/6	n	11/13	STA.Ox	Cpt-m	
1913	ose	2000/23	-	-	1913	C	np	n		STA.Op	PC	

With extrusions to cover Eccleshall, Macclesfield and Buxton.

Weston super Mare. Parts of sheets 111. 112. 121. 122.
Revised 1904-5 — 18 by 27

1	2	3	4	5	6	7	8	9	10	11	12	13
1911	ose.x	-	-	-	1911	A	1/6,2/-,2/6	n	6/11	WES.Ou	Cpt-m	1
1911	ose	-	-	-	1911	A	np	n		WES.Ow	Cu-m	2

With an extrusion to cover Howe Rock. KGM also reports an OS cover entitled *Clevedon District* (not verified). 1. The BL copy is in BL-c (not in Cook and McIntosh (1991)). See figure 14. 2. The component sheet heading remains.

Winchester District. Parts of sheets 123. 124. 134. 135.
Revised 1901 — 27 by 18

1	2	3	4	5	6	7	8	9	10	11	12	13
1910	ose	-	-	-	1910	A	1/6,2/-,2/6	n	12/10	WIN.Ou	Cpt-m	
1910	ose	-	-	-	1910	A	np	n		WIN.Ow	Cu-m	1

1. The component sheet heading remains.

Windsor and Neighbourhood
Revised 1904-6 — 12¼ by 31½

1	2	3	4	5	6	7	8	9	10	11	12	13
1913	ose	-	-	-	1913	C	np	s		-	Cu-m	

Prepared specially for Eton College Officers Training Corps. See figure 19. There appear to have been at least two printings of this map, the earlier being distinguishable from the later by the markedly yellow quality of the green plate.

Worcester and Malvern District
Revised 1903-8 — 20⅜ by 30

1	2	3	4	5	6	7	8	9	10	11	12	13
1912	ose	-	-	-	1912	A	1/6,2/-,2/6	n	6/12	WOR.Ou	Cpt-m	
1912	ose	-	-	-	1912	A	1/6,2/-,3/-	n		WOR.Ov	Cu-m	

York District
Revised 1904-11 — 26 by 22

1	2	3	4	5	6	7	8	9	10	11	12	13
1919	osew	-	-	s	1919	C	1/-	ANg	9/19	YOR.Op	Cpt-m	1
1919	osew	500/23	-	s	1919	C	np	ANg		-	PC	2

Though possessing more of the characteristics of the forthcoming Popular Edition (red main roads, marginalia, no hachures, no parish boundaries, two-inch squaring system) than the coloured Third Edition map (town infill, the unmodified railway line symbol), this map is nonetheless included in this volume because of its derivation from the Second National Revision. See figure 11. 1. With heading "Provisional Popular Edition one-inch map". 2. With heading "Popular Edition one-inch map".

Tourist maps

These two maps were members of a group issued between 1913 and 1922 with enhanced colour schemes. For information on the features that distinguish them the reader is referred to page 18 and appendix 4.

The Lake District

								Revised 1903, 1904		24 by 30
1920	osew	-	-	-	1920	C	np	ANg 6/20	LAK.Oz	Cpt-m
1920	osew	5500/24	1924	-	1920	C	np	ANg	LAK.1z	Cu-m 1

1. With a note concerning the accuracy of contours surveyed on the ground against those which are interpolated. Railway company names reflect the changes made at grouping.

Snowdon District

								Revised 1903, 1904		21⅜ by 30
1920	osew	-	9.19	s	1919	C	np	ANg 2/20	SNO.Oz	Cpt-m

Road edition

The Lake District

								Revised 1903, 1904		22 by 30
1920	osew	-	-	-	1920	C	np	ANg	8.13	Cu-m

OSPR reference not found. Sheet lines are different to those of the tourist map on all four sides. There are four colour plates: black, including contours, water in blue, and road infill in red and orange.

Military map

Admission to the Staff College. Military topography

										11¾ by 10¼
1912	-	-	-	-	-	A	np	s		book

A small sheet covering the North Molton area, printed for the June 1912 examination paper. In *Report on the examination for admission to the Staff College, Camberley, held in June-July, 1912, with copies of the examination papers.* London: HMSO.

3. One-inch Third Edition Map of Scotland

Sheets typically have the heading "Third Edition" top left, the Ordnance Survey heading top centre, and the sheet name and number top right. Standard sheet coverage is 24 by 18 miles.

Sheets 1. 2. *Kirkmaiden & Whithorn* — Revised 1903 — 28 by 12

1	2	3	4	5	6	7	8	9	10	11	12	13
1906	oss	-	-	-	1906	A	1/6,2/-,2/6	w	9/06	2+Ou	Cpt-m	

See also sheet 1.3.7. Overlap: 8 by c.8¾ miles with sheet 1.3.7. The sheet prices have clearly been altered to 1/6,2/-,2/6, apparently by hand.

Sheets 1. 3. Part of sheet 7. *Stranraer & Kirkmaiden* — Revised 1903 — 16 by c.26¾

1	2	3	4	5	6	7	8	9	10	11	12	13
1906	oss	-	-	-	1906	A	1/6,2/-,2/6	w	9/06	3+Ou	Cpt	

See also sheets 1.2 and 7. With an extrusion in sheet 7 to cover Milleur Point. Overlap: 8 by c.8¾ miles with sheet 1.2.

Sheet 4 *Wigtown* — Revised 1903 — 24 by 18

1	2	3	4	5	6	7	8	9	10	11	12	13
1906	oss	-	-	-	1906	A	1/6,2/-,2/6	w	9/06	4.Ou	Cpt-m	

A rare instance of a rights of way notice on a Scottish sheet omitting reference to tracks and footpaths.

Sheet 5 *Kirkcudbright* — Revised 1902-3 — 24 by 18

1	2	3	4	5	6	7	8	9	10	11	12	13
1906	oss	-	-	-	1906	A	1/6,2/-,2/6	w	9/06	5.Ou	Cpt-m	

Sheet 6 *Annan* — Revised 1902 — 24 by 18

1	2	3	4	5	6	7	8	9	10	11	12	13
1905	oss	-	-	-	1905	A	1/6	w	3/05	6.Or	Cpt-m	
1905	oss	2.09	-	2.09r	1908	A	1/6,2/-,2/6	w		6.1u	Cu-m	
1905	oss	2.09	-	2.09r	1908	A	1/6,2/-,3/-	w	-		Cg	

The English area is blank. KGM 6.2u and 6.2v omitted (see page 82).

Sheet 7 *Girvan* — Revised 1902 — 24 by 18

1	2	3	4	5	6	7	8	9	10	11	12	13
1906	oss	-	-	-	1906	A	1/6,2/-	w	3/06	7.Os	Cpt-m	
1906	oss	-	-	-	1906	A	1/6,2/-,3/-	w		7.Ov		

See also sheet 1.3.7. KGM 7.Ov has not been recorded, and thus cannot be verified.

Sheet 8 *Carrick* — Revised 1902 — 24 by 18

1	2	3	4	5	6	7	8	9	10	11	12	13
1905	oss	-	-	-	1905	A	1/6,2/-	w	12/05	8.Os	Cpt-m	
1905	oss	1.09	-	-	1908	A	1/6,2/-,2/6	w	-		PC	1
1905	oss	1.20	-	-	1908	C	np	w	-		Rg	1

KGM 8.Oy and 8.Oz omitted (see page 82). 1. With *Expansion* ↕ left of the legend. See page 134.

Sheet 9 *Maxwelltown* — Revised 1902 — 24 by 18

1	2	3	4	5	6	7	8	9	10	11	12	13
1906	oss	-	-	-	1906	A	1/6,2/-	w	7/06	9.Os	Cpt-m	
1906	oss	4.20	-	-	1906	C	np	w		9.1z	Rg	
1906	oss	2.22	-	-	1906	C	np	w		9.2z	Ag	

Sheet 10 a. *Dumfries* b. *Dumfries and Lockerbie* — Revised 1901-2 — 24 by 18

1	2	3	4	5	6	7	8	9	10	11	12	13
1905	oss.a	-	-	-	1905	A	1/6,2/-	w	11/05	10.Os	Cpt	
1905	oss.a	4.07	-	3.07r	1907	A	1/6,2/-,2/6	w		10.1u	Cu-m	
1905	oss.b	6.13+	5.13	5.13r	1913	C	1/6,2/-,2/6	w		10.2x	Cu-m	
1905	oss.b	6.13+	5.13	5.13r	1913	C	1/6,2/-,3/-	w		10.2y	NLS	
1905	oss.b	1000/24++5.13	5.13	5.13r	1913	C	np	w	-		LDg	

The English area is blank.

Sheet 11 a. *Langholm* b. *Langholm and Newcastleton*   Revised 1901-2   24 by 18

1905	oss.a	-	-	-	1905	A	1/6	w	3/05	11.Or	Cpt-m	
1905	oss.b	1.13	-	9.12r	1913	C	1/6,2/-,2/6	w		11.1x	Cu-m	
1905	oss.b	5.20	-	9.12r	1913	C	np	w		11.2z	NLS	

The English area is blank.

Sheet 12 *Campbeltown*   Revised 1903   24 by 18

1906	oss	-	-	-	1905	A	1/6,2/-	w	8/06	12.Os	Cpt-m	

Sheet 13 see also sheet 21.13.

Sheet 14. Part of sheet 13. *Ayr*   Revised 1902   24 by 18

1906	oss	-	-	-	1906	A	1/6,2/-	w	7/06	14+Os	Cpt-m	
1906	oss.x	nc	-	10.11r	1912	A	1/6,2/-,2/6	w		14+1u	Cu-m	
1906	oss.x	nc	-	10.11r	1912	A	1/6,2/-,3/-	w		14+1v	Og	
1906	oss.x	9.20	-	10.11r	1912	C	np	w		14+2z	Cu-m	

For sheet 13 see also sheet 21.13. The mainland area of sheet 13 forms an extrusion in the south-west.

Sheet 15 a. *Sanquhar* b. *Nithsdale*   Revised 1902   24 by 18

1905	oss.a	-	-	-	1905	A	1/6,2/-	w	2/06	15.Os	Cpt	
1905	oss.b	1.13	-	1.13r	1912	C	1/6,2/-,2/6	w		15.1x	Cu-m	
1905	oss.b	1.22	-	1.13r	1912	C	np	w		-	NLS	
1905	oss.b	1.13,2.22	-	1.13r	1912	-	np	w		15.2z	EXg	

Sheet 16 *Moffat*   Revised 1901-2   24 by 18

1905	oss	-	-	-	1905	A	1/6	w	5/05	16.Or	Cpt-m	
1905	oss	1.13	9.09	9.12r	1913	C	1/6,2/-,2/6	w		16.1x		
1905	oss	1.13	9.09	9.12r	1913	C	1/6,2/-,3/-	w		16.1y	Cu-m	
1905	oss	2.22	9.09	9.12r	1913	C	np	w		16.2z		

KGM 16.1x and 16.2z have not been recorded, and thus cannot be verified.

Sheet 17 a. *Jedburgh* b. *Hawick*   Revised 1901-2   24 by 18

1905	oss.a	-	-	-	1905	A	1/6	w	3/05	17.Or	Cpt-m	
1905	oss.x	7.11	-	-	1911	A	1/6,2/-,2/6	w		17.1u	Ag	
1905	oss.b	9.12+	-	9.12r	1912	C	1/6,2/-,2/6	w		17.2x	PC	
1905	oss.b	6.14++	5.14	5.14r	1914	C	1/6,2/-,2/6	w		-	PC	
1905	oss.b	6.14++	5.14	5.14r	1914	C	1/6,2/-,3/-	w		17.3y	Cu-m	
1905	oss.b	7.20	5.14	5.14r	1914	C	np	w		17.4z	Mg	

The English area is blank.

Sheet 18 *Morebattle*   Revised 1901   24 by 18

1905	oss	-	-	-	1905	A	1/6	w	3/05	18.Or	Cpt-m	
1905	oss	9.12	-	-	1912	C	1/6,2/-,2/6	w		18.1x	RSGS	
1905	oss	9.12	-	-	1912	C	1/6,2/-,3/-	w		18.1y	Rg	

The English area is blank.

Sheet 19. Parts of sheets 20. 27. 28. *Bowmore and Port Askaig*   Revised 1904   21 by 26

1907	oss	-	-	-	1907	A	1/6,2/-,2/6	w	9/07	19+Ou	Cpt	
1907	oss	1.10	-	12.09r	1910	A	1/6,2/-,2/6	w		19+1u	Cu-m	
1907	oss	9.21	-	12.09r	1910	C	np	w		19+2z	Rg	

See also sheets 20 and 28. The sheet lines adopted offer complete coverage of Islay. This is a unique case of a Scottish coloured series sheet with a date of publication rather than a date of printing, in the style of the Large Sheet Series in England and Wales. It is also unusual in that its rights of way notice follows the English model and omits reference to tracks and footpaths.

1	2	3	4	5	6	7	8	9	10	11	12	13

Sheet 20 *Killean*   Revised 1903   24 by 18

1	2	3	4	5	6	7	8	9	10	11	12	13
1906	oss	-	-	-	1906	A	1/6,2/-,2/6	w	9/06	20.Ou	Cpt-m	
1906	oss	8.20	-	-	1906	C	np	w		20.1z	Rg	

See also sheets 19.20.27.28.

Parts of sheets 21. 13. *Island of Arran*   Revised 1903   17 by 24

1	2	3	4	5	6	7	8	9	10	11	12	13
1906	oss.x	-	-	-	1906	A	1/6,2/-,2/6	w	9/06	21+Ou	Cpt-m	
1906	oss.x	5.11	-	4.11r	1911	A	1/6,2/-,2/6	w		21+1u	NLS	
1906	oss	5.13+	-	4.11r	1913	C	1/6,2/-,2/6	w		21+2x	NLS	
1906	oss	9.20	-	4.11r	1913	C	np	w		21+3z	Cu-m	
1906	oss	1000/25	-	4.11r	1913	-	np	w		-	Cu-m	

The sheet lines adopted offer complete coverage of the Island of Arran. For sheet 13 see also sheet 14.13, for sheet 21 see also sheets 22.21 and 29.21.

Sheet 22. Part of sheet 21. *Kilmarnock*   Revised 1902   28 by 18

1	2	3	4	5	6	7	8	9	10	11	12	13
1906	oss	-	-	-	1906	A	1/6,2/-,2/6	w	9/06	22+Ou	Cpt-m	
1906	oss.x	1.12	10.11	10.11r	1912	A	1/6,2/-,2/6	w		22+1u	Cu-m	1
1906	oss.x	1.12	10.11	10.11r	1912	A	1/6,2/-,3/-	w		22+1v	Bc	
1906	oss.x	9.20	10.11	10.11r	1912	C	np	w		22+2z	PC	

Overlap: 4 by 6 miles with sheet 29.21. Enough of sheet 21 was included in an extension to complete coverage of the mainland. 1. A copy (PC) is recorded with a military grid printed in red over an eight-mile square section covering Troon, Irvine and Dundonald, presumably for artillery training purposes. Parts of lettered rectangles M, N, Q and R, each covering an area 16 by 12 miles, are present. Theoretically they are each subdivided into 48 two-mile squares, further subdivided into lettered one-mile quarters. The four rectangles meet at National Grid reference NS 348360, and is thus slightly offset from the sheet's own alpha-numeric squares. There is also a one-inch square diagram divided in each direction into tenths, with the "Point of origin" arrowed in the south-west corner. See appendix 2.

Sheet 23 a. *Hamilton* b. *Lanark*   Revised 1901-2   24 by 18

1	2	3	4	5	6	7	8	9	10	11	12	13
1906	oss.a	-	-	-	1906	A	1/6,2/-	w	7/06	23.Os	Cpt-m	
1906	oss.b	2.14	2.14	2.14r	1914	C	1/6,2/-,2/6	w		23.2x	NLS	
1906	oss.b	2.14	2.14	2.14r	1914	C	1/6,2/-,3/-	w		23.2y	Rg	
1906	oss.b	2.14	2.14	2.14r	1914	C	np	w		23.2z	Gu	

KGM 23.1 (1912) omitted (see page 82).

Sheet 24 *Peebles*   Revised 1901   24 by 18

1	2	3	4	5	6	7	8	9	10	11	12	13
1905	oss	-	-	-	1905	A	1/6	w	3/05	24.Or	Cpt-m	
1905	oss	1.10	1.10	1.10r	1910	A	1/6,2/-,2/6	w		24.1u	Cu-m	
1905	oss	nc	1.10	1.10r	1910	C	np	w		24.1z	Cu-m	

Sheet 25 *Kelso*   Revised 1901-2   24 by 18

1	2	3	4	5	6	7	8	9	10	11	12	13
1905	oss	-	-	-	1905	A	1/6	w	11/05	25.Or	Cpt-m	
1905	oss	1.09	-	-	1907	A	1/6,2/-,2/6	w		25.1u	NLS	1
1905	oss	8.09+	-	7.09r	1909	A	1/6,2/-,2/6	w		25.2u	Cu-m	1
1905	oss	8.09+	-	7.09r	1909	A	1/6,2/-,3/-	w		25.2v	Ob	1
1905	oss	8.20	-	7.09r	1909	C	np	w		25.3z	NLS	

1. With *Expansion* ↕ left of the legend. See page 134.

Sheet 26 *Berwick upon Tweed* Revised 1901-2 24 by 18

1	2	3	4	5	6	7	8	9	10	11	12	13
1905	oss	-	-	-	1905	A	1/6	w	3/05	26.Or	Cpt-m	
1905	oss	1.09	-	-	1907	A	1/6,2/-,2/6	w		26.1u		?1
1905	oss	1.09	-	-	1907	A	1/6,2/-,3/-	w		26.1v	Rg	1

The English area is blank, other than Tweedmouth parish (still marked as Holy Island), Northumberland north of the River Tweed and a few skeletal indications of villages and roads south of the river. KGM 26.1u has not been recorded, and thus cannot be verified. 1. With *Expansion* ↕ left of the legend. See page 134.

Sheet 27 see sheet 19.20.27.28.

Sheet 28 *Jura* Revised 1904 24 by 18

1	2	3	4	5	6	7	8	9	10	11	12	13
1907	oss	-	-	-	1907	A	1/6,2/-,2/6	w	8/07	28.Ou	Cpt-m	

See also sheet 19.20.27.28.

Sheet 29 *Rothesay* Revised 1902-3 24 by 18

1	2	3	4	5	6	7	8	9	10	11	12	13
1907	oss	-	-	-	1907	A	1/6,2/-,2/6	w	6/07	29.Ou	Cpt-m	

From the start it would seem to have been the intention to extend this sheet southwards (see the next), because the extended sheet lines, though not the shading, already appear in the adjoining sheet diagram. KGM 29.Ov omitted (see page 82).

Sheet 29. Part of sheet 21. *Loch Fyne and Firth of Clyde* Revised 1902-3 24 by 24

1	2	3	4	5	6	7	8	9	10	11	12	13
1908	oss	8.13	-	8.13r	1913	C	1/6,2/-,2/6	w		29+1x	Cu-m	
1908	oss	8.13	-	8.13r	1913	C	1/6,2/-,3/-	w		29+1y	Cu-m	
1908	oss	8.13	-	8.13r	1913	C	np	w		29+1z	Ag	

Sheet 29 extended south by six miles to complete coverage of the Island of Bute (also Great and Little Cumbrae), which were otherwise not covered in the coloured edition. Overlap: 4 by 6 miles with sheet 22.21. For sheet 21 see also sheets 21.13, 22.21. KGM 29+Ou omitted (see page 82). The existence of a 1908 printing seems unlikely. The fact that S.C.N. Grant, who assumed the office in 1908, was named Director General in the imprint (when his predecessor Hellard appears on the engraved and coloured Third Editions of both sheets 21 and 29) supports the notion that preparations were made for publication in that year, but it may have been decided to delay printing until the stocks of the 1907 sheet 29 had run down sufficiently. This may not have occurred before 1913, by which time the name should have been altered to C.F. Close.

Sheet 30 a. *Glasgow* b. *Glasgow and Greenock* Revised 1902 24 by 18

1	2	3	4	5	6	7	8	9	10	11	12	13
1905	oss.a	-	-	-	1905	A	1/6,2/-	w	12/05	30.Os	Cpt-m	
1905	oss.a	1.09	-	1.09r	1909	A	1/6,2/-,2/6	w		30.1u	Cu-m	1
1905	oss.a	1.11+	-	11.10r	1911	A	1/6,2/-,2/6	w		30.2u	Cu-m	
1905	oss.b	2.14++	2.14	2.14r	1914	C	1/6,2/-,2/6	w		30.3x	Cu-m	
1905	oss.b	2.14++	2.14	2.14r	1914	C	1/6,2/-,3/-	w		-	RSGS	
1905	oss.b	1.20	2.14	2.14r	1914	C	1/6,2/-,3/-	w		30.4y	Cu-m	2

1. With *Expansion* ↕ left of the legend. See page 134. 2. This issue has the earliest recorded post-war print code, and the only one known to have both sheet prices and a month.year print code.

Sheet 31 *Airdrie* Revised 1901-2 24 by 18

1	2	3	4	5	6	7	8	9	10	11	12	13
1906	oss	-	-	-	1906	A	1/6,2/-	w	6/06	31.Os	Cpt	
1906	oss	8.07	-	6.07r	1907	A	1/6,2/-,2/6	w		31.1u	Cu-m	1
1906	oss	1000/23	-	4.08r	1907	C	np	w		31.3z	Cu-m	

KGM 31.2 state with April 1908 railway revision omitted (see page 82). The existence of many copies of the 8.07 printing in Ellis Martin covers may suggest that it was not issued.

1	2	3	4	5	6	7	8	9	10	11	12	13

Sheet 32 *Edinburgh* Revised 1901 24 by 18

1	2	3	4	5	6	7	8	9	10	11	12	13
1905	oss	-	-	-	1905	A	1/6	w	9/05	32.Or	Cpt-m	
1905	oss	3.09	-	2.09r	1909†	A	1/6,2/-,2/6	w		32.1u	PC	
1905	oss.x	1.12+	-	10.11r	1912	A	1/6,2/-,2/6	w		32.2u	Cu-m	
1905	oss.x	1.12+	-	10.11r	1912	A	1/6,2/-,3/-	w		32.2v	Cu-m	
1905	oss.x	11.20	-	10.11r	1912	C	np	w		32.3z	Rg	
1905	oss.x	1000/23	-	10.11r	1912	-	np	w		32.4z	Cu-m	

KGM 32.5z omitted (see page 82).

Sheet 33. Part of sheet 41. *Haddington* Revised 1901 24 by 21

1	2	3	4	5	6	7	8	9	10	11	12	13
1905	oss	-	-	-	1905	A	1/6	w	9/05	33+Or	Cpt	
1905	oss	2.09	-	2.09r	1908	A	1/6,2/-,2/6	w		33+1[u]	Gu	
1905	oss	7.09+	-	6.09r	1909	A	1/6,2/-,2/6	w		33+2u	Cu-m	
1905	oss	7.09+	-	6.09r	1909	A	1/6,2/-,3/-	w		-	Eg	
1905	oss	3.21	-	6.09r	1909	C	np	w		33+3z	Cu-m	

Sheet 33 was extended north to complete mainland coverage south of the River Forth, and the adjacent islands.

Sheet 34 *Eyemouth* Revised 1901 24 by 18

1	2	3	4	5	6	7	8	9	10	11	12	13
1905	oss	-	-	-	1905	A	1/6	w	3/05	34.Or	Cpt-m	
1905	oss	1.09	-	-	1907	A	1/6,2/-,2/6	w		34.1u	NLS	1
1905	oss.x	3.11+	-	3.11r	1911	A	1/6,2/-,2/6	w		34.2u	PC	1
1905	oss.x	3.11+	-	3.11r	1911	A	1/6,2/-,3/-	w		34.2v	Rg	1

The English area is covered, though this is not reflected in the heading. 1. With *Expansion* ↕ left of the legend. See page 134.

Sheet 35 see sheet 43.35.

Sheet 36 *Kilmartin* Revised 1904 24 by 18

1	2	3	4	5	6	7	8	9	10	11	12	13
1907	oss	-	-	-	1907	A	1/6,2/-,2/6	w	7/07	36.Ou	Cpt-m	
1907	oss	10.20	-	-	1907	C	np	w		36.1z	Cu-m	

Sheet 37 *Inveraray* Revised 1904 24 by 18

1	2	3	4	5	6	7	8	9	10	11	12	13
1908	oss	-	-	-	1908	A	1/6,2/-,2/6	w	3/08	37.Ou	Cpt-m	1
1908	oss	-	-	-	1908	A	1/6,2/-,2/6	w		-	Bc	2
1908	oss	9.21	-	-	1908	C	np	w		37.1z	Cu-m	

1. With *Expansion* ↕ left of the legend. 2. With *Expansion* ↔ below the left end of the legend. See page 134.

Sheet 38 *Loch Lomond* Revised 1903 24 by 18

1	2	3	4	5	6	7	8	9	10	11	12	13
1907	oss	-	-	-	1907	A	1/6,2/-,2/6	w	9/07	38.Ou	Cpt-m	

Sheet 39 *Stirling* Revised 1904 24 by 18

1	2	3	4	5	6	7	8	9	10	11	12	13
1906	oss	-	-	-	1906	A	1/6,2/-,2/6	w	12/06	39.Ou	Cpt-m	
1906	oss	9.10	8.10	8.10r	1910	A	1/6,2/-,2/6	w		39.1u	Cu-m	
1906	oss	9.10	8.10	8.10r	1910	A	1/6,2/-,3/-	w		39.1v	Cu-m	

Sheet 40 *Kinross* Revised 1903-4 24 by 18

1	2	3	4	5	6	7	8	9	10	11	12	13
1907	oss	-	-	-	1907	A	1/6,2/-,2/6	w	7/07	40.Ou	Cpt-m	
1907	oss	1.10	-	12.09r	1910	A	1/6,2/-,2/6	w		40.1u	Cu-m	
1907	oss	1.10	-	12.09r	1910	A	1/6,2/-,3/-	w		40.1v	Cu-m	

1	2	3	4	5	6	7	8	9	10	11	12	13

Sheet 41 *North Berwick* Revised 1904 24 by 18

1	2	3	4	5	6	7	8	9	10	11	12	13
1907	oss	-	-	-	1907	A	1/6,2/-,2/6	w	10/07	41.Ou	Cpt-m	
1907	oss	9.10	-	-	1910	A	1/6,2/-,2/6	w		41.1u	Mg	
1907	oss	9.10	-	-	1910	A	1/6,2/-,3/-	w		41.1v	Rg	

See also sheet 33.41.

Sheets 42. 50 & 51. Part of sheet 43. *Coll & Tiree* Revised 1904 24 by 18

1	2	3	4	5	6	7	8	9	10	11	12	13
1909	oss	-	-	-	1909	A	1/6,2/-,2/6	w	3/09	51+Ou	Cpt-m	1
1909	oss	-	-	-	1909	A	1/6,2/-,2/6	w		-	RSGS	2
1909	oss	10.20	-	-	1909	C	np	w		51+1z	Rg	

See also sheet 43.35. With an inset of Tiree, so in fact the total land coverage of sheets 42 and 50, with part of 43, are here inset on sheet 51. The six-inch diagram is taken from sheet 51, and omits the Tiree sheets. See figure 18. 1. With *Expansion* ↕ left of the legend. 2. With *Expansion* ↔ below the left end of the legend. See page 134.

Sheet 43. Part of sheet 35. *Iona* Revised 1904 24 by 21

1	2	3	4	5	6	7	8	9	10	11	12	13
1907	oss	-	-	-	1907	A	1/6,2/-,2/6	w	8/07	43+Ou	Cpt-m	
1907	oss	-	-	-	1907	A	1/6,2/-,3/-	w		43+Ov	Cu-m	

See also sheet 42.50.51.43. Enough of sheet 35 was included to complete its coverage of the Island of Mull. Colonsay, also present in sheet 35, was not covered in the coloured edition.

Sheet 44 *Mull* Revised 1904 24 by 18

1	2	3	4	5	6	7	8	9	10	11	12	13
1907	oss	-	-	-	1907	A	1/6,2/-,2/6	w	12/07	44.Ou	Cpt-m	1
1907	oss	750/24	-	-	1907	A	np	w		-	Wc	

With an unnoted extrusion from sheet 36 to complete coverage of the Island of Mull. 1. With *Expansion* ↕ left of the legend. See page 134.

Sheet 45 a. *Oban* b. *Loch Etive* Revised 1904 24 by 18

1	2	3	4	5	6	7	8	9	10	11	12	13
1907	oss.a	-	-	-	1907	A	1/6,2/-,2/6	w	7/07	45.Ou	Cpt-m	
1907	oss.b	4.14	2.14	2.14r	1914	C	1/6,2/-,2/6	w		45.1x	NLS	
1907	oss.b	4.14	2.14	2.14r	1914	C	1/6,2/-,3/-	w		45.1y	Cu-m	
1907	oss.b	1100/27+	2.14	2.14r	1914	C	1/6,2/-,3/-	w		45.2y	Cu-m	1

1. Copies of this printing were supplied for use in the University of Durham. The price statement is unlikely to be contemporary; it was probably unaltered from the previous printing.

Sheet 46 a. *Balquhidder* b. *Ben More* Revised 1903 24 by 18

1	2	3	4	5	6	7	8	9	10	11	12	13
1907	oss.a	-	-	-	1907	A	1/6,2/-,2/6	w	6/07	46.Ou	Cpt-m	
1907	oss.b	9.12	9.12	9.12r	1912	C	1/6,2/-,2/6	w		46.1x	Cu-m	
1907	oss.b	9.12	9.12	9.12r	1912	C	1/6,2/-,3/-	w		46.1y	Cu-m	

Sheet 47 a. *Crieff* b. *Comrie and Crieff* Revised 1904 24 by 18

1	2	3	4	5	6	7	8	9	10	11	12	13
1907	oss.a	-	-	-	1907	A	1/6,2/-,2/6	w	12/07	47.Ou	Cpt-m	
1907	oss.b	10.12	9.12	9.12r	1912	C	1/6,2/-,2/6	w		47.1x	RSGS	
1907	oss.b	7.14+	9.12	6.14r	1914	C	1/6,2/-,2/6	w		47.2x	Cu-m	
1907	oss.b	9.20	9.12	6.14r	1914	C	np	w		47.3z	Cu-m	

Sheet 48 *Perth* Revised 1904-5 24 by 18

1	2	3	4	5	6	7	8	9	10	11	12	13
1908	oss	-	-	-	1908	A	1/6,2/-,2/6	w	6/08	48.Ou	Cpt-m	1
1908	oss	-	-	-	1908	A	1/6,2/-,2/6	w		-	Cu-m	2
1908	oss	6.20	-	-	1908	C	np	w		48.1z	Cu-m	

1. With *Expansion* ↕ left of the legend. 2. With *Expansion* ↔ below the left end of the legend. See page 134.

Sheet 49 a. *Arbroath* b. *Arbroath and St. Andrews* Revised 1904-5 24 by 18

1	2	3	4	5	6	7 8	9	10	11	12	13
1908	oss.a	-	-	-	1907	A 1/6,2/-,2/6	w	3/08	49.0u	Cpt	1
1908	oss.a	-	-	-	1907	A 1/6,2/-,2/6	w		-	PC	2
1908	oss.b	9.13	9.13	9.13r	1913	C 1/6,2/-,2/6	w		49.1x	Cu-m	
1908	oss.b	9.13	9.13	9.13r	1913	C 1/6,2/-,3/-	w		49.1y	Rg	

1. With *Expansion* ↕ left of the legend. 2. With *Expansion* ↔ below the left end of the legend. See page 134.

Sheets 50 and 51 see sheet 42.50.51.43.

Sheet 52 *Tobermory* Revised 1905 24 by 18

1	2	3	4	5	6	7 8	9	10	11	12	13
1909	oss	-	-	-	1909	A 1/6,2/-,2/6	w	6/09	52.0u	Cpt	1
1909	oss	6.20	-	-	1909	C np	w		52.1z	NLS	

1. With *Expansion* ↕ left of the legend. See page 134.

Sheet 53 *Ben Nevis* Revised 1904 24 by 18

1	2	3	4	5	6	7 8	9	10	11	12	13
1909	oss	-	-	-	1909	A 1/6,2/-,2/6	w	3/09	53.0u	Cpt-m	1
1909	oss	-	-	-	1909	A 1/6,2/-,2/6	w		-	Gu	2
1909	oss	-	-	-	1909	A 1/6,2/-,3/-	w		-	Mg	
1909	oss	6.20	-	-	1909	C np	w		53.1z	Cu-m	

1. With *Expansion* ↕ left of the legend. 2. With *Expansion* ↔ below the left end of the legend.

Sheet 54 *Rannoch* Revised 1904 24 by 18

1	2	3	4	5	6	7 8	9	10	11	12	13
1908	oss	-	-	-	1908	A 1/6,2/-,2/6	w	3/09	54.0u	Cpt-m	1
1908	oss	-	-	-	1908	A 1/6,2/-,2/6	w		-	Gu	2
1908	oss	-	-	-	1908	A 1/6,2/-,3/-	w		54.0v	Cu-m	

1. With *Expansion* ↕ left of the legend. 2. With *Expansion* ↔ below the left end of the legend.

Sheet 55 *Blair Atholl* Revised 1904 24 by 18

1	2	3	4	5	6	7 8	9	10	11	12	13
1908	oss	-	-	-	1908	A 1/6,2/-,2/6	w	3/09	55.0u	Cpt-m	
1908	oss	8.10	-	7.10i	1910	A 1/6,2/-,2/6	w		55.1u	Cu-m	
1908	oss	8.10	-	7.10i	1910	A 1/6,2/-,3/-	w		55.1v	Cu-m	
1908	oss	1000/23	-	7.10i	1910	A np	w		55.2w	Cu-m	

This is the only Scottish sheet recorded with a railway insertion rather than revision date.

Sheet 56 *Blairgowrie* Revised 1904-5 24 by 18

1	2	3	4	5	6	7 8	9	10	11	12	13
1909	oss	-	-	-	1909	A 1/6,2/-,2/6	w	3/09	56.0u	Cpt-m	
1909	oss	8.10	-	-	1910	A 1/6,2/-,2/6	w		56.1u	NLS	
1909	oss	8.10	-	-	1910	A 1/6,2/-,3/-	w		56.1v	Rg	

Sheets 57. 57A. a. *Forfar* b. *Montrose and Forfar* Revised 1905 24 by 18

1	2	3	4	5	6	7 8	9	10	11	12	13
1909	oss.a	-	-	-	1909	A 1/6,2/-,2/6	w	11/09	57+0u	Cpt	
1909	oss.b	2.14	-	2.14r	1914	C 1/6,2/-,2/6	w		57+2x	PC	
1909	oss.b	2.14	-	2.14r	1914	C 1/6,2/-,3/-	w		57+2y	Cu-m	
1909	oss.b	1.20	-	2.14r	1914	C np	w		57+2z	Bc	

Sheet 57A appears as an extrusion, with the northern length of the border extended into a thirteenth two-inch section. KGM unconfirmed 57.1 state omitted (see page 82).

Sheets 58 and 59 were not published in colour.

Sheet 60 *Rhum* Revised 1905 24 by 18

1	2	3	4	5	6	7 8	9	10	11	12	13
1909	oss	-	-	-	1909	A 1/6,2/-,2/6	w	10/09	60+0u	Cpt	

With unnoted extrusions from sheet 61 to complete coverage of the Eigg and from 70 to complete coverage of Canna. This is unusual for a Scottish sheet in that its rights of way notice omits reference to tracks and footpaths.

Sheet 61 *Arisaig*   Revised 1905   24 by 18

1	2	3	4	5	6	7	8	9	10	11	12	13
1909	oss	-	-	-	1909	A	1/6,2/-,2/6	w	10/09	61.Ou	Cpt-m	
1909	oss	5.20	-	-	1909	C	np	w		61.1z	Rg	

Sheet 62 *Loch Eil*   Revised 1905   24 by 18

1909	oss	-	-	-	1909	A	1/6,2/-,2/6	w	11/09	62.Ou	Cpt-m	
1909	oss	-	-	-	1909	A	1/6,2/-,3/-	w		62.Ov	Rg	

With *Levels of parallel roads* in the north-west corner, first engraved on the outline original of this sheet for inclusion in Sir Henry James, *Notes on the parallel roads of Lochaber.* Southampton: Ordnance Survey, 1874.

Sheet 63 *Glen Roy*   Revised 1905   24 by 18

1909	oss	-	-	-	1909	A	1/6,2/-,2/6	w	11/09	63.Ou	Cpt-m	
1909	oss	-	-	-	1909	A	1/6,2/-,3/-	w		63.Ov	Rg	

With *Levels of parallel roads* in the north-west corner, first engraved on the outline original of this sheet for inclusion in Sir Henry James, *Notes on the parallel roads of Lochaber.* Southampton: Ordnance Survey, 1874.

Sheet 64 *Kingussie*   Revised 1905   24 by 18

1909	oss	-	-	-	1909	A	1/6,2/-,2/6	w	7/09	64.Ou	Cpt	
1909	oss	9.12	-	9.12r	1912	C	1/6,2/-,2/6	w		64.1x	Cu-m	
1909	oss	9.12	-	9.12r	1912	C	1/6,2/-,3/-	w		64.1y	Cu-m	
1909	oss	11.20	-	9.12r	1912	C	np	w		64.2z	Rg	

Sheet 65 *Balmoral*   Revised 1905   24 by 18

1909	oss	-	-	-	1909	A	1/6,2/-,2/6	w	6/09	65.Ou	Cpt	
1909	oss	1.14	1.14	1.14r	1914	C	1/6,2/-,2/6	w		65.1x	Cu-m	
1909	oss	1.14	1.14	1.14r	1914	C	1/6,2/-,3/-	w		65.1y	Cu-m	
1909	oss	1.14	1.14	1.14r	1914	C	np	w		65.1z	Mg	
1909	oss	1000/23	1.14	1.14r	1914	C	np	w		65.2z	Cu-m	

Sheet 66 *Banchory*   Revised 1905-6   24 by 18

1909	oss	-	-	-	1909	A	1/6,2/-,2/6	w	6/09	66.Ou	Cpt-m	
1909	oss	-	-	-	1909	A	1/6,2/-,3/-	w		66.Ov	Cu-m	
1909	oss	250/27	-	-	1909	C	2/-	w		66.1z	Rg	1

1. Price statements were reinstated from 1926. This one reads "Price flat and unmounted 2/-. For Prices mounted and folded see Lists & Catalogue".

Sheet 67 *Stonehaven*   Revised 1905   24 by 18

1909	oss	-	-	-	1909	A	1/6,2/-,2/6	w	9/09	67.Ou	Cpt-m	
1909	oss	-	-	-	1909	A	1/6,2/-,3/-	w		-	Rg	

Sheets 68 and 69 were not published in colour.

Sheet 70 *Minginish*   Revised 1905   24 by 18

1910	oss	-	-	-	1910	A	1/6,2/-,2/6	w	3/10	70.Ou	Cpt-m	
1910	oss	8.20	-	-	1910	C	np	w		70.1z	Cu-m	

Green woodland fill is omitted from all copies seen of this sheet; it should be present in 7B.

Sheet 71 *Glenelg*   Revised 1905   24 by 18

1910	oss	-	-	-	1910	A	1/6,2/-,2/6	w	9/10	71.Ou	Cpt	
1910	oss	9.20	-	-	1910	C	np	w		71.1z	Cu-m	

Sheet 72 *Cluanie* — Revised 1906 — 24 by 18

1910	oss	-	-	-	1910	A	1/6,2/-,2/6	w	3/10	72.Ou	Cpt-m

Some copies were supplied for use in Birmingham University School (copy Bg).

Sheet 73 a. *Fort Augustus* b. *Loch Ness (South)* — Revised 1906 — 24 by 18

1909	oss.a	-	-	-	1909	A	1/6,2/-,2/6	w	12/09	73.Ou	Cpt-m
1909	oss.b	9.12	-	9.12r	1912	C	1/6,2/-,2/6	w		73.1x	Cu-m
1909	oss.b	5.22	-	9.12r	1912	C	np	w		73.2z	NLS

Sheet 74 *Grantown-on-Spey* — Revised 1906 — 24 by 18

1909	oss	-	-	-	1909	A	1/6,2/-,2/6	w	12/09	74.Ou	Cpt-m	
1909	oss	-	-	-	1909	C	1/6,2/-,3/-	w		74.Oy	Cu-m	1
1909	oss	5.22	-	-	1909	C	np	w		74.1z	Cu-m	

1. "Crown Copyright Reserved" appears bottom right instead of bottom centre.

Sheet 75 *Tomintoul* — Revised 1906 — 24 by 18

1909	oss	-	-	-	1909	A	1/6,2/-,2/6	w	12/09	75.Ou	Cpt-m
1909	oss	-	-	-	1909	A	1/6,2/-,3/-	w		75.Ov	Cu-m
1909	oss	5.22	-	-	1909	C	np	w		-	PC

Sheet 76 *Inverurie* — Revised 1905-6 — 24 by 18

1910	oss	-	-	-	1910	A	1/6,2/-,2/6	w	3/10	76.Ou	Cpt-m
1910	oss	-	-	-	1910	A	1/6,2/-,3/-	w		-	Rg
1910	oss	8.20	-	-	1910	C	np	w		76.1z	Cu-m

KGM 76.Oy state omitted (see page 82).

Sheet 77 *Aberdeen* — Revised 1906-7 — 24 by 18

1909	oss	-	-	-	1909	A	1/6,2/-,2/6	w	8/09	77.Ou	Cpt-m
1909	oss	-	-	-	1909	A	1/6,2/-,3/-	w		77.Ov	Rg

Sheets 78 and 79 were not published in colour.

Sheet 80 *Portree* — Revised 1907 — 24 by 18

1910	oss	-	-	-	1910	A	1/6,2/-,2/6	w	9/10	80.Ou	Cpt-m
1910	oss	9.20	-	-	1910	C	np	w		80.1z	Cu-m

Sheet 81 *Applecross* — Revised 1907 — 24 by 18

1910	oss	-	-	-	1910	A	1/6,2/-,2/6	w	6/10	81.Ou	Cpt-m
1910	oss	5.22	-	-	1910	C	np	w		81.1z	Cu-m

Sheet 82 *Lochcarron* — Revised 1907 — 24 by 18

1910	oss	-	-	-	1910	A	1/6,2/-,2/6	w	6/10	82.Ou	Cpt-m
1910	oss	-	-	-	1910	A	1/6,2/-,3/-	w		-	Bc

Sheet 83 *Dingwall and Inverness* — Revised 1908-9 — 24 by 18

1913	oss	-	-	s	1913	C	1/6,2/-,2/6	w	2/13	83.Ox	Cpt-m
1913	oss	-	-	s	1913	C	np	w		83.Oz	Cu-m

Sheet 84 *Nairn and Moray Firth* — Revised 1908-9 — 24 by 18

1913	oss	-	-	s	1913	C	1/6,2/-,2/6	w	3/13	84.Ox	Cpt-m

1	2	3	4	5	6	7	8	9	10	11	12	13

Sheet 85 unnamed [*Rothes*] Revised 1908 24 by 18

1	2	3	4	5	6	7	8	9	10	11	12	13
1911	oss.x	-		-	s	1911	A 1/6,2/-,2/6	w	11/11	85.Ou	Cpt-m	
1911	oss.x	-		-	s	1911	A 1/6,2/-,3/-	w		85.Ov	Cu-m	
1911	oss.x	6.22		-	s	1911	C np	w		85.1z	Cu-m	

Ellis Martin covers with name *Rothes and District* were issued for this sheet.

Sheet 86 *Huntly* Revised 1906-7 24 by 18

1	2	3	4	5	6	7	8	9	10	11	12	13
1911	oss	-		-	-	1911	A 1/6,2/-,2/6	w	5/11	86.Ou	Cpt-m	
1911	oss	-		-	-	1911	A 1/6,2/-,3/6	w		-	Rg	1

1. The 3/- price appears as 3/6, no doubt the consequence of a poorly erased "6".

Sheet 87 *Peterhead* Revised 1907 24 by 18

1	2	3	4	5	6	7	8	9	10	11	12	13
1910	oss	-		-	-	1910	A 1/6,2/-,2/6	w	10/10	87.Ou	Cpt-m	
1910	oss	-		-	-	1910	A 1/6,2/-,3/-	w		-	Rg	

Sheets 88 and 89 were not published in colour.

Sheet 90 *Rudha Hunish* Revised 1907 24 by 18

1	2	3	4	5	6	7	8	9	10	11	12	13
1910	oss	-		-	-	1910	A 1/6,2/-,2/6	w	11/10	90.Ou	Cpt	
1910	oss	6.20		-	-	1910	C np	w		90.1z	Rg	1

1. Green woodland fill is omitted (J9).

Sheets 91. 100. *Gairloch* Revised 1907 24 by 18

1	2	3	4	5	6	7	8	9	10	11	12	13
1910	oss	-		-	-	1910	A 1/6,2/-,2/6	w	11/10	91+Ou	Cpt-m	
1910	oss	-		-	-	1910	C np	w		91+Oz	Cu-m	

Sheet 100 is inset.

Sheet 92 *Inverbroom* Revised 1907 24 by 18

1	2	3	4	5	6	7	8	9	10	11	12	13
1910	oss	-		-	-	1910	A 1/6,2/-,2/6	w	11/10	92.Ou	Cpt	
1910	oss	3.20		-	-	1910	C np	w		92.1z	Cu-m	

Sheet 93 *Alness* Revised 1909 24 by 18

1	2	3	4	5	6	7	8	9	10	11	12	13
1913	oss	-		-	s	1913	C 1/6,2/-,2/6	w	2/13	93.Ox	Cpt-m	

Sheet 94 *Cromarty and Tain* Revised 1909 24 by 18

1	2	3	4	5	6	7	8	9	10	11	12	13
1913	oss	-		-	s	1913	C 1/6,2/-,2/6	w	3/13	94.Ox	Cpt-m	
1913	oss	6.22		-	s	1913	C np	w		94.1z	NLS	

Sheet 95 unnamed [*Elgin*] Revised 1908 24 by 18

1	2	3	4	5	6	7	8	9	10	11	12	13
1911	oss.x	-		-	s	1911	A 1/6,2/-,2/6	w	11/11	95.Ou	Cpt	
1911	oss.x	-		-	s	1911	A 1/6,2/-,3/-	w		95.Ov	Rg	

Ellis Martin covers with name *Elgin and District* were issued for this sheet.

Sheet 96 a. *Banff* b. *Cullen and Banff* Revised 1907-8 24 by 18

1	2	3	4	5	6	7	8	9	10	11	12	13
1910	oss.a	-		-	-	1910	A 1/6,2/-,2/6	w	12/10	96.Ou	Cpt-m	
1910	oss.b	9.12		-	9.12r	1912	C 1/6,2/-,2/6	w		96.1x	Ag	
1910	oss.b	9.12		-	9.12r	1912	C 1/6,2/-,3/-	w		96.1y	Cu-m	

Sheet 97 *Fraserburgh* Revised 1907 24 by 18

1	2	3	4	5	6	7	8	9	10	11	12	13
1910	oss	-		-	-	1910	A 1/6,2/-,2/6	w	9/10	97.Ou	Cpt-m	
1910	oss	9.12		-	9.12r	1912	C 1/6,2/-,2/6	w		97.1x	NLS	
1910	oss	9.12		-	9.12r	1912	C 1/6,2/-,3/-	w		97.1y	Cu-m	

Sheets 98 and 99 were not published in colour.

Sheet 100 see sheet 91.100.

Sheet 101 *Ullapool*   Revised 1908   24 by 18

| 1910 | oss | - | - | s | 1910 | A | 1/6,2/-,2/6 | w | 12/10 | 101.Ou | Cpt-m |
| 1910 | oss | 5.20 | - | s | 1910 | C | np | w | | 101.1z | Cu-m |

Sheet 102 *Lairg*   Revised 1910   24 by 18

| 1913 | oss | - | - | s | 1913 | C | 1/6,2/-,2/6 | w | 3/13 | 102.Ox | Cpt-m |
| 1913 | oss | - | - | s | 1913 | C | 1/6,2/-,3/- | w | | 102.Oy | Rg |

Sheet 103 *Helmsdale and Dornoch*   Revised 1909   24 by 18

| 1913 | oss | - | - | s | 1913 | C | 1/6,2/-,2/6 | w | 3/13 | 103.Ox | Cpt |
| 1913 | oss | - | - | s | 1913 | C | 1/6,2/-,3/- | w | | 103.Oy | Rg |

Sheets 104 to 106 were not published in colour.

Sheet 107 *Lochinver*   Revised 1908   24 by 18

| 1911 | oss | - | - | s | 1911 | A | 1/6,2/-,2/6 | w | 3/11 | 107.Ou | Cpt-m |
| 1911 | oss | - | - | s | 1911 | C | np | w | | 107.Oz | Cu-m |

Sheet 108 *Altnaharra*   Revised 1908   24 by 18

| 1911 | oss | - | - | s | 1911 | A | 1/6,2/-,2/6 | w | 3/11 | 108.Ou | Cpt-m |
| 1911 | oss | 5.20 | - | s | 1911 | C | np | w | | 108.1z | Gu |

Sheet 109 *Kildonan*   Revised 1909   24 by 18

| 1913 | oss | - | - | s | 1913 | C | 1/6,2/-,2/6 | w | 3/13 | 109.Ox | Cpt |

Overlap: c.6⅝ by 18 miles with sheet 110.

Sheet 110 *Latheron*   Revised 1910   24 by 18

| 1913 | oss | - | - | s | 1913 | C | 1/6,2/-,2/6 | w | 3/13 | 110+Ox | Cpt |

Overlap: c.6⅝ by 18 miles with sheet 109. Despite its appearance on most indexes, sheet 110 was published west of its true position in order to maximise its land coverage.

Sheets 111 and 112 were not published in colour.

Sheet 113 *Cape Wrath*   Revised 1908   24 by 18

| 1911 | oss | - | - | s | 1911 | A | 1/6,2/-,2/6 | w | 3/11 | 113.Ou | Cpt-m |
| 1911 | oss | 4.20 | - | s | 1911 | C | np | w | | 113.1z | Rg |

With insets of Sula Sgeir and Rona. There is no green woodland plate.

Sheet 114 *Tongue*   Revised 1908   24 by 18

| 1911 | oss | - | - | s | 1911 | A | 1/6,2/-,2/6 | w | 3/11 | 114.Ou | Cpt |
| 1911 | oss | 9.20 | - | s | 1911 | C | np | w | | 114.1z | NLS |

Sheet 115 *Reay*   Revised 1909-10   24 by 18

| 1913 | oss | - | - | s | 1913 | C | 1/6,2/-,2/6 | w | 6/13 | 115.Ox | Cpt-m |

Sheet 116 *Wick and Thurso*   Revised 1909   24 by 20

| 1913 | oss | - | - | s | 1913 | C | 1/6,2/-,2/6 | w | 6/13 | 116+Ox | Cpt |

With an unnoted extension into sheet 117 to complete coverage of Dunnet Head.

Sheets 117. 118. Parts of sheets 119. 120. *Orkney Islands (South)*   Revised 1910   35½ by 27
1913   oss   -   -   s   1913   C   1/6,2/-,2/6   w   11/13   117+Ox   Cpt
There is no green woodland plate.

Sheets 121. 122. Parts of sheets 119. 120. *Orkney Islands [North]*   Revised 1910   35½ by 27
1913   oss   -   -   s   1913   C   1/6,2/-,2/6   w   11/13   122+Ox   Cpt
There is no green woodland plate.

Sheets 123. 124. 125. 126. Parts of sheets 127. 128. *Shetland Islands (South)*
                                                                                                                 Revised 1910   27¼ by 34⅞
1913   oss   -   -   s   1913   C   1/6,2/-,2/6   w   12/13   126+Ox   Cpt
There is no green woodland plate. Fair Isle (sheet 123), Foula (on sheet 125) and Ve Skerries are inset.

Sheets 129. 130. 131. Parts of sheets 127. 128. *Shetland Islands (North)*
                                                                                                                 Revised 1910   28⅝ by 36
1913   oss   -   -   s   1913   C   1/6,2/-,2/6   w   12/13   130+Ox   Cpt-m
There is no green woodland plate. Out Skerries are inset. With extrusions to cover Muckle Roe, Whalsey, the east end of Fetlar, and Esha Ness.

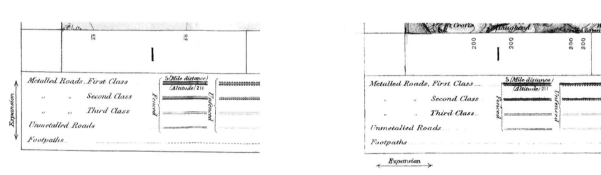

Figure 21 "Expansion", with its double headed arrow, in its vertical and horizontal positions. The meaning of this is unknown.

District maps

Aberdeen District   Revised 1905-7   29 by 20
1913   oss   -   -   -   1913   C   1/6,2/-,2/6   w   6/13   ABD.Ox   Cpt-m

Glasgow District   Revised a. 1901-2 b. 1902   29¼ by 19⅛
1914   oss.a   -   -   s   1914   C   1/6,2/-,2/6   g   5/14   GLD.Ox   Cpt-m
1914   oss.a   -   -   s   1914   C   1/6,2/-,3/-   g   -   Eg
1914   oss.b   -   -   S   1920   C   np   ANg   GLD.1z   Cu-m   1
One of a group of maps issued between 1913 and 1922 with enhanced colour schemes (see page 18 and appendix 4). 1. The heading "(Third Edition)" is deleted; there is a new heading "Edition of 1921".

Loch Lomond District. Parts of sheets 37. 38. 29. 30.   Revised 1902-4   27 by 20
1908   oss   -   -   -   1908   A   1/6,2/-,2/6   n   7/08   LLD.Ou   Cpt-m
With an inset of the northern continuation of Loch Lomond. See figure 4. This is the only recorded Scottish sheet with a narrow (approximately quarter-inch) border. Ellis Martin incorporated "Sheets 37 & 38" into his cover design for this map. It was common practice to include the component sheet numbers of district maps on H.3 standard cover designs, but was distinctly abnormal thereafter, and especially so on covers carrying an index diagram.

Tourist maps

These seven maps were members of a group issued between 1913 and 1922 with enhanced colour schemes. For information on the features that distinguish them the reader is referred to page 18 and appendix 4.

Burns' Country   Revised 1902   22 by 32
1921 oss   -   -   -   1920   C np   ANg 1921/2 16.5   Cpt-m

Deeside   Revised 1894, 1905-6   34 by 22
1920 oss   -   -   -   1920   C np   ANg 6/20   16.5   Cpt-m
With extrusions to cover Tomintoul and Aboyne.

Lower Strath Spey   Revised 1894   26 by 36
1921 oss   -   -   s   1920   C np   ANg 1921/2 16.5   Cpt-m
If the revision date is to be believed, this is the product of the first, not the second revision.

Oban   Revised 1895, 1905   22 by 32
1920 oss   -   -   -   1920   C np   ANg 6/20   16.5   Cpt

Rothesay & Firth of Clyde   Revised 1895, 1904   24 by 34
1920 oss   -   -   -   1920   C np   ANg 1922/1 16.5   Cpt-m

Scott's Country   Revised 1901-2   32 by 22
1921 oss   -   -   -   1920   C np   ANg 1921/1 16.5   Cpt-m

The Trossachs & Loch Lomond   Revised 1895, 1904   34 by 28
1920 oss   -   -   -   1920   C np   ANg 1920/3 16.5   Cpt-m

Military maps

Scottish Command Training Map, 1911. Parts of sheets 21. 22. 13. 14.   Revised 1902 c.24 by c.25¾
1911 oss   -   -   -   1911   A np   s   -   PC
With prohibited areas and specified locations overprinted in red. The northern limit of the map is the same as that of sheets 21 and 22. The imprint is in the "English" style.

Admission to the Staff College. Tactics   c.8¾ by 6
1912 -   -   -   -   -   A np   s   -   book
A small sheet covering the East Kilbride area, printed for the June 1912 examination paper. In *Report on the examination for admission to the Staff College, Camberley, held in June-July, 1912, with copies of the examination papers.* London: HMSO.

4. One-inch Third Edition map of Ireland : small sheet series

It may seem odd to word the heading of this section "Third Edition" and "small sheet series", since only three sheets published in Southampton are recorded that advanced beyond the coloured edition of 1901-07 based on the first revision, and none of them have third edition headings. But they merit their status as third edition sheets, being based on the second national revision which began in Ireland in 1908, and, as in England and Wales, are most conveniently distinguished from the edition that followed them by emphasising the difference in sheet size. They have a list of the counties covered top left, the Ordnance Survey of Ireland heading top centre, and the sheet name and number top right. Standard sheet coverage is 18 by 12 miles. Sheets produced in Dublin after 1922 which display second revision dates are listed in supplement 2.

Sheets 1 to 35 are not recorded in colour.

Sheet 36 *Belfast*   Revised 1912   18 by 12
1914   osi   11.19   -   s   1919   C   1/-,1/6,2/6   gw   24.A.3.2   Cu-m
1914   osi   11.19   -   s   1919   C   np   gw   24.A.3.2   RGS
With the graticule border of the engraved original, surrounded by the standard alpha-numeric border divided into two-inch blocks. Without contours. The imprint is apparently that of the 1914 outline edition original, and no coloured issue earlier than 1919 has been recorded. It would be usual for a printing date also to have been present. With the publication of LSS sheet 16.17 in 1918, it is hard to determine what justification the OS had in 1919 for printing this sheet at all.

Sheets 37 to 59 are not recorded in colour.

Sheet 60. Part of sheet 61. *Newry and Castlewellan*   Revised 1912   22 by 12
1914   osi   250/32   -   s   1912   C   np   ANn   24.A.3.3   OSNI
With an alpha-numeric squaring system, and contours in brown. The imprint is that of the 1914 engraved outline edition of sheet 60, and no coloured issue earlier than this of 1932 has been recorded. Only three years later it was superseded by a new map, with the same sheet lines on three sides but extended nine miles further south to complete coverage of the Carlingford Lough area. This was partially revised in 1935 and published as *The Mourne Mountains* by the Ordnance Survey of Northern Ireland in their One-inch Popular Edition. It was a district map, with contours in brown and coloured with layers, not hachures (pre-war printings 750/35, 2500/35).

Sheets 62 to 128 are not recorded in colour.

Sheet 129 *Baltinglass*   Revised 1911   18 by 12
1913   osi   2.13   -   s   1913   C   1/-,1/6,2/-   n   24.A.3.1   Dtf
1913   osi   2.14+   -   2.14rs   1914   C   1/-,1/6,2/-   n   7/14   24.A.3.1   Dtf
1913   osi   2.14+   -   2.14rs   1914   C   np   n   24.A.3.1   Ob
Without contours. The imprint relates directly to this coloured issue, not the engraved original: thus the presence of the word "printed" instead of "published" would appear to be an error. See figure 17.

Sheets 130 to 205 are not recorded in colour.

District map

Belfast District   Revised 1900-1   28 by 18
1912   osi   -   -   -   1912   A   1/6,2/-,2/6   n   11/12   24.A.7   Cpt
This is not a third edition map, being derived from the first national revision, but it is included here for its interesting parallels. In its design and specification it approaches more closely than any other Irish map the contemporary coloured Third Edition in England and Wales. The colours used are the same, including, probably for the first time on an Irish one-inch map, contours in red. Detail differences include submarine contours measured in fathoms, against contours in bed of sea measured in feet.

Military maps

a. *Manœuvre Map Ireland. 1912. Kilworth* b. *Manœuvre Map Ireland. 1913. Kilworth*
Parts of sheets 165. 166. 176. 177. 187. 188.   No revision date   25 by 19
1912   osi.a   -   -   -   -   A   np   s   -   PC
1913   osi.b   -   -   -   -   C   np   s   -   PC
The maps were "Printed at the Ordnance Survey Office, Southampton". They are borderline cases for inclusion in this list, but they are probably based on the second national revision which had covered this area in 1909-10, but may, nonetheless, derive directly from the outline rather than the coloured map. With coloured hachures and road infill; contours, water and woodland are on the black plate. With a one-inch alpha-numeric squaring system overprinted in green. Government ground is overprinted in green, manoeuvre area particulars in blue, brown, red, out of bounds areas in yellow. Maps in covers may have leaflets pasted on their inside faces, one giving instructions on the use and mental subdivision of the squaring system, the other a reference list of the overprinted colours and their meaning.

Supplement 1. *Northern Ireland after 1922*

These are the only issues recorded (in addition to 60.61 already listed) covering Northern Ireland to be published after 1922. They still carry first revision dates, but it is quite probable that the 1945 printings at least carried updated information derived from the 1936-38 revision of Northern Ireland. They seem to have been printed as stop gap measures prior to the publication of OSNI Popular Edition sheets.

Sheet 35 *Dungannon*   Revised 1899-9   18 by 12
1902   osi   245/Cr   -   -   1904   A   np   w   24.A.4.1   RGS   1
1. The original printing was from a transfer to stone in 1904. This printing is coloured, without hachures and with contours in brown. There is a "Provisional Edition" heading.

Sheet 47 *Armagh*   Revised 1900   18 by 12
1902   osi   100/34+   -   -   1903   A   np   w   24.A.2.1   NYp   1,2
1902   osi   345/Cr+   -   -   1945   C   np   w   24.A.4.2   RGS   1,3
1. The original printing was from a transfer to stone in 1903. 2. The full print code string is 2.07,100/34. 3. This printing is coloured, without hachures and with contours in brown.

Supplement 2. *Ireland after 1922*

No Irish coloured small sheets have yet been recorded that were reprinted in Dublin before 1938. From then on there were well over seventy new printings, usually containing new railway revision, the last apparently being in 1956. Several carry no full revision date at all. Others retain the first revision dates of the Southampton originals published between 1902 and 1907. Those published during the 1950s also carry partial revision dates.[185] The remainder are listed below: they have similar partial revision dates, but their principal revision dates have been updated from first to second revision, which *de facto* gives them third edition status. It has yet to be established how reliable these modified revision dates are.

As it happens Ordnance Survey of Ireland were also publishing one-inch outline sheets during the 1950s with similar partial revision dates. The extent of this work and how much of it was common to the work on the coloured map are matters yet to be fully investigated, but the indications so far are that there was not a joint programme of publishing an outline and a coloured version of each sheet required, though there was indeed considerable overlap. There was also one essential distinction, that the relevant outline sheets already were third edition.

Sheets 1 & 5 *Carndonagh*   Revised 1911, partly revised 1953   18 by 17
-     osi   -   -   1949r   1953   c   np   n   24.B.1.3   Ob

Sheet 70 *Dundalk*   Revised 1912, partly revised 1953   18 by 12
-     osi   7.04,2.07 -   1949r   1953   c   np   w   24.B.1.3   Ob

Sheet 101 *Trim*   Revised 1914, partly revised 1952   18 by 12
-     osi   7.07   -   1949r   1952   c   np   n   24.B.1.3   Ob

Sheet 131 *Mullagh*   Revised 1912, partly revised 1952   18 by 12
-     osi   3.09   -   1949r   1952   c   np   n   24.B.1.3   Ob

Sheets 140. 141 *Kilrush*   Revised 1911, partly revised 1951   24 by 12
-     osi   -   -   1949r   1951   c   np   n   24.B.1.3   Ob

Sheet 142 *Foynes*   Revised 1912, partly revised 1956   18 by 12
-     osi   -   -   1949r   1946   c   np   n   24.B.1.4   Ob
With first and second class roads in red.

Sheet 143 *Limerick*   Revised 1911, partly revised 1951   18 by 12
-     osi   4.20   -   1949r   1951   c   np   n   24.B.1.3   Ob
-     osi   -   -   1949r   1951   c   np   n   24.B.1.4   Bg   1
1. With classified roads in red.

Sheet 147 *Kilkenny*   Revised 1910, partly revised 1952   18 by 12
-     osi   8.05,1.08 -   1949r   1952   c   np   n   24.B.1.3   Ob

Sheet 148 *Bunclody*   Revised 1910, partly revised 1952   18 by 12
-     osi   2.06,12.08 -   1949r   1952   c   np   n   24.B.1.3   Ob

Sheets 150. 151 *Listowel*   Revised 1911, partly revised 1952   24 by 12
-     osi   7.07   -   1949r   1952   c   np   n   24.B.1.3   Ob

Sheet 153 *Rathkeale*   Revised 1910, partly revised 1952   18 by 12
-     osi   1.07   -   1949r   1952   c   np   n   24.B.1.3   Ob

---

[185] A provisional listing of these sheets may be found in Roger Hellyer, "A cartobibliography of the one-inch map of Ireland, in colour, 1901-1956", *Sheetlines* 63 (2002), 12-38.

1	2	3	4	5	6	7	8	9	10	11	12	13

Sheets 160. 171 *Dingle* — Revised 1908, partly revised 1952 — 18 by 18

| - | osi | 11.07 | - | 1949r | 1952 | c | np | n | | 24.B.1.3 | Ob | |

Sheet 162 *Tralee* — Revised 1909, partly revised 1952 — 18 by 12

| - | osi | 11.07 | - | 1949r | 1952 | c | np | n | | 24.B.1.3 | Bg | |

Sheet 164 *Rath Luirc* — Revised 1909, partly revised 1952 — 18 by 12

| - | osi | 1.08++ | - | 1949r | 1952 | c | np | n | | 24.B.1.3 | Ob | |

The full print code string is 1.06,3.06,1.08.

Sheet 166 *Clonmel* — Revised 1910, partly revised 1952 — 18 by12

| - | osi | 4.18++ | - | 1949r | 1952 | c | np | n | | 24.B.1.3 | Ob | |

The full print code string is 6.06,10.06,4.18.

Sheets 168 *Waterford* **179** *Tramore* — Revised 1909, partly revised 1952 — 18 by 19

| - | osi | 8.08 | - | 1949r | 1952 | c | np | n | | 24.B.1.3 | Ob | |

Sheets 169. 170. 180. 181 unnamed [*Wexford*] — Revised 1909, partly revised 1952 — 24 by 18

| - | osi | 2.08 | - | 1949r | 1952 | c | np | n | | 24.B.1.3 | Ob | |

Sheet 173 *Killarney* — Revised 1908, partly revised 1953 — 18 by 12

| - | osi | 7.07 | - | 1949r | 1953 | c | np | n | | 24.B.1.3 | Ob | |

Sheet 174 *Millstreet* — Revised 1909, partly revised 1953 — 18 by 12

| - | osi | - | - | 1949rs | - | c | np | g | | 24.B.1.2 | Ob | |

With a Third Edition heading. The legend notes contours in black, but they are not on the map.

Sheet 184 *Kenmare* — Revised 1908, partly revised 1952 — 18 by 12

| - | osi | 2.06,12.08 | - | 1949r | 1952 | c | np | n | | 24.B.1.3 | Ob | |

Sheet 185 *Ballymakeery* — Revised 1909, partly revised 1952 — 18 by 12

| - | osi | - | - | 1949r | 1952 | c | np | n | | 24.B.1.3 | Ob | |

Sheet 187 *Cork* — a. Revised 1909 b. Revised 1909, partly revised 1952 — 18 by 12

| 1945 | osi.a | - | - | 1945r | 1945 | c | 1/-,1/6 | n | | 24.B.1.2 | RGS | 1 |
| - | osi.b | - | - | 1949r | 1952 | c | np | n | | 24.B.1.2 | Ob | 1 |

1. With a Third Edition heading. See also figure 20.

Sheets 191 & 197 Part of Sheet 198 *Kenmare River and Castletown Bearhaven* — Revised 1908, partly revised 1952 — 18 by c.19

| - | osi | 9.07 | - | 1949r | 1952 | c | np | n | | 24.B.1.3 | Ob | |

With an inset of Dursey Head.

Sheet 192 *Glengarriff* — Revised 1908, partly revised 1952 — 18 by 12

| - | osi | 12.48++ | - | 1949r | 1952 | A | np | n | | 24.B.1.3 | PC | |

The full print code string is 6.06,9.07,12.48.

Sheet 200. 205 *Skibbereen* — Revised 1899, partly revised 1952 — 18 by 16

| - | osi | - | - | 1949r | 1952 | c | np | w | | 24.B.1.2 | Ob | |

With Third Edition heading, though still with a first revision date!

Sheets 201. 202 *Clonakilty* — Revised 1908, partly revised 1956 — 24 by 12

| - | osi | - | - | 1949r | 1908 | c | np | n | | 24.B.1.4 | Ob | |

With first and second class roads in red.

5. One-inch Third Edition Map of Ireland : large sheet series

All the maps listed in this section are members of a group of maps issued between 1913 and 1922 with enhanced colour schemes.[186] Unlike most previous Irish maps in colour, contours are included, though still in black. Only one of the 1918 sheets appeared in the publication reports, and that as late as September 1919. In fact all three were in print before 23 July 1918, when they were added to a Military Survey index.[187] As early as late 1919 any idea of continuing with this edition as a national series appears to have been abandoned, and even the two numbered sheets were being advertised as district maps. The OS *Catalogue of......Ireland. To 1st April 1920* merely marked them as in print on the large sheet series index. Sheets typically have "(Third Edition)" after the Ordnance Survey of Ireland heading, top left, and the sheet number top right. Sheet names appear top centre. The words "large sheet series" do not appear on maps, though occasionally on indexes or in catalogues etc. Standard sheet coverage was to be 27 by 18 miles, though the sheets issued were to other dimensions.

Sheets 1 to 15 were not published.

Sheets 16 & 17. *Belfast*   Revised 1910-2   36 by 21

1918	osi	-	-	+	1918	C 1/6,2/-,3/-	ANg	26.3	Cpt-m
1918	osi	500/27	-	+	1918	C 1/6,2/-,3/-	ANg	26.3	PC
1918	osi	1000/31+	-	+	1918	C 1/6,2/-,3/-	ANg	26.3	PC

OSPR reference not found. See figures 8 and 20. Sheets 16 and 17 appear separate on indexes, and combining them caused sheet 16 to lose its overlap with 15, and to be extended three miles north. There were apparently more than one printing of the first state, with distinct variations in colour tints between copies, especially the blue water plate. The map was further revised in 1936 and reissued by the Ordnance Survey of Northern Ireland as sheet 7 in their One-inch Popular Edition. It thus remained in print until superseded by Third Series mapping in 1963. It was probably also issued with military grid in 1927, and certainly in GSGS 3917 with War Office Irish Grid in 1932 (print code WO 3000/32 (coloured contours), reprinted as WO 1500/39 (uncoloured contours), copies BL-d). An outline printing with water in blue was also issued, lacking the squaring system across the face of the sheet (copy PC).

Sheets 18 to 79 were not published.

Sheet 80 *Cork*   Revised 1908-10   24 by 34

1918	osi	-	-	s	1918	C 1/6,2/-,2/6	g	9/19	26.1	Cpt-m 1
1918	osi	-	-	s	1918	C 1/6,2/-,2/6	ANg		26.3	PC 1
1918	osi	1946	-	s	1918	c 1/6,2/-,2/6	g		26.1	Dtf 2
1918	osi	1946	-	s	1946	c 2/-	g		26.1	PC 2,3
1918	osi	1949	-	s	1949	c 2/-	g		26.1	Dtf 2,3
1918	osi	1949	-	s	1949	c np	g		26.1	Dtc 2,3

The sheet was issued with military grid in 1925 (print code 3.25, not found), and in GSGS 3943 with War Office Irish Grid in 1934 (print code WO 1400/34, copy BL-d). It was also reprinted (without sheet number) in 1940 by the Ordnance Survey in Dublin for the Department of Defence, overprinted with their 5000 yard grid in red (copy Dtc). 1. The 2/6 cost of the "folded in sections" map was anomalous in 1918, or simply erroneous. The existence of a sheet both with and without a squaring system is very unusual. 2. The sheet number is deleted. 3. The Third Edition heading is also deleted.

Sheets 81 to 85 were not published.

---

[186] For information on the features that distinguish them see pages 18 to 21, and appendix 4.
[187] A copy of the index is in the CCS Archive, in the Map Library, Cambridge University Library.

District maps

Dublin District   a. Revised 1898 b. No revision date   24 by 26

1918	osi.a	-	-	s	1918	C	1/6,2/-,3/-	ANg		26.4	Cpt	
1918	osi.a	1929	-	s	1918	c	2/-,3/-,4/-	ANg		26.4	Dtf	
1918	osi.a	1933	-	s	1918	c	2/-,3/-,4/-	ANg		26.4	Dm	
1918	osi.a	1944	-	1944rs	1944	c	2/-,3/-,4/-	ANg		26.4	Cu-m	1
1947	osi.b	-	1942	1947rs	1947	c	2/-	ANg		26.4	PC	
1948	osi.b	-	1942	1947r	1948	c	2/-	AN		26.4	Mg	2

OSPR reference not found. With an inset of Lambay Island. The 1898 revision date is unchanged from that on the *Dublin District* map of 1904. The Third Edition heading may reflect the product of the second national revision of 1914 in the SSS sheet 101 area. There were apparently more than one printing of the first state, with distinct variations in colour tints between copies, especially the hachures and the green woodland plate. The map's appearance on the index in the OS *Catalogue of......Ireland. To 1st April 1920* was inaccurate, because it was marked as coincident with LSS sheet 51. A further attempt on a wartime cover at depicting its coverage was just as erroneous (see figure 20). Its sheet lines in fact derive from the 1904 *Dublin District* map which covered an area 24 by 24 miles unrelated to SSS sheet lines: the 1918 map has a two mile extension to the north. The alpha-numeric system is unchanged but for the addition of an "X" division at the top. 1. The railway revision note is in red. 2. With a simple alpha-numeric border, with no diced latitude and longitude sector. The original legend was replaced with one intended for the SSS coloured map, thus depicting incorrect railway symbols and no stations. Otherwise with OSI marginalia replacing the original.

Killarney District   20 by 27¼
a. Revised 1908 b. No revision date c. Revised 1899, partly 1951 d. Revised 1909, partly 1953

1913	osi.a	-	-	s	1913	C	1/6,2/-,2/6	g	9/13	26.2	Cpt	
1944	osi.b	-	-	1944rs	1944	c	1/6,2/-,2/6	g		26.2	PC	1
1946	osi.b	-	1942	1946rs	1946	c	2/-	g		26.2	Cu-m	
1946	osi.b	-	1942	1946rs	1949	c	2/-	g		26.2	LVg	
1946	osi.b	-	1942	1946rs	1949	c	np	g		26.2	Cu-m	
nd	osi.c	-	-	1949rs	1949	c	np	g		26.2	PC	
nd	osi.d	-	-	1949rs	1949	c	np	g		26.2	Cu-m	

With an extrusion to cover Killorglin. Classified as "New coloured series" in the OS *Catalogue of......Ireland. To 1st April 1920*. There is an implicit association between this 1913 map and the 1918 large sheet series: main roads in red and railway lines of two or more tracks in solid black are just two of several common elements that distinguish both from the earlier small sheet coloured map. Another feature they share is the new style border that was standard on the Irish half-inch and large sheet one-inch, and on the majority of small-scale mapping throughout Great Britain after the First World War. It made its first appearance on the one-inch map with *Killarney* (see footnote 71 on page 18, and figure 13 where the border as on sheets 16 & 17 is illustrated). 1. The railway revision note is in red.

Appendices

Appendix 1. *Outline editions*

1. Black Outline Edition One-inch Map

Without contours, with water in black. England and Wales sheets are derived from the coloured large sheet series; those of Scotland from the engraved third edition, so play no real part in this volume, but are listed here for completeness sake. Most appear in the supplements to the catalogue between 1918 and 1920 (OSPR), and are thus in the copyright collections; a few were not listed, and thus it is possible that there are still further sheets awaiting discovery. The "Black Outline Edition One-inch Map" heading is placed top right, replacing "(Large Sheet Series)", and a note is added between the index of adjoining sheets and the imprint: *An edition of this map is published in colours*. The price statement is altered to "Price 1/- net". Sheet 38 does not carry these alterations. Some copies have been recorded issued in contemporary OS white or buff covers (see figure 3).

England and Wales (LSS)
57 sheets recorded: 1, 2, 3, 4, 6, 8, 13, 14, 15, 16, 17, 18, 19, 20, 21, 22, 27, 28, 36, 37, 38, 42, 43, 44, 45, 46, 48, 52, 53, 59, 66, 68, 73, 78, 79, 86, 93, 94, 95, 96, 98, 99, 103, 104, 105, 106, 107, 108, 111, 112, 114, 115, 116, 124, 125, 126, 150.
   Sheets 38 (copy Og) and 48 (copy BL) are lacking in OSPR.

Scotland
79 sheets in 78 recorded: 1, 2, 8, 11, 14, 17, 18, 19, 21, 22, 23, 24, 25, 26*, 27, 29, 30, 31, 32, 33, 34, 35, 36, 37, 38, 39, 40, 41, 42.50, 43, 44, 45, 46, 47, 48, 49, 51, 55, 56, 57, 57A, 58, 59, 60, 63, 64, 66, 67, 68, 70, 72, 73, 75, 76, 77, 79, 85, 87, 91, 92, 94, 95, 96, 97, 98, 100, 102, 103, 104, 105, 106, 107, 108, 109, 110, 111, 113, 114.
   Lacking in OSPR: sheets 35, 66, 68, 100, 111 (in private collections), 58 (copy EXg), 67, 76 (copies Wc), 79 (copy Cu). *Sheet 26 in this style is a Fourth Edition sheet.

2. Outline with water in blue, contours in red

England and Wales (LSS)
4 sheets recorded: 30, 31, 97, 124.
   See the cartobibliography for source references. Copies of sheets 11, 15, 21 have also been reported, but the present (2003) inaccessibility of the RGS collections renders confirmation impossible.

3. Outline with water in blue

Ireland (LSS) sheet 16.17 *Belfast*.
   Without squaring system. It has yet to be established whether this sheet was made available to the public, or whether sheet 80 was also printed. The only known copy is in a private collection.

4. A special printing from the black plate only (therefore no water, hachures or contours), with a heading overprinted in red *Old Large Sheet Series 1-inch. Fully coloured outline made up from small sheets by transfer from copper (engraved)*

England and Wales (LSS) sheet 30.
   See the cartobibliography for source references.

Appendix 2. *Military maps*

1. Sheets recorded overprinted with military squaring systems

a. Based on the second national revision
England & Wales (LSS) sheets 107, 115, 115 (another system), 124, 135; Scotland sheet 22.21.[188]
      The detail of the squaring systems is described above in the footnotes to each map.

b. Based on the third national revision
Aldershot District (North), 1914, *Aldershot District (South),* 1914.[189]
      Some copies of the standard coloured map are overprinted in red with a military grid, continued from the north sheet onto the south, divided into twelve-mile and quartered two-mile squares.

2. GSGS 2766, ?1915, is an identification trace related to the England and Wales LSS, with 2000 yard squares, for training in the use of artillery squaring systems on Western Front mapping (copy BL-d).

3. The sheets of the 1:25,344 *Map of East Anglia* were numbered as geographic quarters of England and Wales LSS sheets. Publication began in 1914, and the GSGS number 3036 was allocated to the series in 1915. The name was later altered to *Map of the Eastern Counties* to reflect the growth in its coverage. The associated identification trace with 2½ inch squares is GSGS 3293, 1916.

Appendix 3. *Sheets showing the 25 feet contour*

The 25 feet contour was limited to areas of Lancashire, Yorkshire and Lincolnshire only.

England and Wales (LSS)
18 sheets: 24, 26, 27, 28 (around Hornsea Mere), 29, 31, 32, 33, 34, 37, 38, 39, 47, 48, 55, 56, 64, 65.
District map: *York District.*

Appendix 4. *Maps printed with enhanced colour schemes*

a. Based on the second national revision
Killarney District, 1913; The Lake District specimen, 1913;[190] *Glasgow District,* 1914; *Dorking and Leith Hill District,* 1914; *Ilkley District,* 1914; Sheet 16.17 *Belfast,* 1918; Sheet 80 *Cork,* 1918; *Dublin District,* 1918; *Snowdon District,* 1920; *The Lake District,* 1920; *Deeside,* 1920; *Oban,* 1920; *The Trossachs & Loch Lomond,* 1920; *Glasgow District : Edition of 1921; Scott's Country,* 1921; *Burns' Country,* 1921; *Lower Strath Spey,* 1921; *Rothesay & Firth of Clyde,* 1920.

b. Based on the third national revision
Aldershot (North), 1914, *Aldershot (South),* 1914; Sheet 144 *Plymouth,* 1914, Sheet 145 *Torquay & Dartmouth,* 1914, Sheet 120 *Bridgwater & Quantock Hills,* 1916;[191] *New Forest,* 1920; *Isle of Wight,* 1921; *London,* 1921.

---

[188] All known copies of these maps are in private collections.
[189] The only known copies of these maps are in private collections.
[190] Plate XXIV in Colonel C.F. Close, *Text book of topographical and geographical surveying.* Revised by Captain E.W. Cox. London: HMSO, 1913.
[191] Sheets 144, 145 and 120 are unpublished maps on Popular Edition sheet lines. Sheet 145 is in the RGS (OS specimen no.49); the others are in private collections.

Appendix 5. *Sheets with railway station symbols*

The standard method of depicting railway stations at the start of third edition publication was by the use of black rectangles, placed on whichever side of the line a ticket office was located. Railway station symbols overlaying the railway line, in the form of an open circle or, for larger stations, a rectangle, began to appear in 1910, and exceptionally earlier. They were inconsistently added to third edition mapping, and may appear in the legend or on the map face, or both. In a very few cases a red infill was added, as became standard on Popular Edition maps. Some Scottish sheets carrying railway station symbols cover areas with no railways: one has railway but no stations. Station symbols do not necessarily appear on all printings of the sheets listed below.

Sheets with open circle railway station symbols

England and Wales (SSS)
Sheet 286.

England and Wales (LSS)
37 sheets recorded: 1, 3, 9, 19, 24, 25, 26, 29, 30, 31, 34, 35, 36, 43, 52, 58, 66, 67, 68, 69, 70, 78, 79, 80, 85, 89, 90, 91, 92, 100, 101, 121, 140, 141, 148, 149, 150.
District maps: *Dorking and Leith Hill District, Ilkley District, Snowdon District, York District.*
     Ilkley District was reprinted with station symbols with red infill.

Scotland
21 sheets recorded: 83, 84, 85, 93, 94, 95, 101, 102, 103, 107, 108, 109, 110, 113, 114, 115, 116, 117+, 121+, 123+, 129+.
District maps: *Glasgow District, Lower Strath Spey.*
     Glasgow District : Edition of 1921 was printed with station symbols with red infill.

Ireland (SSS)
3 sheets: 36, 60.61, 129.

Ireland (LSS)
2 sheets: 16.17, 80.
District maps: *Dublin District, Killarney District.*

Appendix 6. *Developments in the Ellis Martin cover design*

Set out here in tabular form is the information provided in footnote 173 on page 81. See the footnote for additional detail, including sheet number lists, and figure 10 for illustrations of the design.

	Colours	Border	Cover type	Location of sheet number	Top right sheet number	Price
1	black, red	none	bookfold	below scale statement	no	2/- cloth
2	black, red	none	bookfold	on index diagram	no	2/- cloth
3	black, red	none	end cards	on index diagram	no	1/6,2/-,3/-
4	brown, dark red	dark red	end cards	on index diagram	no	1/6,2/-,3/-
5	brown, dark red	dark red	end cards	top of index diagram	no	1/6,2/-,3/-
6	brown, dark red	dark red	end cards	top of index diagram	yes	1/6,2/-,3/-
7	brown, dark red	dark red	end cards	top of index diagram	yes	2/-,3/-,4/-
8	as 7, with refinements in lettering style of sheet number and name					

     A few type 6/?7 covers exist with the sheet number still on the face of the index diagram.

Appendix 7. *Sheet line co-ordinates*

Brian Adams

This appendix details the fundamental data used to construct early one-inch map series, and lists the rectangular construction co-ordinates of their basic sheet line systems. The sheet lines are given two-letter codes as shown on the sheet indexes herewith, and the co-ordinates are listed against these codes.

Codes commencing E, I or S are feet east when +, feet west when −
         F, G, J, T are feet north when +, feet south when −
Those with lower case letters are only applicable to the Large Sheet series.

Due to the methods and materials then in use, displaced and extended sheets often lack specific sheet line co-ordinates and no attempt has been made to list these. Astute readers will realise that this would appear to apply to the large sheet series (including the Popular Edition), made up as they are with quarters and halves of small sheets; however, the regular sheets of these series are constructed to specific sheet lines although the actual mapping may not be laid down accurately thereto. Thus a difference of 550 feet has been seen between the co-ordinates of the same feature on two overlapping sheets.

For the development of the Old Series sheet system see Adams (1994) or a summary in Hellyer (1999) pages xi, xii. Sheet line co-ordinates of Old Series quarter-sheets north of the Preston - Hull line are identical with those of the equivalent England & Wales sheets listed below. Those for the Popular Edition of England & Wales are to be found in Hodson (1999) Appendix 7, whilst those for Scotland can be obtained from the present appendix compiler through the publishers. Subsequent editions have their co-ordinates printed upon them.

The formulae for conversion of rectangular co-ordinates to and from geographical co-ordinates (latitudes and longitudes) are to be found in *Survey Computations* (second edition, HMSO 1932) pages 108, 116.

FUNDAMENTAL ELEMENTS APPLICABLE TO ALL AREAS :-

Horizontal Datum	OSGBI 1858
Spheroid	Airy
Unit	Foot of O_1
False Co-ordinates	None
Scale Factor	Unity

O_1 is the Ordnance Survey standard 10 foot bar

1 foot of O_1 = 0·304 800 749 1 international metre

ENGLAND, WALES and ISLE of MAN

	Projection	Cassini's
	True Origin	Delamere (triangulation station originally Delamere Forest, 53° 13' 17".274 N, 2° 41' 03".562 W)
	Sheet size	Small sheets: 18 × 12 miles (95040 × 63360 feet)
		Large sheets: 27 × 18 miles (142560 × 95040 feet)

EA	−	906 570	Eg	−	288 810	EL	+	138 870	Ep	+	566 550
EB	−	811 530	EH	−	241 290	El	+	186 390	EQ	+	614 070
EC	−	716 490	Eh	−	193 770	EM	+	233 910	Eq	+	661 590
ED	−	621 450	EI	−	146 250	Em	+	281 430	ER	+	709 110
Ed	−	573 930	Ei	−	98 730	EN	+	328 950	ES	+	804 150
EE	−	526 410	EJ	−	51 210	En	+	376 470	Es	+	851 670
Ee	−	478 890	Ej	−	3 690	EO	+	423 990	ET	+	899 190
EF	−	431 370	EK	+	43 830	Eo	+	471 510	Et	+	946 710
EG	−	336 330	Ek	+	91 350	EP	+	519 030	EU	+	994 230

FA	−	1249 940	FK	−	616 340	FT	−	46 100	GC	+	524 140
FB	−	1186 580	FL	−	552 980	FU	+	17 260	GD	+	587 500
FC	−	1123 220	Fl	−	521 300	Fu	+	48 940	Gd	+	619 180
FD	−	1059 860	FM	−	489 620	FV	+	80 620	GE	+	650 860
FE	−	996 500	FN	−	426 260	FW	+	143 980	GF	+	714 220
FF	−	933 140	FO	−	362 900	FX	+	207 340	GG	+	777 580
Ff	−	901 460	Fo	−	331 220	Fx	+	239 020	Gg	+	809 260
FG	−	869 780	FP	−	299 540	FY	+	270 700	GH	+	840 940
FH	−	806 420	FQ	−	236 180	FZ	+	334 060	GI	+	904 300
FI	−	743 060	FR	−	172 820	GA	+	397 420	GJ	+	967 660
Fi	−	711 380	Fr	−	141 140	Ga	+	429 100			
FJ	−	679 700	FS	−	109 460	GB	+	460 780			

SCOTLAND

Projection	Bonne's	
True Origin	57° 30' N, 4° W (Nairnshire, near Croy)	
Sheet size	24 × 18 miles (126720 × 95040 feet)	

SA − 804 669	SD − 424 509	SG − 44 349	SJ + 335 811
SB − 677 949	SE − 297 789	SH + 82 371	SK + 462 531
SC − 551 229	SF − 171 069	SI + 209 091	SL + 589 251

TA − 1098 523	TH − 433 243	TO + 232 037	TV + 897 317
TB − 1003 483	TI − 338 203	TP + 327 077	TW + 992 357
TC − 908 443	TJ − 243 163	TQ + 422 117	TX + 1087 397
TD − 813 403	TK − 148 123	TR + 517 157	TY + 1182 437
TE − 718 363	TL − 53 083	TS + 612 197	TZ + 1277 477
TF − 623 323	TM + 41 957	TT + 707 237	
TG − 528 283	TN + 136 997	TU + 802 277	

IRELAND

Projection	Bonne's	
True Origin	53° 30' N, 8° W (in Lough Ree)	
Sheet size	18 × 12 miles (95040 × 63360 feet)	

IA − 597 280	IE − 217 120	II + 163 040	IM + 543 200
IB − 502 240	IF − 122 080	IJ + 258 080	IN + 638 240
IC − 407 200	IG − 27 040	IK + 353 120	
ID − 312 160	IH + 68 000	IL + 448 160	

JA − 787 960	JH − 344 440	JO + 99 080	JV + 542 600
JB − 724 600	JI − 281 080	JP + 162 440	JW + 605 960
JC − 661 240	JJ − 217 720	JQ + 225 800	JX + 669 320
JD − 597 880	JK − 154 360	JR + 289 160	JY + 732 680
JE − 534 520	JL − 91 000	JS + 352 520	
JF − 471 160	JM − 27 640	JT + 415 880	
JG − 407 800	JN + 35 720	JU + 479 240	

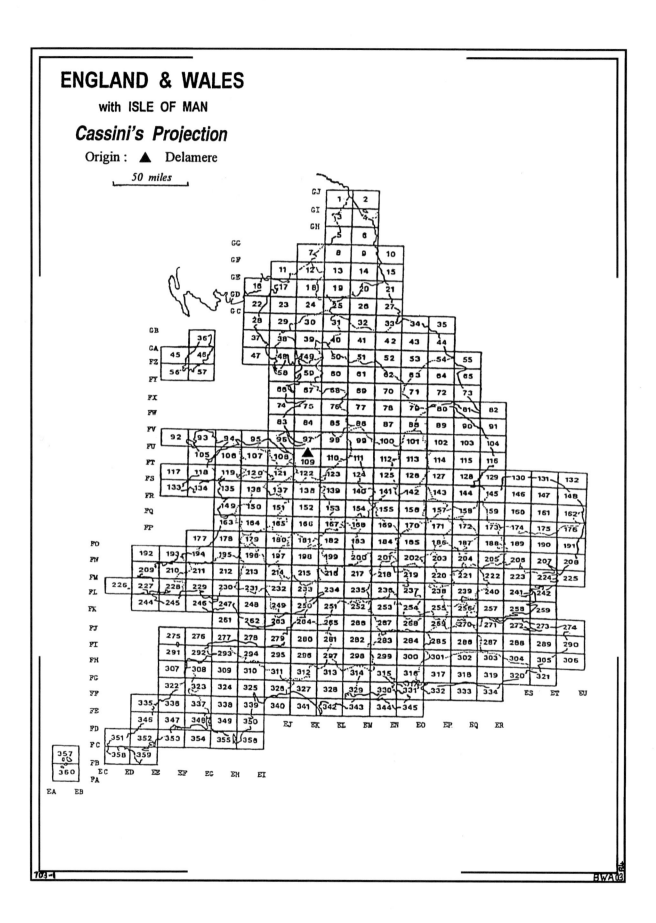

ENGLAND & WALES

with ISLE OF MAN

Cassini's Projection

Origin : ▲ Delamere

50 miles

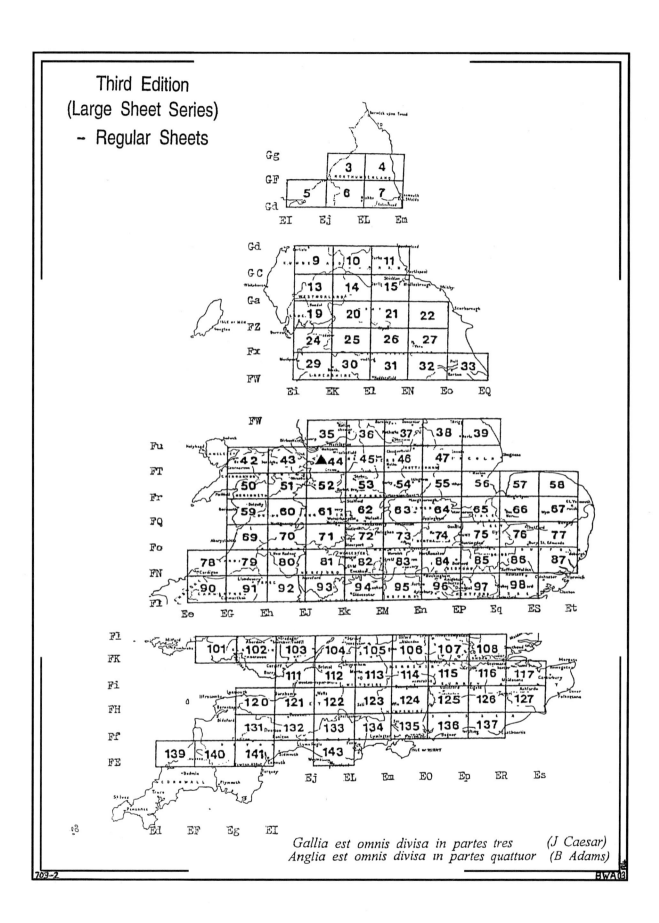

Third Edition
(Large Sheet Series)
- Regular Sheets

Gallia est omnis divisa in partes tres   (J Caesar)
Anglia est omnis divisa in partes quattuor   (B Adams)

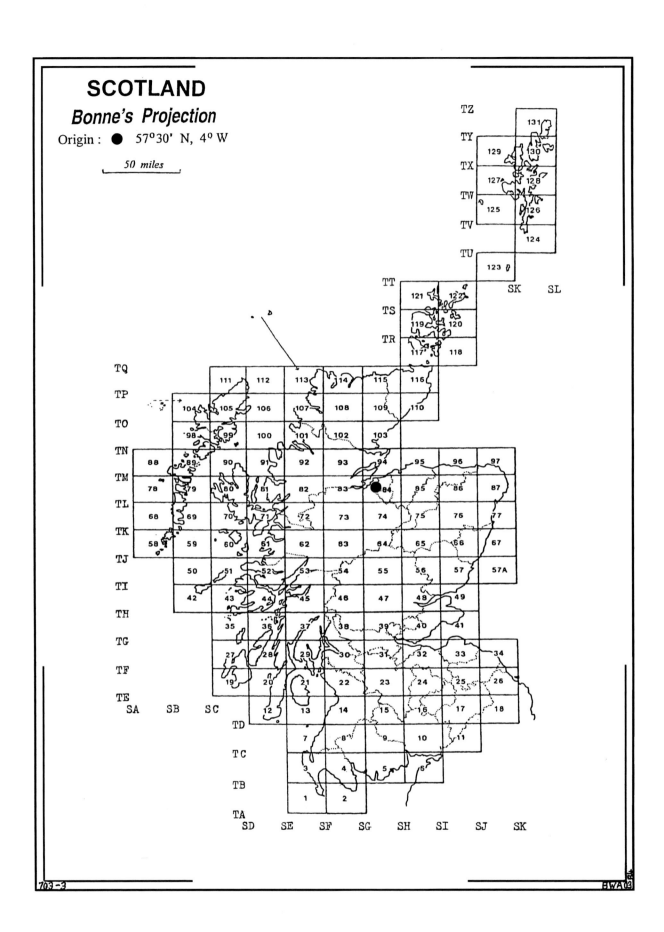

SCOTLAND

Bonne's Projection

Origin : ● 57°30' N, 4° W

|— 50 miles —|

703-3

BWA03

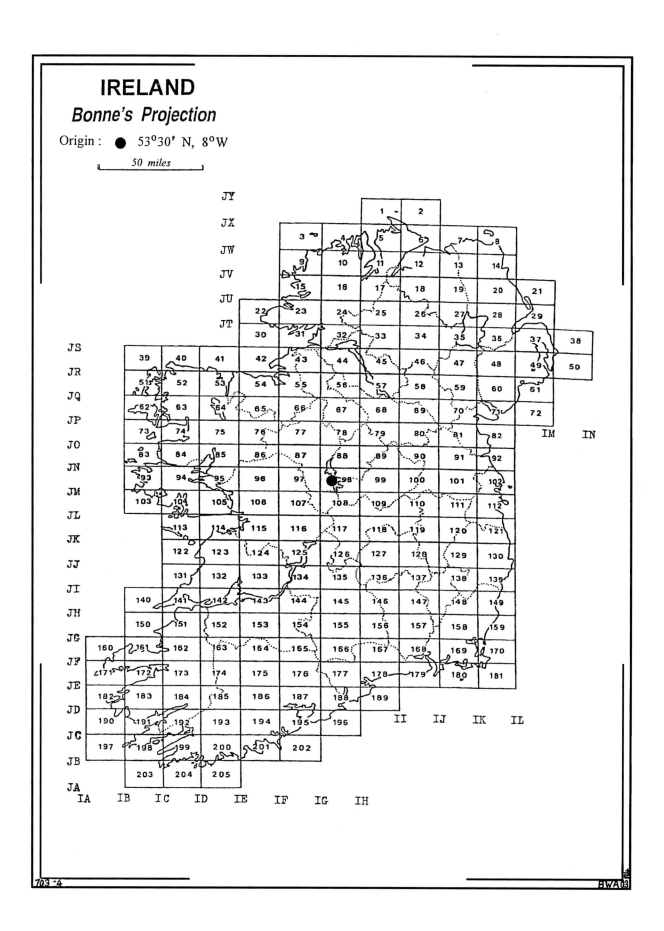

IRELAND

Bonne's Projection

Origin : ● 53°30' N, 8°W

50 miles

Appendix 8. *Instructions for the revision of the one-inch map, 1909*

The Instructions of 1901 have been quoted above at length (pages 40-53). In 1909 they were replaced by a fresh set, which differs in that it includes also instructions to draughtsmen and the procedure to be adopted when the latest version of the one-inch is more recent than the latest version of the six-inch. Much of the substance of the Instructions of 1901 was repeated in 1909, but a few 'new passages' have been included here. The document opens with the substance, and sometimes the actual wording, of the circular of 8 April 1909, cited above (page 6).[192]

Churches, chapels and cathedrals
s.91. 'Cathedrals may be shown to scale if large enough for the object to be plain on the map; otherwise they should be shown by the Church symbol.'
s.93. 'Churches and Chapels should be shown by symbol where space permits. The distinguishing name "Ch.", "Church", "Chap." or "Chapel" will not be written.
   '"Cath." or "Cathedral" may be written where there is room.'

County boroughs
s.90. 'The county dash will be shown round County Boroughs; but as the latter are not administrative counties there will be no need to alter the character of writing of such boroughs, nor to alter the tablet. The county dash will not be shown round boroughs, like Lichfield, which form part of the administrative County in which they are situated.'

Gates on roads
s.19. 'All gates which bar the passage along roads should be shown.'

Golf courses
s.20. 'Golf Courses which are sufficiently large and important should be shown. It is usual to describe those inland as Golf Courses; the term "Links" should be reserved generally for those on the sea coast, or in Scotland for those where the name is applicable.'

Letter boxes
s.43. 'L.B. may be written in villages where no post or telegraph office exists; in all other cases L.B. will only be written beyond the limits of towns and villages and if more than one mile from a post office.'

Parish and village names
s.106. 'The name of a Civil Parish will be written in Roman print to the parish village situated within its area, or failing that to the parish church if there is one. In the absence of both parish and village and church the Parish name will be written across the area in sloping hair line Egyptian. By the term "Parish Village" or "Parish Church" is understood a village, hamlet, collection of houses, &c., or church bearing the same name as the parish. All other village names will be in stump.'

Piers
s.16. 'The word "pier" will not be written when the object is sufficiently distinct and clear to the average user of the map; but in the case of important piers used by the travelling or touring public, the word may be written if there is room.'

---

[192] Col S.C.N. Grant, *Instructions for the revision of the 1-inch map*, 1909: copy in PRO OS 45/9.

Post and telegraph offices

s.109. 'Insert T over or under a village name when it contains a Post and Telegraph Office; P when a Post Office only. Insert T for a Post and Telegraph Office at a station; if a Telegraph Office only and within about half a mile of a P.O., write T to the village name to cover both offices; if over about ½ a mile from a P.O., T may be written at the station, and P at the village. If P or T near the village name is misleading as to the position of the office, write near the object.'

Railways and stations

s.47. 'Railways of importance which are under construction will be shown on plots, provided that no part of a railway is to be shown until the earthwork is so far advanced as to leave no doubt as to the alignment.'

s.48. ['Rail Motor Car Services' in margin] 'For the purpose of the 1-inch map, stopping places for passenger traffic on lines of railway are described either as "Stations" or "Halts". The term "Station" will only be applied where permanent station buildings, booking office, station officials, &c exist; for all other forms of stopping places "Halt" will be used.'

Roads and paths

The section on road classification is similar to that of 1901.

s.67. '... Only footpaths that are habitually used by the public are to be shown, but no question as to footpaths being public should be raised, as the O.S. does not concern itself with rights of way.'

s.68. 'The cases of footpaths required to be added to the 1-inch map should be rare, but where this is necessary, a coloured dotted line should be drawn along the footpath on the 6-inch plot.'

Schools

s.69. 'The word school should only be written in isolated positions.'

Smithies

s.70. 'All smithies at which horses can be shod, not situated in villages, are to be shown.'

Windmills and windpumps

s.75. 'Windmills are shown (by symbol) if room permits, and the purpose for which they are used should be noted; if the windmill be permanently disused the symbol and name, if any, should be removed; but if the object be a prominent landmark the symbol may be retained, and "old windmill" written if there is room.'

s.76. 'Windpumps, &c., in isolated positions will be shown, provided there is room. If very numerous show the most important.'

Appendix 9. *Chronology*

NB the titles of maps listed here may be abbreviated: their full form is given in the cartobibliography.

1872
July   One-inch New Series of England and Wales authorised by the Treasury

1892
April   Production of a coloured one-inch map recommended by the Baker Committee

1894
March   Colonel John Farquharson appointed Director General

1896
?December   Published *Aldershot District*, the first Revised New Series map to appear in colour

1897
September   Publication of one-inch Revised New Series, in colour, begun

1899
March   Colonel Duncan A. Johnston appointed Director General

1901   Second National Revision England and Wales, and Scotland begun

1902   Publication of one-inch coloured map of Ireland begun

1903
March   Publication of OS half-inch map (SSS) begun
                Publication of Bartholomew's half-inch map of Great Britain completed
July   Publication of one-inch Third Edition outline map of England and Wales begun
August   Publication of one-inch Third Edition outline map of Scotland begun
November   Publication of one-inch Third Edition map of England and Wales (SSS), in colour, begun
                Published SSS 317.332
December   Published SSS 300

1904
January   Published SSS 253, 316.331, 344+
February   Published SSS 267, 299, 301, 302, 318.333
March   Publication of one-inch Revised New Series, in colour, completed
April   Published SSS 315
July   Published SSS 254
August   Published SSS 268, 269, 286, 330. Reprinted SSS 300
September   Published SSS 283
October   Published SSS 284, 285, *Aldershot District*
November   Published SSS 255
December   Published SSS 270, 329.343

1905
                Colonel R.C. Hellard appointed Director General
January   Reprinted *Aldershot District* (not verified)
February   Reprinted SSS 317.332, 318.333
March   Publication of one-inch Third Edition map of Scotland, in colour, begun
                Introduction of narrow borders and redesigned marginalia on SSS
                Published SSS 236, 238, 239, 256; Scotland 6, 11, 17, 18, 24, 26, 34

April	Major C.F. Close appointed head of Topographical Section, General Staff
	Reprinted SSS 316.331
May	Published Scotland 16
June	Published SSS 257, 314. Reprinted SSS 267, 302
July	Published SSS 282. Reprinted SSS 285
?August	"mounted" (on cloth) price added to maps
August	Published SSS 303. Reprinted SSS 268, 269, 299
September	Published SSS 218, 298, 319.334; Scotland 32, 33.41. Reprinted SSS 283, 301, 315
October	Published SSS 219, 221, 237, 240, 252, 266, 287, *Aldershot (North), Aldershot (South)*
	Reprinted SSS 286
November	Published SSS 25, 235; Scotland 10, 25. Reprinted SSS 253, 254, 255, 329.343
December	Published SSS 251, 271, 272, 304, 320; Scotland 8, 30

1906

January	Published SSS 288. Reprinted SSS 238, 284, 318.333
February	Published SSS 234; Scotland 15. Reprinted SSS 270
March	White covers replace red on OS small-scale maps
	Published SSS 30, 92.93, 94.106, 119, 120, 135, 136, 149, 217, 313, 328.342
	Published Scotland 7; Reprinted SSS 239, 266
April	Reprinted SSS 344+
May	Published SSS 258.259. Reprinted SSS 270, 330, *Aldershot (North), Aldershot (South)*
June	Published SSS 216, 250, 273+, 305+, *Salisbury Plain*; Scotland 31. Reprinted SSS 257
July	Publication of OS half-inch map (LSS) begun
	Published SSS 220, 223; Scotland 9, 14.13, 23. Reprinted SSS 256, 314
?July	"folded in Sections" price added to maps
August	Published Scotland 12
September	Published SSS 26, 222, 241.242, *Wareham*; Scotland 1.2, 1.3.7, 4, 5, 20, 21.13, 22.21
October	Published SSS 96, 185
November	Published SSS 18, 19, 95.107, 105.118, 203, 204, 224.242, 233. Reprinted SSS 300
December	Publication of Large Sheet Series publication of England and Wales (LSS) begun
	Published SSS 63, 202, 281, 327.341; LSS 17; Scotland 39
?December	"net" added to map prices

1907

	Published SSS 205, 232 (month unknown)
January	Published SSS 249.263. Reprinted SSS 240
February	Reprinted SSS 219, 285, 319.334, *Aldershot (North)*
March	Published SSS 42, 108, 117+, 137, 150, 265, 297. Reprinted SSS 221, 269
April	Reprinted SSS 271, 287, 303; Scotland 10
June	Published LSS 12, 14, 15, 21; Scotland 29, 46
July	Published SSS 152; Scotland 36, 40, 45. Reprinted SSS 299, 317.332
August	Published SSS 138; LSS 16, 18, 20, 23; Scotland 28, 43.35. Reprinted Scotland 31
September	Published LSS 13, 19, 22, 97; Scotland 19+, 38. Reprinted *Wareham*
October	Published LSS 95, 96, 98, 99, 104; Scotland 41. Reprinted *Aldershot (South)*
November	Published LSS 112
December	Published LSS 1, 2, 3, 4, 5, 6, 7, 8, 9, 94, 122; Scotland 44, 47

1908

	Colonel Samuel Charles Norton Grant appointed Director General
	Second National Revision of Ireland begun
	Scotland 29.21 prepared, but apparently not published
February	Published 10, 11, 111, 121, 143
March	Published LSS 27, 28, 32, 33, 87, 106, 123, 133; Scotland 37, 49
May	Published LSS 85, 86
June	Published Scotland 48

July	Published LSS 51, 61, 62, 84; *Loch Lomond*
August	Published LSS 43, 52, 60
October	Published LSS 39, 74, 103, 135
November	Published LSS 109
December	Published LSS 38, 44, 53, 88, 105, 107, 108, 113, 151

1909

	Publication of one-inch Third Edition outline map of Ireland begun
	Published LSS 118, 128. Reprinted *Salisbury Plain* (month unknown)
January	Reprinted Scotland 8, 25, 26, 30, 34
February	Reprinted Scotland 6, 33.41
March	Published LSS 48, 63, 64, 73, 144; Scotland 42+, 53, 54, 55, 56. Reprinted Scotland 32
April	Reprinted LSS 108, 111
May	Published LSS 152
June	Station symbol (circle or oblong) appears in legend of SSS 286
	Published LSS 55, 146; Scotland 52, 65, 66
	Reprinted SSS 286, *Aldershot (North);* LSS 109
July	Published LSS 77, 83; Scotland 64. Reprinted LSS 43; Scotland 33.41
August	Published LSS 134; Scotland 77. Reprinted LSS 88; Scotland 25
September	Published LSS 45, 47, 54, 110, 114; Scotland 67
October	Published LSS 115; Scotland 60, 61. Reprinted *Aldershot (South), Salisbury Plain*
November	Published LSS 50, 116, 120, 124, 126; Scotland 57.57A, 62, 63
December	Published LSS 42, 75, 76, 117, 125, 127, 136, 137, 145; Scotland 73, 74, 75

1910

	Second National Revision of Scotland completed
January	Reprinted LSS 39; Scotland 19+, 24, 40
February	Published LSS 46, 74, 138, 139
March	Published LSS 59, 72, 82, 93, 132, 142; Scotland 70, 72
April	Reprinted LSS 135
May	Published LSS 56, 65, 131
June	Published LSS 71, 119; Scotland 81, 82
July	Published LSS 81, 105, 129. Reprinted LSS 17, 107, 133
August	Published LSS 41, 57. Reprinted LSS 106; Scotland 55, 56
September	Replacement of all published SSS by LSS completed
	Published LSS 40, *Cambridge;* Scotland 71, 80, 97. Reprinted Scotland 39, 41
October	Published Scotland 87. Reprinted LSS 45, 87, 122, 123, 134, 144
November	Published Scotland 90, 91.100, 92. Reprinted LSS 118
December	Published LSS 37, 58, 66, 67, 68, *Winchester;* Scotland 96, 101

1911

	Publication of one-inch Fourth Edition outline map of England and Wales begun
	Station symbol (circle or oblong) added to map or legend
	Reprinted LSS 142; Scotland 14.13 (month unknown)
January	Reprinted LSS 113; Scotland 30
February	Sheet names omitted or deleted – first noted instance LSS 85
	Reprinted LSS 48, 85
March	Map covers with location maps introduced
	Published LSS 102, 118, 141, 149, 150, *Oxford;* Scotland 107, 108, 113, 114
	Reprinted Scotland 34
May	Published *Ipswich;* Scotland 86
	Reprinted LSS 6, 19, 125, 151, 152; Scotland 21.13
June	Published LSS 101, 130, *Weston super Mare.* Reprinted LSS 121, 126
July	Published LSS 147, 148. Reprinted *Aldershot (North);* LSS 94; Scotland 17

August	Colonel Charles Frederick Close appointed Director General

August | Colonel Charles Frederick Close appointed Director General
Reprinted LSS 110, 115, 117, 119, 146
September | Reprinted LSS 112
October | Published LSS 140. Reprinted LSS 44
November | Published Scotland 85, 95. Reprinted LSS 62, 75

1912

Second National Revision of England and Wales completed
Publication of one-inch Fourth Edition outline map of England and Wales abandoned
Publication of one-inch Third Edition outline map of Scotland completed
Reprinted *Aldershot District* (not verified, month unknown)

January | Published LSS 78, 80, 90, 96. Reprinted LSS 42; Scotland 22.21, 32
February | Sheet names restored – first recorded instance LSS 73
Reprinted LSS 7, 53, 73
March | Published LSS 70, 92, 100, *Brighton, Hastings, Land's End, Sidmouth*
Reprinted LSS 50, 64, 65
April | Reprinted LSS 55, 56, 58, 66, 67, 68, 72, 84
May | ARRR replaced by CCR, in large lettering – first recorded instance on LSS 77
Reprinted LSS 54, 57, 74, 77, 95, 106, 114, 116, 127, 135
June | Published *Newquay, Worcester*
Reprinted LSS 22, 47, 48, 51, 63, 76, 81, 82, 87, 94, 99, 107, 113, 123, 124, 136, 145
Reprinted *Oxford*
July | Published *Maidenhead*. Reprinted LSS 28, 32, 39, 86, 103, 128, 137, 138
August | Published LSS 69, *Reading, Rugby*. Reprinted *Aldershot (South)*; LSS 27, 37, 46
September | Reprinted LSS 105, 108, 120, 144; Scotland 17, 18, 46, 64, 73, 96, 97
October | Published LSS 79, 89, 91, *London (North), London (South)*
Reprinted *Salisbury Plain*; LSS 33, 85, 129; Scotland 47
November | Published LSS 128; *Belfast*. Reprinted LSS 38
December | Reprinted *Cambridge*

1913

Publication of one-inch Third Edition outline map of England and Wales completed
January | Reprinted Scotland 11, 15, 16
February | Published Scotland 83, 93. Reprinted *Maidenhead;* Ireland SSS 129
March | Published *Folkestone;* Scotland 84, 94, 102, 103, 109, 110
May | Lettering size of CCR reduced – earliest recorded instance LSS 45
Reprinted LSS 45; Scotland 21.13
June | Published LSS 49, *Pwllheli;* Scotland 115, 116, *Aberdeen*
Reprinted *Land's End;* Scotland 10
July | Published LSS 26. Reprinted LSS 61, 74
August | Reprinted LSS 52, 92; Scotland 29.21 (see 1908)
September | Published LSS 31; *Killarney*. Reprinted Scotland 49
November | Published LSS 24, 25, *Staffordshire Potteries;* Scotland 117+, 121+
December | Published LSS 29, 30, 34, 35, 36; Scotland 123+, 129+. Reprinted LSS 14, *Sidmouth*

1914

Second National Revision of Ireland abandoned
January | Reprinted LSS 20, 21, 44, 83, 96, 98; Scotland 65
February | Reprinted Scotland 23, 30, 57.57A; Ireland SSS 129
March | Reprinted LSS 18, 22, 41, 71, 112, 118, 133, *Ipswich*
April | Reprinted LSS 12, 15, 134; Scotland 45
May | Published *Glasgow*. Reprinted LSS 125
June | Published *Dorking*. Reprinted LSS 99; Scotland 17

July	Published *Ilkley*. Reprinted LSS 42, 62, 108, 126, 131; Scotland 47
August	Reprinted LSS 9, 95, 126
September	Reprinted LSS 16, 85, 86, 88, 89, 90, 94, 103
October	Reprinted LSS 22, 91, 106
November	Reprinted LSS 8, 10, 11, 33, 53
December	Intermediate revision of published mapping stopped
	Reprinted LSS 135

1914 or 15	Coloured SSS (Revised New Series and Third Edition) withdrawn from sale

1916	Probable year of price increase of "folded in sections" maps, SSS to 2/6, LSS to 3/-

1917	Republished LSS 1, 3 with coverage of Scotland (month unknown)
	LSS 5 prepared with coverage of Scotland, but apparently not published

1918	
	Black Outline Edition (BOE) version of England and Wales LSS begun
April-June	Published BOE 36, 44, 68, 73, 79, 94, 96, 98, 104, 107, 108, 112, 115, 116, 126, 150
Pre-23 July	Published Ireland LSS 16.17, 80, *Dublin*
July-Sept	Published BOE 1, 2, 3, 4, 6, 13, 14, 15, 16, 18, 19, 20, 78, 86, 93, 95, 103, 106, 111, 114, 124, 125
Oct-Dec	Published BOE 8, 17, 21, 22, 27, 28, 37, 42, 43, 45, 46, 99, 105

1919	
February	Published BOE 52, 53
March	Published BOE 59, 66
?	BOE 38, 48 copies released, apparently not published (month unknown)
May	Ellis Martin appointed to OS staff as "Designer" (9 May)
June	Publication of one-inch Popular Edition of England and Wales begun
September	Published *York*. Ireland LSS 80 announced (published 1918)
November	Reprinted Ireland SSS 36

1920	
	Published *Lake District* (Road edition) (month unknown)
January	Price rises, resulting in the omission of prices from map faces (announced 26 January)
	Reprinted Scotland 8, 30, 57.57A
February	Published *Snowdon*
March	Reprinted Scotland 92
April	Reprinted LSS 13, 17, 30, 42, 43, 47, 126, *Rugby, Sidmouth;* Scotland 9, 113
May	Reprinted Scotland 11, 61, 101, 108
June	Published *Lake District; Deeside, Oban.* Reprinted *Ilkley;* Scotland 48, 52, 53, 90
July-Sept	Published *The Trossachs*
July	Reprinted Scotland 17
August	Reprinted LSS 25; Scotland 20, 25, 70, 76
September	Reprinted LSS 19; Scotland 14.13, 21.13, 22.21, 47, 71, 80, 114
October	Reprinted LSS 6, 27; Scotland 36, 42+
November	Reprinted LSS 1, 3, 16, 40, 50, 59; Scotland 32, 64
December	Reprinted LSS 7, 18, 26, 51, 69

Post-WW1 undated reprints, c.1920-21. These are all unpriced, thus their issue presumably follows the price increase of January 1920 when it became OS practice to remove the price from maps.

> Reprinted LSS 10, 12, 15, 21, 24, 29, 31, 34, 35, 43, 44, 45, 46, 48, 53, 54, 55, 56, 63, 64, 65, 74, 80, 87, 107, 116, 128, 136, 138, *Brighton, Cambridge, Dorking, Folkestone, Weston super Mare, Winchester;* Scotland 23, 24, 29.21, 65, 83, 91.100, 107, *Glasgow;* Ireland SSS 36, 129

1921
Jan-March   Published *Scott's Country*
January   Reprinted LSS 9, 23, 28, 61
February   Reprinted LSS 20
March   Reprinted Scotland 33.41
April-June   Published *Burns' Country, Lower Strath Spey*
August   Reprinted LSS 36, 41, 45
September   Reprinted Scotland 19+, 37
December   Republished LSS 5, with coverage of Scotland (see 1917)

1922
Jan-March   Published *Rothesay*
January   Reprinted Scotland 15
February   Reprinted LSS 7; Scotland 9, 15, ?16
May   Reprinted LSS 4; Scotland 73, 74, 75, 81
June   Reprinted Scotland 85, 94
Late 1922   Print codes no longer contain the month of issue (last recorded in any series 11.22)
             Reprinted *Dorking* (month unknown)

1923   Reprinted LSS 29, 30, *London (South), Staffordshire Potteries, York*
             Reprinted Scotland 31, 32, 55, 65

1924
             Reprinted *Lake District;* Scotland 10
April-June   Publication of one-inch Popular Edition of Scotland begun

1925   Reprinted *Dorking;* Scotland 21.13

1926
             Sheet prices restored
July-Sept   Publication of one-inch Popular Edition of England and Wales completed

1927   Reprinted *Salisbury Plain; Hastings;* Scotland 45, 66; Ireland LSS 16.17

1929   Reprinted *Dublin*

1931   Reprinted Ireland LSS 16.17

1932
             Reprinted Ireland SSS 60.61
April-June   Publication of one-inch Popular Edition of Scotland completed

1933   Reprinted *Dublin*
1937   Ireland LSS 16.17 replaced by OSNI Popular Edition 7
1944   Reprinted *Dublin, Killarney*
1945   Reprinted Ireland SSS 35, 47, 187
1946   Reprinted *Cork, Killarney*
1947   Reprinted *Dublin*
1948   Reprinted *Dublin*
1949   Reprinted *Cork, Killarney*
1951-56   Reprinted Ireland SSS carrying second revision and partial revision dates

Bibliography

Adams, B., "'Parallel to the meridian of Butterton Hill' – do I laugh or cry?", *Sheetlines* 38 (1994), 15-19. Correction in *Sheetlines* 50 (1997), 58-59.

Browne, J.P., "Ellis Martin and the rise of map cover art", *The Map Collector* 35 (1986), 10-14.

Browne, J.P., *Map cover art*. Southampton: Ordnance Survey, 1991.

Close, Col C.F., *Ordnance Survey maps of the United Kingdom. A description of their scales, characteristics, &c.* London: HMSO, 1913.

Cook, K.C. and McIntosh, R.P., *A preliminary list of Ordnance Survey one-inch district and tourist maps and selected precursors in the British Library.* London: Charles Close Society, 1991.

Dean, R.J. [ed.], "Notes and queries : Third Edition coloured large sheet series", *Sheetlines* 13 (1985), 21.

Hellyer, R., "Sheet lines: some notes on GSGS 3917 and other one-inch large sheet maps of Ireland", *Sheetlines* 43 (1995), 4-24.

Hellyer, R., *Ordnance Survey small-scale maps : indexes 1801-1998.* Kerry: David Archer, 1999.

Hellyer, R. and Oliver, R.R., "The One-inch Third Edition Map of England and Wales, in colour : small sheet series", *Sheetlines* 57 (2000), 8-20.

Hellyer, R., "A cartobibliography of the one-inch map of Ireland, in colour, 1901-1956", *Sheetlines* 63 (2002), 12-38.

Hodson, A.Y., *Popular maps : the Ordnance Survey Popular Edition one-inch map of England and Wales 1919-1926.* London: Charles Close Society, 1999.

Messenger, K.G., "The OS one-inch maps of England & Wales, Third Edition (Large Sheet Series)", *Sheetlines* 7 (1983), 6-9.

Messenger, K.G., *The Ordnance Survey one-inch map of England and Wales Third Edition (Large Sheet Series) : a descriptive and cartobibliographical monograph.* London: Charles Close Society, 1988. Supplement: *Additions and corrections*, April 1989.

Messenger, K.G., *A guide to the Ordnance Survey one-inch map of Scotland Third Edition in colour.* London: Charles Close Society, 1991.

Mumford, I., "New light on an early decorative cover", *Sheetlines* 35 (1993), 44-45.

Nicholson, T.R., "The Ordnance Survey and smaller scale military maps of Britain 1854-1914", *Cartographic Journal* 25 (1988), 109-127.

Nicholson, T.R., "A major military "special" : the 2-inch/mile map *War Department Land on Salisbury Plain,* 1899-1914, and its companions", *Sheetlines* 39 (1994), 20-27.

Nicholson, T.R., *The birth of the modern Ordnance Survey small-scale map : the Revised New Series colour printed one-inch map of England and Wales 1897-1914.* London: Charles Close Society, 2002.

Oliver, R.R., "Kenneth Guy Messenger", *Sheetlines* 38 (1994), 1-4. (Obituary).

Oliver, R.R., "Design and content changes on one-inch mapping of Britain, 1870-1914", *Sheetlines* 62 (2002), 6-23.

Oliver, R.R., "The one-inch revision instructions of 1896", *Sheetlines* 66 (2003), 11-25.

Olivier, Sir S. (chairman), *Report of the departmental committee on the sale of small-scale Ordnance Survey maps; with appendices.* London: HMSO, 1914. (Copy PRO OS 1/6/5).

Stubbs, P., "One inch 3rd Edition (Large Sheet Series) – prices in retailers covers", *Sheetlines* 41 (1994), 32-33. (Containing the text of a letter from Guy Messenger to Peter Stubbs).